ANDREW SULLIVAN

SAME-SEX MARRIAGE: PRO AND CON

Andrew Sullivan is a senior editor at The New Republic, a magazine he edited from 1991 to 1996, and the U.S. columnist for the Sunday Times of London. He holds a B.A. in modern history and modern languages from Oxford University and a Ph.D. in political science from Harvard University. He lives in Washington, D.C.

ALSO BY ANDREW SULLIVAN

Virtually Normal: An Argument about Homosexuality

SAME-SEX MARRIAGE: PRO AND CON

A READER

SAME-SEX MARRIAGE:
PRO AND CON

A READER

ANDREW SULLIVAN

WITH RESEARCH ASSISTANCE BY JOSEPH LANDAU

VINTAGE BOOKS / A DIVISION OF RANDOM HOUSE, INC. / NEW YORK

A VINTAGE ORIGINAL, APRIL 1997
FIRST EDITION

Copyright © 1997 by Andrew Sullivan

All rights reserved under International and Pan-American
Copyright Conventions. Published in the United States by
Vintage Books, a division of Random House, Inc., New York,
and simultaneously in Canada by Random House of Canada
Limited, Toronto.

Library of Congress Cataloging-in-Publication Data
Same-Sex Marriage: Pro and Con : a reader /
edited and with an introduction by Andrew Sullivan.
— 1st ed.
p. cm.
"A Vintage original."
ISBN 0-679-77637-0
1. Gay marriage.   2. Homosexuality—Religious aspects.
3. Gay couples—Legal status, laws, etc.
I. Sullivan, Andrew, 1963–
HQ76.25.F677   1997
306.84'8—dc21   96-51881
CIP

Pages 367–373 constitute an extension of this copyright page.

Printed in the United States of America
1 3 5 7 9 8 6 4 2

FOR ALL THOSE, GAY AND STRAIGHT,

WHO HAVE FOUND THE STRENGTH

AND THE LOVE TO SUSTAIN THE

INSTITUTION OF MARRIAGE.

ACKNOWLEDGMENTS

This book would not have been possible without Joseph Landau, my research assistant. In many ways, this book is as much his work as it is mine. He is an adventurous researcher, a tireless administrator, a constant source of ideas and arguments, and also a good friend. I cannot thank him enough.

I would also like to thank professor Bill Eskridge of Georgetown University, whose pioneering research in the history of same-sex marriage gave us many of the leads we followed; *The New Republic* for generously giving me a base from which to work; Evan Wolfson for his courage, advice, and companionship; and the following people, who, in small ways and large, helped bring this together: professors Marcel Tetel and Dale Martin, Rabbi Margaret Moers Wenig, Chloe Tribich, Brian Jacobson, Steve Glass, Debra Durocher, Charlotte Patterson, Jordan Sable, Beatrice Dohrn, Gillian Chi, Pepper Schwartz, Mark Spengler, Stuart Spencer, Daniel McGlinchey, Robert Raben, Roy Tsao, and Guy Wilson. I am also indebted to Jane Garrett and Marty Asher for their faith in the project from the beginning and their patience in bringing it to fruition. The errors, of course, remain my own.

CONTENTS

Contents

Contents

Contents

Contents

Chapter Eight: A Slippery Slope? The Polygamy and Adultery Debate 273

Chapter Nine: Whose Life Is It Anyway? The Real World of Love and Marriage 295

Contents

Chapter Ten: After Hawaii, What? The Future of the Legal and Political Battle 327

"We deal with a right to privacy older than the Bill of Rights—older than our political parties, older than our school system. Marriage is a coming together for better or for worse, hopefully enduring, and intimate to the degree of being sacred. It is an association that promotes a way of life, not causes; a harmony in living, not political faiths; a bilateral loyalty, not commercial or social projects. Yet it is an association for as noble a purpose as any involved in our prior decisions . . ."

—From Justice Douglas's ruling for the majority,
U.S. Supreme Court,
Griswold v. *Connecticut,* June 1965

Perhaps I should begin by telling a story.

A good friend of mine grew up in a small town on the panhandle of Florida. It's a classically Southern town with conservative politics and a solidly Democratic tradition, and during the course of the last few years, I came to visit a few times and got to know my friend's family a little. The town, like many in the region, is racially divided, with one part almost entirely black and the other almost entirely white. You literally cross railroad tracks from one neighborhood to the other, and the black section is still colloquially known as "the quarters." Nevertheless, since the 1960s the public schools have been integrated, and race relations today seem relatively civil.

The process of integration, however, had been anything but easy. One night, on a visit with my friend's family, the conversation turned toward those years, and, after a few drinks, I asked my friend's father about them—and why they had been so traumatic. And what he told me was not something I had expected. "Well," he said, "it was a mixture of things. Politics—and worrying about your children's education and so on. But the thing people were most worried about was not integrating the schools as such—or the quality of the education they would get. They were worried that once they started integrating the schools, the kids would get to know one another better; and then maybe some of them would fall in love—and then maybe some of them would get married. That's what they were really worried about."

Marriage, it seems, has always been at the heart and center of political trauma. As a civil institution, it was instituted many centuries ago to solve political problems—to annex one family to another, to settle dynastic disputes, to distribute property. But since then it has also been the occasion for dramatic and sometimes violent political conflict. Churches have been created, monarchs deposed, civil wars initiated, and civil rights movements ignited by the struggle to control one of the most central institutions in most people's lives. From Romeo and Juliet to *Loving v. Virginia,* marriage has been a place where broader social divides and quarrels have been fought over and settled. So it is, perhaps, no accident that, in the last decade of the twentieth century, the institution of marriage has intersected with yet another major social convulsion. The same-sex marriage debate, indeed, is perhaps best seen not as some modern aberration in our peculiar culture wars but as yet another instance of how a particularly divisive social issue—this time the place of homosexuals in society—has collided once again with the social institution that defines for many people the most meaningful part of their lives.

So two histories and two meanings interact in these pages: the history and meaning of marriage and the history and meaning of homosexuality. In the passages that follow, you will see all of these histories and meanings fought over. Marriage is alternately praised and derided as a lynchpin of procreation, love, power, economics, convenience, morality, civil rights. And homosexuality similarly evokes opposing judgments: it is seen as a perversion; a source of identity, love, and desire; a freely chosen lifestyle, a fabricated personality, a revolution against the status quo. And when these two contested areas are brought together, this matrix of interpretation is multiplied even more, so that, at times, it may seem as if no one is even speaking about the same thing.

Yet certain fundamental issues are discernible. Because marriage is such a central institution in so many people's lives, because it forms such an integral part of our own self-understanding, any change in it opens up a host of questions about what the union of two people means, what it has become, and what it could stand for—for everybody. And that is partly what is at stake here. When homosexuals seek the right to marry, heterosexuals who oppose same-sex marriage have to ask themselves what exactly it is that they're so eager to retain. And this questioning process can be a disconcerting process. It is at moments like this that we realize that marriage itself has changed. From being an institution governed by men, it has been placed on a radically more egalitarian footing. From being a contract for life, it has developed into a bond that is celebrated twice in many an American's lifetime. From being a means to bringing up children, it has become primarily a way in which two adults affirm their emotional commitment to one another. From being an institution that buttresses certain previous bonds—family, race, religion, class—it has become, for many, a deep expression of the modern individual's ability to transcend all of those ties in an exercise of radical autonomy. When we talk about the same-sex marriage debate, then, we are also talking about the marriage debate. Which is why the issue has so captured the broader public imagination, and why it will resonate for many years to come.

And yet it is also true that as well as being a debate about all of us, the same-sex marriage debate is also about a small minority of us. And because marriage is an institution so close to people's hearts, this debate has been particularly fraught. Including homosexuals within marriage, after all, would be a means of conferring the highest form of social approval imaginable. Bestowing or accepting such approval is not easy for any of the parties involved, given the human temptation, and often the need, to define oneself in contradistinction to others. Even now, across America and the world, young men and women still brace themselves before bringing home to their parents a girlfriend or boyfriend of another race or religion or class. Parents whose tolerance of other traditions and communities is unquestioned in general often find themselves balking when the meaning of their own family—particularly in the form of a wedding ceremony—is brought into the equation. If the issue is still contentious within a heterosexual context, it is no surprise that it should be explosive when homosexuality is involved.

And in a broader political setting, where the meaning of culture and nation are at stake, the tensions can be even greater. So in the history of race relations in the United States, approval of citizenship for African Americans was one thing, but equal economic opportunity was very much another. And it took decades for the full integration of the military and public schools and public accommodations to take place—areas, again, where the symbolism of the national identity was at stake. The fact that the constitutionality of interracial marriage was the last of these civil milestones to be established is therefore far from remarkable. The symbolic power of marriage, it turns out, is even deeper than that of citizenship, even starker than that of military glory, even clearer than that of public space. It is the institution where public citizenship most dramatically intersects with private self-definition. It is where people have historically drawn the line.

So in racial matters it was the last citadel of white supremacy to fall. But even then, it did not collapse entirely. Legality—and constitutionality—did not mean approval. The polls tell an interesting story. In 1968, the year that interracial marriage became legal across the United States, a Gallup poll found that some 72 percent of Americans still disapproved of such marriages, even if they were prepared to tolerate them. It wasn't until 1991 that a majority existed to approve them—by a narrow margin of 48 to 42 percent. Since then, there has been a standstill in American opinion on the issue. (Among blacks, on the same Gallup poll, there has even been a *decline in* approval rates from 70 to 63 percent.) To this day a significant minority of Americans—around 30 percent—disapprove of interracial marriage, even though they are prepared to see it legal. And the number of white and black Americans who would disapprove of such a marriage in their own family is undoubtedly a larger number still.

And so the notion that same-sex marriage is a simple matter of public debate, or is somehow inevitable, was never likely to be borne out. Like interracial marriage and the national debate over race, same-sex marriage stands at the very heart of the issue of accepting homosexuality in America yet remains the most elusive prize of all. So Americans are far more comfortable with workplace protections for homosexuals than they are with same-sex marriage; and far more comfortable with housing protection. In 1996, according to a Newsweek poll, some 84 percent of

Americans favored protecting homosexuals from discrimination in employment, and 80 percent supported such protection in housing. (The momentum in favor of those changes is considerable: only 56 percent of Americans favored such protections twenty years ago.) A large majority supports inheritance rights for gay spouses—61 to 29 percent—and a narrow majority even supports social security benefits for gay spouses—48 to 43 percent. And yet a clear majority—58 to 33 percent—still opposes legalizing same-sex marriage. Why? Perhaps because Americans rightly intuit, as they intuited with interracial marriage, that granting homosexuals entrance into this institution is tantamount to complete acceptance of homosexuality by American society. No other measure would signal approval in such a stark and unambiguous way. And many heterosexual Americans are not yet ready to go quite that far. They are prepared to tolerate, yes, even, in some ways, approve. But they are not yet ready to say that their heterosexual relationships are equivalent to homosexual ones; that their loves and gay loves are worth the same respect. That, it seems to me, is the issue that same-sex marriage starkly presents and that Americans are now furiously and anxiously trying to resolve.

But that doesn't mean that America will never legalize same-sex marriage—or that the issue is always going to be anathema to the center of American politics and culture. A glance at the interracial marriage analogy is revealing again. The polls show that hostility to same-sex marriage in 1996 is markedly less profound than hostility to interracial marriage was in 1968. And this despite the fact that, in terms of legal status, same-sex marriage is far more tenuous today than interracial marriage was in 1968. How to account for this extraordinary discrepancy? Growing levels of tolerance and liberalism in all facets of American life, perhaps. But one feature of American society today is more telling than any other. In 1985 a Newsweek poll found that only 22 percent of Americans had a friend or acquaintance whom they knew to be homosexual. Today the statistic is 56 percent. Thirty-one percent report knowing a gay person at work, and 18 percent know one in their own family. It is surely this new, and dramatic, integration of homosexuals into heterosexual society that accounts for the current levels of tolerance and approval—especially within families. And this, I think, is significant, because it is within families that fundamental issues, such as marriage, are clearly most contentious; and within families that such issues are ultimately resolved.

These family arguments were never as common with interracial marriage in the 1960s, since blacks and whites were more estranged from each other then than gays and straights are today. And this is especially true when you think of how many black families had white family members, and vice versa in 1968, compared with how many straight families knowingly have gay members today. The effects of this degree of integration on the acceptance of homosexuals in American society could be dramatic.

But, of course, volatility can work both ways. The Defense of Marriage Act of 1996 revealed how politically dangerous it is for most politicians to endorse anything as contentious an issue as same-sex marriage. And hefty majorities remain opposed to legalization. In many ways, although on the surface the issue of homosexuality may appear to be more flexible than race is, it is, at a deeper level, far more intractable. With race, after all, there is a broad public consensus that the inherent distinction at stake is not a matter of morals. Very few people argue that because a person is black, he or she is for that reason incapable of the moral and civil responsibilities of marriage. With homosexuality, of course, that is precisely the issue. Morals matter deeply in this debate, and religion matters, perhaps, more deeply than anything else.

So the objection to same-sex marriage cannot be dismissed out of hand as equivalent to the objection to interracial marriage, since it begs a different argument about the nature of homosexuality itself. And that argument, in turn, makes the resolution of this civic discussion that much more emotional and difficult to resolve, because it inevitably involves religious convictions that cannot, by their very nature, be subjected to reason. Faith is not equivalent to a prejudice; neither, unfortunately, is it equivalent to an argument. And although religion can legitimately be excluded in a strict sense from our civic discourse (there is, after all, a separation of Church and State in America), it cannot be excluded from the culture that informs and shapes politics. Sixty-seven percent of Americans in the Newsweek poll reported that same-sex marriage violated their religious beliefs. Even among those who favored civil same-sex marriage, 56 percent said that it violated their religion. Religious belief was easily the most common objection cited for opposing the legalization of same-sex marriage. That is an issue that cannot be ignored.

So this debate has to operate on a whole variety of levels. The issue of same-sex marriage is a civil rights matter and a religious matter. It is a question of politics and a question of culture. It interacts with people as citizens and as parents, as lovers and as relatives, as people of faith and as people of reason. It requires from each of us the most patient of dialogues and the most exacting of distinctions. Hence the structure of this book. The motivating thought behind the selection of passages is to serve the purpose of helping us make those distinctions, to be surprised by the evidence, to be alert to the possibilities of argument, to be open to debate at every level. To get to the bottom of this debate, we have to talk theology as well as politics; we have to talk about life as well as law. So the book is framed around a variety of discrete questions—historical and religious, legal and political, cultural and sociological—and a variety of separate discourses. Every now and again, the same issue—polygamy, say, or child rearing—will crop up in a different context, but that only goes to show that each of these discourses is another way of addressing the same fascinating, if elusive, questions.

And in this diverse debate, the very methodologies are equally diverse. You will find here a celebrity interview, a political treatise, a book review, and a social science survey. There are anthropological reports and historical monographs, doctrinal statements and magazine editorials, parliamentary debates and op-ed articles. There are even poems and advice columns. Each of these, I am trying to say, has its place in the discussion that is going on. And each may show us a truth, or a shard of a truth, that can help deepen our understanding of what is at stake, or how people feel, or where the crux of an argument may lie. With any luck, these separate ways of looking at the issue can inform or deepen one another. That, at least, is my hope.

I cannot pretend, of course, that I am a neutral observer to this debate, as any reader will soon discover. I have been as engaged as anyone in this argument for the last eight years or so. But I hope that I have been able to put that partisanship aside in assembling the selections that follow. There are plenty of sentiments here with which I vigorously disagree. Nevertheless in each chapter, I have attempted to establish some semblance of balance. Including anti–same-sex marriage material was in some ways the most difficult part of the project—not because I have an aversion to it, but because, for a long time, the opposition didn't even feel the need to articulate itself. Recently, that has changed dramatically, especially as the Hawaii decision and its possible consequences have sunk in. No doubt there will be an even greater outpouring of objections as events proceed. But readers will notice that the majority of the "con" material has been published within the last eighteen months or so.

One final prediction. In going through the vast range and depth of materials in this book—not to mention the acres of materials that didn't make it into the last cut—I have come to see how vital and symbolic a debate this is. It will not, I hope, be seen as yet another tributary in the rivers of identity politics. It is about our national politics as a whole. In some ways, it's typical of the kind of argument that will increasingly define the way we conduct our political affairs. As our national political parties converge ideologically and our national politicians focus on such technical issues as a balanced budget, the future of social security, or the contours of managed health care, the deeper political discussions are taking place in the cultural sphere. How do we effectively counter the divisions of race? What are the consequences for society of greater equality between the sexes? Is assisted suicide moral? Should abortion be legal? These are the matters that are really shaping the future of American society; and same-sex marriage is surely at the heart of that debate. It strikes at the core of the quintessentially modern problem: Should the law reflect our common moral values—or our widening moral pluralism? Or is there a way in which we can square these circles and bring our old values to apply to our new diversity?

That's why this debate is ultimately about more than marriage and more than homosexuality. As an argument, it is a crucible for the future shape of democratic liberalism. On the one hand, there is the unanswerable demand of a group of citizens to be treated equally by the government to which they pay taxes and bear allegiance. On the other, there is the common belief that to grant this right to the homosexual population would be to fatally undermine the meaning of the society to which those citizens belong. How to reconcile such irreconcilable demands? That, essentially, is the challenge of modern politics. Meeting that challenge is, in part, the aspiration of this book.

SAME-SEX MARRIAGE: PRO AND CON

A READER

CHAPTER ONE

For the First Time Ever?
SAME-SEX MARRIAGE IN HISTORY

One of the recurring clichés of the same-sex marriage debate is that the very notion of such a thing is a radical departure from anything entertained before in human history. Nothing, however, could be further from the truth. In many cultures and in many eras, the issue has emerged—and the themes of the arguments are quirkily similar. Same-sex love, as Plato's Symposium *shows, is as ancient as human love, and the question of how it is recognized and understood has bedeviled every human civilization. In most, it has never taken the form of the modern institution of marriage, but in some, surprisingly, it has. In seventeenth-century China and nineteenth-century Africa, for example, the institution seems identical to opposite-sex marriage. In other cultures (see the debate between Brent Shaw and Ralph Hexter) the meaning of same-sex unions remains opaque and complex. In Native American society, marriage between two men was commonplace, but its similarity to contemporary lesbian and gay marriages is far from evident. And today in Denmark and Sweden different compromises have been made that affect the meaning of marriage itself.*

Judge for yourself what this might mean for our current convulsion. One thing emerges clearly: this issue is not a modern invention. The need to balance human dignity and social norms is as old as civilization itself. Although much of the past history of this debate has been buried until recently, it has begun to emerge again with all the passion that now crackles through modern Western culture.

The Speech of Aristophanes
PLATO

From the Symposium, *by Plato, translated by Alexander Nehamas and Paul Woodruff, 1989*

In a dialogue on the meaning of love, Plato writes a masterpiece for his sometime sparring partner, the playwright Aristophanes, to explain the mystery of our desire for one other person. This passage follows Aristophanes's myth about the origins of human beings. In the beginning, Aristophanes conjectures, humans were essentially two people combined, each with two heads, four feet and four arms. There were three sexes: those with two male halves, those with two female halves, and those with one of each (the "androgynous" sort). At one point, however, Zeus, to punish humans for misbehaving, cut each human in two. Since then, each half wanders the earth in search of its lost other half, creating homosexual men, lesbians, and heterosexuals. Notice how same-sex love is put on the same plane as opposite-sex love, but also see how marriage is not identified with it.

Each of us, then, is a "matching half" of a human whole, because each was sliced like a flatfish, two out of one, and each of us is always seeking the half that matches him. That's why a man who is split from the double sort (which used to be called "androgynous") runs after women. Many lecherous men have come from this class, and so do the lecherous women who run after men. Women who are split from a woman, however, pay no attention at all to men; they are oriented more towards women, and lesbians come from this class. People who are split from a male are male-oriented. While they are boys, because they are chips off the male block, they love men and enjoy lying with men and being embraced by men; those are the best of boys and lads, because they are the most manly in their nature. Of course, some say such boys are shameless, but they're lying. It's not because they have no shame that such boys do this, you see, but because they are bold and brave and masculine, and they tend to cherish what is like themselves. Do you want me to prove it? Look, these are the only kind of boys who grow up to be politicians. When they're grown men, they are lovers of young men, and they naturally pay no attention to marriage or to making babies, except insofar as they are required by local custom. They, however, are quite satisfied to live their lives with one another unmarried. In every way, then, this sort of man grows up as a lover of young men and a lover of Love, always rejoicing in his own kind.

And so, when a person meets the half that is his very own, whatever his orientation, whether it's to young men or not, then something wonderful happens: the two are struck from their senses by love, by a sense of belonging to one another, and by desire, and they don't want to be separated from one another, not even for a moment.

These are the people who finish out their lives together and still cannot say what it is they want from one another. No one would think it is the intimacy of sex—that mere sex is the reason each lover takes so great and deep a joy in being with the other. It's obvious that the soul of every lover longs for something else; his soul cannot say what it is, but like an oracle it has a sense of what it wants, and like an oracle it hides behind a riddle. Suppose two lovers are lying together and Hephaestus stands over them with his mending tools, asking, "What is it you human beings really want from each other?" And suppose they're perplexed, and he asks them again: "Is this your heart's desire, then—for the two of you to become parts of the same whole, as near as can be, and never to separate, day or night? Because if that's your desire, I'd like to weld you together and join you into something that is naturally whole, so that the two of you are made into one. Then the two of you would share one life, as long as you lived, because you would be one being, and by the same token, when you died, you would be one and not two in Hades, having died a single death. Look at your love, and see if this is what you desire: wouldn't this be all the good fortune you could want?"

Surely you can see that no one who received such an offer would turn it down; no one would find anything else that he wanted. . . .

A Groom of One's Own?

BRENT D. SHAW

Same-Sex Unions in Pre-Modern Europe: A Response

RALPH HEXTER

From The New Republic, *July 18 and 24, 1994; and October 3, 1994*

The publication of Yale historian John Boswell's book Same-Sex Unions in Pre-Modern Europe *created a furor in 1994. The media hyped the notion that Boswell had discovered same-sex marriage rites from the ancient world, although his own work made far more sophisticated claims. Instead of extracting from the book itself, I've reprinted here a penetrating review that outlines the book's main arguments and attempts to refute them. It is followed by Ralph Hexter's response to the review, which shows that an accurate reading of the past can often be a complex undertaking. Boswell, alas, was too ill at that point to respond to the review of his work.*

A GROOM OF ONE'S OWN?

We find ourselves, all of us, in a historical crisis of gender. It has produced highly charged arguments over "Amendment 2" to the constitution of Colorado, and over the various legal actions that have stemmed from that controversial initiative. In Ontario, Canada, it has produced acerbic debate and the defeat of a legislative bill that would have recognized same-sex unions as "marital" in nature, and would have granted them comparable rights and duties. No small part of the disputation is about definitions—What is a family? What is a marriage?—and about the social and political consequences of these definitions.

The relationship of historians and their work to this crisis is fraught and dangerous. The stakes are high. And so the appearance of a large book by a well-known historian from Yale University on what are, he says, historical precedents for homosexual marriages in Christian society and their official recognition by the Christian church, is bound to find a large readership and to stoke a vigorous debate. The publisher's announcement excitedly warns that the work is "bound to be as controversial as the publication of the Dead Sea Scrolls." For John Boswell claims to have discovered a series of medieval manuscripts that record Christian church ceremonials for creating and blessing "same-sex unions"—for what were, in effect, marriages between men.

Apart from a foray into the problem of abandoned infants in ancient and early-modern European society, Boswell is best known for his investigation of the problematic relations between male homosexuals and the Christian church. His *Christianity, Social Tolerance and Homosexuality: Gay People in Western Europe from the Beginning of the Christian Era to the Fourteenth Century,* which appeared in 1980, was a learned and groundbreaking investigation of a subject that the author rightly categorized as "taboo." More than twelve years in the researching and writing, his new book on same-sex unions is similarly intended to reshape our interpretations of the past and our practices in the present.

Boswell attempts to demonstrate that "gay marriage ceremonies" were an accepted part of the early Christian church, and that the rituals that formalized such marriages were only later deliberately and consciously effaced by the church. He laudably provides the reader with transcriptions of the documents in the original Greek, along with his own English translations of them. No less laudably, he guides the reader through interpretations of his material that differ from his own.

Since the material that Boswell has uncovered is unfamiliar and impressive and controversial, it is perhaps best to give the reader some sense of it—his own English version of the text of one of these ceremonies. What follows is from an eleventh-century Greek manuscript labeled Grottaferrata Γ.Β.Π, and I have inserted some of the significant original Greek words in transcription.

Office for Same-Sex Union
[Akolouthia eis adelphopoiesin]

I.

The priest shall place the holy Gospel on the Gospel stand and they that are to be joined together place their right hands on it, holding lighted candles in their left hands. Then shall the priest cense them and say the following:

II.

In peace we beseech Thee, O Lord.

For heavenly peace, we beseech Thee, O Lord.

For the peace of the entire world, we beseech Thee, O Lord.

For this holy place, we beseech Thee, O Lord.

That these thy servants, N. and N., be sanctified with thy spiritual benediction, we beseech Thee, O Lord.

That their love [*agape*] abide without offense or scandal all the days of their lives, we beseech Thee, O Lord.

That they be granted all things needed for salvation and godly enjoyment of life everlasting, we beseech Thee, O Lord.

That the Lord God grant unto them unashamed faithfulness [*pistis*] and sincere love [*agape anhypokritos*], we beseech Thee, O Lord. . . .

Have mercy on us, O God.

"Lord, have mercy" shall be said three times.

III.

The priest shall say:

Forasmuch as Thou, O Lord and Ruler, art merciful and loving, who didst establish humankind after thine image and likeness, who didst deem it meet that thy holy apostles Philip and Bartholomew be united, bound one unto the other not by nature but by faith and the spirit. As Thou didst find thy holy martyrs Serge and Bacchus worthy to be united together [*adelphoi genesthai*], bless also these thy servants, N. and N., joined together not by the bond of nature but by faith and in the mode of the spirit [*ou desmoumenous desmi physeis alla pisteis kai pneumatikos tropi*], granting unto them peace [*eirene*] and love [*agape*] and oneness of mind. Cleanse from their hearts every stain and impurity and vouchsafe unto them to love one another [*to agapan allelous*] without hatred and without scandal all the days of their lives, with the aid of the Mother of God and all thy saints, forasmuch as all glory is thine.

IV.

Another Prayer for Same-Sex Union

O Lord Our God, who didst grant unto us all those things necessary for salvation and didst bid us to love one another and to forgive each other our failings, bless and consecrate, kind Lord and lover of good, these thy servants who love each other with a love of the spirit [*tous pneumatike agape heautous agapesantas*] and have come into this thy holy church to be blessed and consecrated. Grant unto them unashamed fidelity [*pistis*] and sincere love [*agape anhy-*

pokritos], and as Thou didst vouchsafe unto thy holy disciples and apostles thy peace and love, bestow them also on these, O Christ our God, affording to them all those things needed for salvation and life eternal. For Thou art the light and the truth and thine is the glory.

v.

Then shall they kiss the holy Gospel and the priest and one another, and conclude.

It is this ceremonial, and blessings like these, that Boswell claims to be part of a lost, or deliberately suppressed, tradition of church-legitimized same-sex marriages between men.

Boswell's argument stands or falls on his interpretation of a series of documents relating to a singular ritual practiced in the Christian church during antiquity and the high middle ages, principally in the lands of the eastern Mediterranean. The bonds between men that are confirmed in these church rituals are cautiously (and a little coyly) labeled by him as "same-sex unions." For his arguments to have the force that he wishes them to have, however, the words "same-sex" and "union" must be construed to mean "male homosexual" and "marriage." If they signify other sorts of associations that happened to be same-sex in gender, or unions that were meant for purposes other than marriage or a permanent affective union, then his claims fail.

For this reason, the narrative chapters of his book are ancillary, in that they digress on other aspects of the general problems of marriage and family formation in a way that is designed to support Boswell's claims about the supposed same-sex marriage rituals. His larger investigation of the nature of "heterosexual" marriage and love, and their attendant vocabulary in the Greco-Roman world, is undertaken to demonstrate that his interpretation of the "same-sex union" rituals is the most probable one.

Given the centrality of Boswell's "new" evidence, therefore, it is best to begin by describing his documents and their import. These documents are liturgies for an ecclesiastical ritual called *adelphopoiesis* or, in simple English, the "creation of a brother." Whatever these texts are, they are not texts for marriage ceremonies. Boswell's translation of their titles (*akolouthia eis adelphopoiesin* and parallels) as "The Order of Celebrating the Union of Two Men" or "Office for Same-Sex Union" is inaccurate. In the original, the titles say no such thing. And this sort of tendentious translation of the documents is found, alas, throughout the book. Thus the Greek words that Boswell translates as "be united together" in the third section of the document quoted above are, in fact, rather ordinary words that mean "become brothers" (*adelphoi genesthai*); and when they are translated in this more straightforward manner, they impart a quite different sense to the reader.

Whatever effect these liturgical ceremonials were intended to achieve, it is clear that they used ecclesiastical formalities to make two men "brothers," and employed various rituals and symbolic claims to confirm this relationship within the confines of the church. All of Boswell's documents relate to practices rooted in the societies of Greece, the Balkans and the eastern Mediterranean between the twelfth and sixteenth centuries— though, as he rightly argues, they surely reflect practices that were current from periods dating back to the end of the Roman empire, and probably earlier. The original documents that he cites are therefore in Greek, the ecclesiastical lingua franca of the eastern Mediterranean. The only Western versions of them are translations made into Latin from the original Greek prayer and liturgical books—wherein, notably, it seems that the Latin translators did not understand the purpose of the originals very well.

The ecclesiastical rituals that bless *adelphopoiesis,* or the making of a brother, include prayers and invocations of Christian virtues, particularly *agape,* or the Christian concept of love. They note that conditions of peace, not conditions of hate or vituperation, should exist between the two parties. Appeal is also made to pairs of men in the Christian tradition who were thought to exemplify these virtues: Philip and Bartholomew, among the disciples of Christ, and Serge and Bacchus, among the martyrs of the early church. Other elements of the ceremonial include, most significantly, the shaking or "juncture" of right hands; the exchanging of tokens; the mutual bestowing of a ritualistic kiss; and the holding of a celebratory feast or banquet to mark the occasion.

Such agreements and rituals are "same-sex" in the sense that it is two men who are involved; and they are "unions" in the sense that the two men involved are co-joined as "brothers." But that is it. There is no indication in the texts themselves that these are marriages in any sense that the word would mean to readers now, nor in any sense that the word would have meant to persons then: the formation of a common household, the sharing of everything in a permanent co-residential unit, the formation of a family unit wherein the two partners were committed, ideally, to each other, with the intent to raise children, and so on.

Although it is difficult to state precisely what these ritualized relationships were, most historians who have studied them are fairly certain that they deal with a species of "ritualized kinship" that is covered by the term "brotherhood." (This type of "brotherhood" is similar to the ritualized agreements struck between members of the Mafia or other "men of honor" in our own society.) That explains why the texts on *adelphopoiesis* in the prayer-books are embedded within sections dealing with other kinship-forming rituals, such as marriage and adoption.

Giovanni Tomassia in the 1880s and Paul Koschaker in the 1930s, whose works Boswell knows and cites, had already reached this conclusion.

This likely interpretation is made more likely by an extensive modern study of which Boswell appears to be unaware. In 1987 Gabriel Herman, a professor of history at the Hebrew University in Jerusalem, published *Ritualized Friendship and the Greek City.* In that book, and in several papers and articles on the subject published in leading journals of history and literature, Herman has analyzed the phenomenon of fictive "brotherhood" and "friendship" in the context of the world of the Greek city-state, and also in the cultures of the ancient Near East and in the regions that would later become parts of Slavonic Europe. In Herman's studies one finds all the phenomena regarded as indicative of "same-sex marriage" by Boswell: the ritual of the handshake, the exchange of tokens and right hands (*dexiai*), the declaration of love and friendship and of "no hostility or animosity" between the two parties, the exchange of a ritualistic kiss and the celebration of a common feast or banquet at the time of the formation of the compact.

Such ceremonials created ritualized friends who often spoke of each other as "brothers" and forged a close bond of brotherhood between themselves. They were "made brothers" rather than "brothers by nature." Hence the terminology, in Boswell's documents, of *adelphopoiesis,* or the ritual connected with "the making of a brother," and the phrases in his liturgical documents that specify that the two men "are not joined by the bond of nature, but rather by means of faith / trust and spirit," or similar words. This is why the documents contain references to the right of "protective asylum" (*asylon anepereastos*) and "safe conduct" (*asphaleia*) as divine attributes.

The kinds of words used to express the new relationship of "brothers" (words that are also found in Boswell's ecclesiastical rituals) were employed precisely because the men often entered into these relationships not out of love, but out of fear and suspicion. Hence the effusive emphasis on safety and trust. These relationships form as close a parallel in social institutions and practices as one could wish to have as background to the church ceremonials described in the texts cited by Boswell. Although such rituals did create fictive kinship links between the parties to them, these links were never mistaken or confused with the union of marriage. They were not undertaken primarily for erotic or affective reasons, for household formation, nor, even theoretically, for the procreation of children and the continuation of household lines.

There is only one segment of one document in Boswell's book that contains part of a liturgical service designed for a marriage ceremony: the fifth and sixth sections of the Grottaferrata manuscript of the eleventh century. Its words, which do refer to a wedding (*gamos*) and to the ceremonial use of crowns (*stephanoi*) in the ritual "crowning" of the bride and groom, give Boswell grounds to expatiate on the significance of these terms and the ceremonials involved. But there is no mention here of a same-sex union. From even a cursory reading of all of the documents, it is apparent that the original text of the "making of a brother" ceremony terminates at the end of section four of the manuscript in question. What Boswell prints as section five and section six of this document, as if they were a seamless continuation of the ritual of *adelphopoiesis,* belong in fact to an entirely different and separate document, which was indeed connected with a ceremony of marriage. The questionable joining of the two documents as if they were one enables Boswell to appeal throughout his main text to the totality of the documents as if they are all variant types of a marriage ceremonial, which they are not. . . .

*   *   *

The practices and the rituals performed by the men in Boswell's documents, and also the emotional and erotic connections that are so richly described by him, may seem unusual or frightening to us, given our codes of civility, morality and masculinity. There is a nice irony here: the ancient and medieval world about which Boswell writes was not riven by the same anxieties and repressions that mark our own. In that world, public and affective bonds between men were typical, even banal. But this is not the same thing as the legitimization, or the sacralization, of homosexuality. The "new" documents that Boswell has unearthed are nothing more than a few additional texts that shed more light on a primitive and basic power linkage between men in the ancient Mediterranean, and the rituals attendant on its formation.

By the time Boswell's ecclesiastical documents celebrated or blessed this type of personal arrangement, it had been brought at least partially under the aegis of the Christian church. As the structures of the law and the civil institutions of the state became more dominant, particularly in Western Europe, the church wished to divest itself of a ceremonial that was intended to substantiate a type of personal power that, in synchrony with the state, it now excoriated. Ritualized friendship naturally survived much longer in parts of the eastern Mediterranean, and especially in the mountainous regions of the Balkans, where more primitive forms of personal power have tended to subsist. There might well have been homoerotic elements to some of these "brotherhood" relationships, and a rather alien Greek ritual may have been misunderstood by some of its Latin translators; both of those possibilities deserve more attention than they have received by historians. But same-sex marriages forged with the approval of the Christian church, and with its rituals? No. Such a reading is very misleading.

The data of the past may not be all that happy for the liberationist movement of our time. Why else would those movements come into being? But what the sources record is, for better or for worse, what the sources record. A good part of what they record, certainly, is made up of systematic and successful repressions; but tinkering with the moral balance of the past is a disservice to the study of history and to the reform of society. The past is dead. We cannot change it. What we can change is the future; but the way to a better future requires an unsentimental and accurate understanding of what happened in the past, and why. A more civil and humane modernity will not be achieved by tendentious misreadings of antiquity.

SAME-SEX UNIONS IN PRE-MODERN EUROPE: A RESPONSE

I am responding to Brent D. Shaw's recent review of John Boswell's book, *Same-Sex Unions in Premodern Europe*. I write as a professor of Classics, a medievalist and a longtime friend and associate of John Boswell. The best refutations of Shaw's criticisms, of course, are to be found in the book itself. But Shaw gives so distorted an account of the book that many readers may be disinclined to make that discovery themselves.

Shaw's first (mis)step is to describe *Same-Sex Unions* as a book about "male homosexual marriages," as if he were reviewing recent popular accounts, even comic strips, rather than a scholarly work. Shaw seems to abandon criticism for mind-reading when he asserts that "the bonds between men that are confirmed in these church rituals are cautiously (and a little coyly) labeled by him as 'same-sex unions.'" It is distinctly odd to accuse the author of *Christianity, Social Tolerance, and Homosexuality: Gay People in Western Europe from the Beginning of the Christian Era to the Fourteenth Century* (1980) of coyness. Boswell has never pulled punches. If he thought that the best, most inclusive description of what he was writing about were "gay marriage," he would have used it. It is precisely that label that he wishes to test, with a completely open mind, and he wishes to give readers the information, and the context, with which to come to their own conclusions.

Boswell's use of the broader term "union" is in part heuristic; to stimulate his readers to follow his discussion of the changing habits and ideals of hetero- and homosexual "partnerships" across centuries and thus be prepared to appreciate the full range of possibilities in other societies in their own terms. The answer to the question he expected readers to focus on—"Was it a marriage?"—"depends," he says, "to a considerable extent on one's conception of marriage. . . . It was unequivocally a marriage" if one believes marriage to be "a permanent emotional union acknowledged in some way by the community," his characterization of the common current conception. What it was for members of earlier societies is trickier to ascertain, and while Boswell tries to give a sense of the range of the possibilities, even ambiguities, in different times and places, he is clear that "same-sex unions were . . . neither a threat to nor a replacement of heterosexual marriage."

Shaw's strategy is to adopt a tone of authoritative dismissal, as if Boswell were either too stupid or too politically engaged to realize what errors he was making. Readers should not be misled by this tone: Shaw is not an authority on Christian doctrine or liturgy, nor is he in any sense a medievalist. Moreover, his knowledge of Greek, like that of so many Classicists, is rooted in Classical, not patristic and medieval, usage; and he gives no evidence of any familiarity with other languages Boswell has and uses (inter alia Hebrew, Arabic, and above all for this study, Old Church Slavonic).

What strikes the reader familiar with *Same-Sex Unions* is that virtually all of Shaw's caveats and criticisms derive from Boswell's own argumentation. Shaw presents as if it were a revelation that *adelphopoiesis* "in simple English" is "creation of a brother," and concludes that Boswell's title for the ceremony, "Office of Same-Sex Union," "is inaccurate." As if Boswell didn't spend dozens of pages discussing the problems of translation, and this problem in particular. Any reader of *Same-Sex Unions* would learn what the "literal" meaning of the term is, and would be able to weigh whether this would be the best rendering or not. Indeed, so sensitive is Boswell to the issues surrounding this translation that he takes the term as an exemplary case in his appendix of translations (No. 5), and in a note experiments with both literal and more tendentious language.

Shaw's view that *adelphopoiesis* must mean "the making of brothers" is about as absurd as if I were to argue that "husband" couldn't mean "male partner in a heterosexual marriage" because its etyma would force it to mean "householder." Or more suggestively (though such analogies are always difficult), a French Shaw of the thirty-fifth century might well argue that, based on his Cassell's, a late-twentieth-century English text with the phrase "gay man" should be translated *homme joyeux*. Indeed, if one were to be absolutely literal, only your parents could "make" you a "brother." Obviously, the term is being used figuratively. The question is, in what way? And Boswell, not Shaw, gives his reader abundant evidence and sophisticated linguistic guidelines to draw his or her own conclusions.

Early on Shaw pontificates: "From even a cursory reading of all the documents, it is apparent that the original text of the 'making of a brother' ceremony [in a certain eleventh-century Grottaferrata manuscript] terminates at the end of section four. . . ." Boswell discusses the problematics of this text and compares it, for both commonality and singularity, with many other manuscript versions of the ceremony. Without going into the issue of putative originality (a typically Classicist concern that is particularly inappropriate to the study of evolving medieval reality), there is no doubt that this manuscript has what Boswell presents. He made two trips to Grottaferrata to see this manuscript, and took the precaution of photographing it. Shaw clearly knows nothing about this original material other than what he can derive from Boswell's own notes, which should be praised, not criticized, for pointing out problems and exploring the limits of certainty. This is, obviously, an unusual manuscript, but despite what Shaw implies, even the strongest version of Boswell's argument doesn't rise or fall on the inclusion of its final prayers. Here Shaw simply fails to mention such things as the organization of ceremonies within liturgical manuscripts, iconography and, above all, historical data.

But Shaw already dismissed "the narrative chapters . . . [as] ancillary," so he doesn't need to consider the actual descriptions of real historical people joined in union across the centuries. In the words of Montaigne, who witnessed the *adelphopoiesis* ceremony performed in Rome in 1581, *"ils s'espousoint masle à masle à la messe"* ("they married, one man to another, at mass"). Apparently contemporary authorities didn't interpret the ceremony as the "ritualized" friendship Shaw would have us believe it is, unless we are also to believe that such friendships called for the burning that we know at least some of those who participated in the ceremony suffered in the sixteenth century.

It is this issue of "ritualized friendship" that brings us to a point that Shaw stage manages in such a way as to, he must hope, completely undermine any reader's confidence in Boswell as a scholar. Shaw adduces "an extensive modern study of which Boswell appears to be unaware. In 1987 Gabriel Herman ... published *Ritualized Friendship and the Greek City.* . . . In Herman's studies one finds all the phenomena regarded as indicative of 'same-sex marriage' by Boswell." Whether Boswell knows this book or not, I cannot say. As a Classicist, I know it, and it is a fine study of "ritualized friendship" from Homeric society through the city states and into the Hellenistic states Alexander left behind. It ends, however, several hundred years before Boswell's major focus begins. Herman never addresses the particular ceremony that Boswell examines.

If Boswell had presented Herman's findings to his reader, the only value would have been to show up the differences between the institution that Herman describes and the medieval Christian ceremony. The essential point of the institution described by Herman is that the participating parties belong to different groups: *xenia* is an alliance between two men who are foreigners (or in some sense members of politically or socially opposed groups). This is not the hallmark of the medieval ceremony of union that Boswell describes. Shaw does not know it, but there is another ceremony in many of these same liturgical manuscripts that is intended to cement peace between two parties who have been enemies. It is completely distinct from *adelphopoiesis.* . . .

Readers should consider Shaw's views in light of Boswell's book, not in place of it.

A Strange Brotherhood

MICHEL DE MONTAIGNE

From his Travel Journal, *March 18, 1581*

> *In his journal of 1580–1581 (not published until two centuries later) the French skeptic and essayist Montaigne records a remarkable incident, as Ralph Hexter noted in the previous excerpt. Montaigne learned of same-sex marriages celebrated in a nuptial mass in Rome, but the participants had been subjected to vicious persecution.*

On the 18th the ambassador of Portugal made obeisance to the Pope for the kingdom of Portugal on behalf of King Philip— the same ambassador who was here to represent the deceased king and the Cortes opposed to King Philip.

On my return from Saint Peter's I met a man who informed me humorously of two things: that the Portuguese made their obeisance in Passion week; and then, that on this same day the station was at San Giovanni Porta Latina, in which church a few years before certain Portuguese had entered into a strange brotherhood. They married one another, male to male, at Mass, with the same ceremonies with which we perform our marriages, read the same marriage gospel service, and then went to bed and lived together. The Roman wits said that because in the other conjunction, of male and female, this circumstance of marriage alone makes it legitimate, it had seemed to these sharp folk that this other action would become equally legitimate if they authorized it with ceremonies and mysteries of the Church. Eight or nine Portuguese of this fine sect were burned. . . .

Deviant Marriage Patterns in Chinese Society
JAMES MCGOUGH

From Normal and Abnormal Behavior in Chinese Culture, *edited by Arthur Kleinman and Tsung-Yi Lin, 1981*

Husbands, Boys, Servants
BRET HINSCH

From Passions of the Cut Sleeve, *by Bret Hinsch, 1990*

Historian James McGough here details how the growing economic power of women in nineteenth- and early twentieth-century southern China enabled many to form relationships outside of conventional marriage—and some to set up same-sex marriages. In Fukien Province in seventeenth-century China, same-sex marriages between gay men seem to have been common, if not fully accepted, as well. Bret Hinsch supplies the details of one of the actual ceremonies in Fukien.

DEVIANT MARRIAGE PATTERNS
IN CHINESE SOCIETY

There were few alternative life-styles for women in traditional Chinese Society. Apart from the officially endorsed role of wife and mother, there were few ways a woman could make a living. . . .

One alternative was domestic service in another family. Women who worked as domestic servants sometimes renounced "normal" marriage and family life, and instead banded together for moral and other kinds of support.

Another alternative was made possible by other forms of wage labor; something that became much more prevalent with increased foreign investments in China in the last century. Once factory jobs were available in any numbers, women had greatly increased sources of income, and could be much more independent of the family system.

This happened, for instance, [according to scholar Hu P'u-an,] in the silk producing areas around Canton:

> In P'an-yu the land is fertile, and the people mainly make their living from silk production. Whether rich or poor, the daughters of the families there all know how to pick mulberry leaves and how to reel off silk from cocoons. In one day they can earn as much as eight or nine *chiao,* but at the least three or four *chiao.* The standard of living in rural areas is of course not as high as in the cities, and this amount is enough for self-sufficiency, and even for a bit of surplus. Such girls, then, have a means of support, and regard marriage as the most shameful of human affairs. Thus they form pacts not to marry. If they are forced to marry by their parents, they do not move to reside with the husband. These latter, after marriage, do not

have intercourse with the husband, and the next day return to their natal family, to be companions to their sisters and female cousins. This means that they are lost to the husband's family.

It is in this context that we find transactional social forms that are similar to, or are, marriage. The nonmarrying pacts were in the form of groups, or associations, of girls. They all entered into a kind of sworn sisterhood, called a "golden orchid society," "mutual admiration society," or "workmates' society."

In some cases two individuals would establish such a bond, [Hu writes,] and unite as a pair:

> In the drawing up of the contract, both sides must agree, much as in the legal form of contracts. If both parties are interested, then one will prepare . . . gifts of respect, to symbolize her sentiments. If the other side accepts them, this constitutes consent. If not then it is refusal. When the contract is written up and put into effect, and if they have any savings, they invite friends for a night's feast, and the friends all congratulate them. After this they are inseparable, day and night, and happier than any married couple. After the contract has been established, if there is any difference of opinion, and one of them wishes to go back on the agreement, then they must submit to the judgment of one of their sisterhood leaders. Usually the punishment is some kind of beating or disgrace. Thus it has become a kind of customary law.
>
> As far as their cohabitation is concerned, though they cannot completely live as man and wife, yet they can actually have the pleasure that men and women do, either through massage and caresses, or through using mechanical aids. This is not a refined account, and it is difficult for a gentleman to speak of it. These women even select descendants, instituting a daughter to succeed to their estate, and later their adopted

daughter will also enter into one of these compacts, as though there were a daughter-in-law, and it is really just as in blood relationships. This is really strange.

Ch'en Tung-yuan attributed the custom to the unsettled economic situation: "To refrain from marrying because of lesbianism is really unnatural, and very harmful to the woman's health, but after the great changes in the circumstances of earning a livelihood, women not getting married at the proper time, and falling into lesbianism, has become much more widespread, and is truly a big problem."

Institutionalized same-sex unions for men were evidently much less widespread, though these are precisely the kinds of unions that one would expect to be least talked about and written about. This is a general problem in the study of many aspects of social life in traditional China. Only a small portion of the people were literate, and the use and contents of literary works were heavily influenced by socio-political factors. It is no accident that the standard histories and other works tend to ignore non-standard social forms and processes, and have very little that is reliable to say about non-elite social life.

This has been acknowledged by historians as a great pity, but not something about which anything could be done. More recently, however, more attention has been paid to the use of such things as short stories and plays as sources of historical material for the study of the "other side" of the traditional society. What little I have found on male-male marriages comes in part from a short story by Li Yu (1611–1679). For our purposes an important aspect of Li's literary philosophy is that he advocated a sort of "literature for the masses." Essays and other standard works were to be kept apart from stories and drama. The former were expected to be profound and even difficult; they were for the literate. The latter, on the contrary, were expected to be clear and simple, since they were intended for the illiterate as well as the literate. Furthermore, Li advocated a kind of realism; an author of plays and stories should stick to colloquial language and to realistic details, avoiding the fantastic and things outside of one's own experience and observation.

One of the stories of Li's collection titled *The Silent Play* (*Wu-sheng Hsi*) is about a young, brilliant, and handsome scholar in P'u-t'ien Hsien, Hsing-hua Prefecture, Fukien, during the late Ming period, named Wei Chi-fang, who married a young boy. Wei had earlier married a woman, who died after giving him a son. Having fulfilled his Confucian duty to provide offspring, he decided to remarry, this time to a young homosexual. The term for "remarriage" used here is *hsu-hsuan,* "to replace the string on one's lute," a common if somewhat literary term for remarriage. After a number of false starts, Wei finally managed to pay a brideprice of 500 taels, the two went through a marriage ceremony, and took up residence as man and "wife."

The background information provided by the author is very interesting. Fukien was said to be a center of homosexuality in China, and such marriages were said to be fairly common, with payment of brideprice:

> In Fukien it happens that homosexuals pay a brideprice, but usually it's no more than symbolic; several tens of taels at most, but sometimes as little as several taels. It is a symbol of entreaty.

> One must understand that with Fukien homosexuals, as in marrying women, first marriages are distinguished from later ones. For a virgin, men are prepared to pay a much higher brideprice, and to carry out a complete and proper wedding ceremony. If, then, one is not strict in controlling young boys, and they are seduced by someone, then they are called "fallen flowers." They do not become completely

worthless, but a buyer will generally be interested only in a casual and temporary relationship, and will not enter into a permanent marriage relationship, and he will not select the boy to come to live with him.

What is of interest is the institutionalization and permanence of such relationships. There is some fragmentary information tending to support Li's claim that there were institutionalized, marriage-like, male homosexual unions in China. A much later writer, Yao Ling-hsi, says

> The term "little brothers" (*hsiung-ti erh*) is the same as the Fukienese "bond younger brother" (*ch'i-ti*). . . . Homosexuals raise them like younger brothers. . . . Fukienese homosexuals consider themselves as brothers.

This term *ch'i*, "contract," "bond," shows up in many "deviant" social transactions. It is used for a kind of adoption found in many areas of China; it was used in connection with the consensual union described above under the term *p'ing-t'ou*. It indicated a kind of consensual union in Taiwan, and Hsu K'o says that "bond brother," *ch'i-ti*, means male prostitute in Cantonese. Indeed, this term (*kai-dai* in Cantonese) is common invective in Hong Kong today, used as a derogatory term for homosexuals.

It seems fairly clear to me, then, that there were at least in late Ming and Ch'ing China institutionalized relationships between males in some areas, and that these relationships were often expressed in terms of marriage and carried out in some of the social forms connected with "regular" marriage. . . .

HUSBANDS, BOYS, SERVANTS

We have a description of an actual ceremony for swearing friendship from the works of the invaluable Li Yu. Two men sacrifice a carp, a rooster, and a duck. They then exchange their exact times of birth, smear each other's mouths with the blood of the victims, and swear eternal loyalty to each other. The ceremony concludes with feasting on the sacrificial victims. Afterward they address each other as older brother (*xiong*) and younger brother (*di*). The similarity of this practice to the Fujianese [Fukienese] custom of male marriage is obvious, with similar terminology and an important ritual component. Li Yu even suggests erotic overtones to the subsequent encounters of these sworn brothers. And yet the Fujianese marriage ceremony went beyond this earlier custom by abandoning the earlier ritual of brotherhood and adopting the language and ceremonies of heterosexual marriage.

According to the terms of the Fujianese male marriage, the younger *qidi* would move into the *qixiong*'s household. There he would be treated as a son-in-law by his husband's parents. Throughout the marriage, many of which lasted for twenty years, the *qixiong* was completely responsible for his younger husband's upkeep. Wealthy *qixiong* even adopted young boys, whom the couple raised as sons. Usually, these marriages would eventually have to be dissolved because of the familial responsibilities of procreation. As a character in the early-Qing-dynasty short story "Chronicle of Sacrificing Love" ("Qing lie ji") rhetorically asks, "In all history when has there ever been a precedent for two men to live out their lives together?" Similarly, in Langxian's short story "Pan Wenzi" from *Shi dian tou*, two young men who decide to live out their lives together go back on their decision just before their respective fiancées are about to pressure them into heterosexual marriage. To men of the late Ming and early Qing, emotional and sexual relationships with other men could be intense and even enduring, yet they could not exclude heterosexuality.

At the end of a male marriage in Fujian [Fukien], the older husband paid the necessary price to acquire a suitable bride for his beloved *qidi*. Shen Defu marveled at the heights of devotion reached by these couples. Star-crossed lovers who encountered difficulties even strode together into the sea to drown in each other's arms. . . .

A Curious Married Couple
THE EDITORS

From Fincher's Trades' Review, *July 25, 1863*

> *This Philadelphia-based journal, directed at emigrant workers from Britain, included this story of an Englishwoman, Mary East, and her wife of thirty-four years. The only catch was that Ms. East was living undercover as one James How. Notice the matter-of-fact tone of the reporting—wry, but certainly not shocked.*

In 1731, a girl named Mary East was engaged to be married to a young man for whom she entertained the strongest affection; but upon his taking to evil courses, or, to tell the whole truth, being hanged for highway robbery, she determined to run no risk of any such disappointment from the opposite sex in future. A female friend of hers having suffered in some similar manner, and being of the like mind with herself, they agreed to pass for the rest of their days as man and wife, in some place where they were not known. The question of which should be the husband was decided by lot in favor of Mary East, who accordingly assumed the masculine habit, and under the name of James How, took a small public house at Epping for himself and consort. Here, and subsequently at other inns, they lived together in good repute with their neighbors for eighteen years—during which neither experienced the least pang of marital jealousy—and realized a considerable sum of money. The supposed James How served all the parish offices without discovery, and was several times a foreman of juries. While occupying the *White Horse* at Poplar, however, his secret was discovered by a woman who had known him in his youth; and from that time the happy couple became the victims of her extortion. First five, then ten, then one hundred pounds were demanded as the price of her silence, and even these bribes were found to be insufficient. At last, however, the persecutor pushed matters too far, and killed the goose that laid such golden eggs. James brought the whole matter before a magistrate, and attired, awkwardly enough, in the proper garments of her sex, herself witnessed against the offender, who was imprisoned for a considerable term. Exposure, however, of course followed upon the trial, and the *White Horse* had to be disposed of, and the landlord and landlady to retire from public life into retirement. After thirty-four years of pretended matrimony, Mrs. How died; the disconsolate widower survived long afterwards, but never again took to himself another spouse. Neither husband nor wife had ever been seen to dress a joint of meat; nor did they give entertainment to their friends like other couples; neither, although in excellent circumstances (having acquired between three and four thousand pounds) did they keep man-servant or maid-servant, but Mary East served the customers and went on errands, while her wife attended solely to the affairs of the house.

A Note on "Woman Marriage" in Dahomey
MELVILLE J. HERSKOVITS

From Africa, *1937, Vol. 10*

A short scholarly note on a widespread practice observed in parts of West Africa in the early part of this century: one wealthy, infertile woman marrying another woman to produce offspring via a surrogate father.

Reports of the occurrence of "woman marriage" in parts of Africa as far distant from one another as northern and southern Nigeria, the Anglo-Egyptian Sudan, and the Union of South Africa indicate the possibility that there may be other instances of this institution that have gone unrecorded. The purpose of this paper is therefore to call attention to this striking phase of social organization by describing the form which "woman marriage" takes in Dahomey, presenting data collected in the field in 1931. In doing this, attention will be paid to such aspects of the social setting in which this kind of marriage is lodged as may be needed to allow it best to be understood, while some of the attitudes which arise from it will also be indicated.

Before proceeding to give the details of Dahomean "marriages" between women, however, the prior accounts may be reproduced in some detail, so that comparisons by the reader may be facilitated. The first quotation to be given, from [anthropologist C. K.] Meek, describes the institution as it exists in northern Nigeria:

> There is a curious and ancient custom found among some of the Yoruba, Yagba, Akoko, Nupe, and Gana-Gana communities—that of a woman going through a regular form of matrimony with other women. In the Osi district a barren woman will formally marry a young girl and hand her over to her husband with a view to bearing children—as Hagar was given by Sarah to Abraham. But a more striking example of this type of marriage is where a wealthy woman, who may or may not be normally married to a man, contracts a marriage with a young girl to whom she subsequently allows a *cicisbeo* to have access, the resultant children belonging to the female "husband." This is a common practice among the Yoruba, Nupe, Akoko, and Gana-Gana, and the female "husband" will even pay men to have connection with her young "wife." In some cases she exacts gifts of farm-service from the *cicisbei*. All the ceremonial of marriage is observed in these marriages of women to women, and a bride-price is even paid to the young girl's father. The usual rules of divorce apply. The legal "husband" can divorce her "wife" and recover her dowry, and if the young girl runs off with a man she can claim the resultant children as her own. The marriage of women to women is not regarded with disfavour, and the chiefs will even consent to their daughters being married in this way. . . .

Dahomean marriages take thirteen different forms. They are divided into two general classes, one called *akwénýsî*, "woman-with-money," comprising those forms where the marriage-dues are paid by the spouse to the bride's father; the other, termed *xadudó*, "friend-custody," where these payments are not made. Expressed in another way, the first class includes those forms of marriage whose resultant offspring are under the control of the father; the second category being composed of those matings where the mother retains control of her children. Interestingly enough, though a woman who "marries" another must make all the payments and perform all the duties required in any marriage of the first class, the spirit of such a marriage is so foreign to what is regarded as normal procedure that every Dahomean with whom the matter of marriage-types was discussed placed this form in the second category rather than the one in which strictly and legally speaking it should belong.

The name given this form of marriage is *gbɔsú dɔ́nɔ́ gbɔsî*, "giving the goat to the buck." It occurs but rarely among commoners, but is frequent in upper class families, particularly among royalty, with girls of commoner or slave status figuring most often as the female mates. It is based directly upon the fact that women sometimes become independently wealthy. . . .

As has been stated, when a woman of means asks and is given a girl from a family other than her own to be her "wife," she supports all the payments and gifts decreed for this form of marriage as though she were a man. She causes a house to be built near her own, and installs the young woman there. She is regarded by the inhabitant of this house as her husband, and is actually called "husband" by her "wife." From among her male acquaintances, or perhaps from among the men of her husband's family, she chooses one to whom she "gives" the young woman she has "married." He is told that the girl is his to live with, that he may come to her as often as he likes, but that he may not take her to his own compound. The man is under no obligations of any sort, either toward the parents of the girl or toward the woman who has given her to him. All the obligations entailed in marriage have been discharged by the "husband" of the girl, while, as for this woman, her recompense is had in the children to be born of her "wife."

It now becomes clear why this type of marriage is given the name it bears. It could not be explained more concisely than in the terms stated by the Dahomeans: "When a goat becomes large, one does not ask which buck has caused her to conceive." . . .

A Normal Man
WALTER L. WILLIAMS

From The Spirit and the Flesh,
by Walter L. Williams, 1986

Here is an account of the astonishingly common same-sex marriages in Native American culture. Notice, however, that some stigma still attached to them, if only in the kidding that often went along with the acquisition of a male "wife."

In 1542, one of the earliest Spanish explorers in Florida, Cabeza de Vaca, reported on his previous five years among the Timucua Indians: "During the time I was thus among these people I saw a devilish thing, and it is that I saw one man married to another." The sources are extremely unsatisfactory in describing these relationships, but the fact that these relationships exist is noted for several tribes, usually by a brief statement saying that the berdache "lived together with a man, as his wife." This was noted as the socially accepted practice for some berdaches among the Ojibwa, Winnebago, Lakota, and Yuma. It was said that the only male homosexual behavior among the Quinault Indians involved those who had relationships with the *keknat-sa'nxwix* ("part woman male").

In a massive survey of northern California Indian cultures conducted in the 1930s, all but one of the groups who recognized a berdache status also recognized his marriage to a "normal man." Next to doing women's work and acting androgynously, sexual behavior with a man is the most commonly noted characteristic of berdache status. This aspect is even more widespread among berdaches than a special ceremonial role.

An ethnographer of the Omahas wrote in the 1880s: "*Min-gu-ga* [*mexoga*] took other men as their husbands. Frank La Fleche knew one such man, who had had several men as his husbands. . . . [They] are publicly known, and do not appear to be despised or to excite disgust." Among the Southern Maidus, a traditionalist informant in the 1920s explained in a respectful manner about *osa'pu:* "They just grew that way, being half-man and half-woman," and in a similar matter-of-fact way said "he lives with a man. . . . No contempt was shown them." The berdache's sexuality is accepted in the same way as his androgyny; both are seen as reflections of his spirit, his basic nature. . . .

Marriage between a berdache and a man existed in the context of the general position of marriage in aboriginal American Indian society. Although wide ranges of activities are open for both women and men, there is in most Native American societies a basic division of labor into two halves. This is usually referred to as a "division of labor by sex." By dividing the necessary tasks into "men's work" and "women's work," each person has to learn only half of the jobs available. This is important to small-scale societies that do not have much role specialization. It is, however, more accurate to call this pattern a division of labor by *gender*, because people can take on a gender role that is divergent from their genital sex.

Within a marriage in a gender-divided economy, there can be only two roles: husband and wife. The sex of the person who takes these roles may vary, but the roles generally do not. This is an additional reason that two berdaches would not marry, and two masculine men would not marry. Masculine men might have sex, which is their private business, but marriage is a public matter and an economic concern.

Each person has something to gain by entering a marriage. They gain the expertise of the other in tasks that are different from their own skills. Why should two hunters marry, if neither of them is good at gathering plants? The closest exception to this rule is among the Navajos. When *nadle* marry, they dress like men. A Navajo informant explains, "If they marry men, it is just like two men working together." Yet it must be remembered that *nadle* also do women's work, so such a marriage is still viable. Economically, the husband has both a wife and a husband, which partly explains the reputation these marriages have for economic success.

When people get married, they gain another advantage: the economic security that comes with a wider circle of relatives. Nothing is worse in a kin-based society than to be without kin. Marriage creates an alliance of families, whereby one has twice as many relatives on which to draw for support. In the context of a subsistence economy, with a division of labor by gender, it makes sense that such an economy would be family centered. Families provide extra productive labor and take care of the aged.

Marriages between men and berdaches fit into this pattern. In such a marriage, the man takes the husband role, and the berdache takes the wife role. Recognizing the fluidity of women's and men's roles and the mixed-gender status of the berdache means that there can be considerable variation from this simply stated dichotomy. The Navajo example just cited illustrates the variation in spousal relationships and the mixed-gender status of *nadle*.

In a marriage between a man and a berdache, the berdache supplies women's work and a network of kin, like any other wife. Lakota chief Crazy Horse, for example, had one or two *winktes* for wives, along with his female wives. A berdache wife offered the same economic advantages of any other polygynous marriage. While it is true that a berdache cannot reproduce, many of the reports of such marriages mention that the husband already had children, either through a previous marriage or by taking a berdache as a second or third wife. But with adoption being so commonly accepted, children may even be gained by the berdache. Thus, the same advantages of heterosexual marriage also accrue to the man who marries a berdache.

The two roles of husband and berdache are not to be confused. After I had been living in the household of a well-known *winkte* on a particular reservation for a while, a medicine man told me in private, "People say———is a 'he-she' and you must be his lover." They did not say I was a "he-she," because he was clearly the androgynous one. Personal character and gender role, not sexual behavior per se, distinguish the *winkte* role.

S exual behavior of berdaches is often considered a serious reflection of their spiritual natures. But for other people, it can be an object of humor. . . .

Kidding is often directed more toward the husbands than toward berdaches themselves. According to a Crow berdache, "If a Crow man moved in with me, other men would tease him. They wouldn't tease me, because they all know what I am." The joking toward the husband could also be due to the reputation that berdaches have for being highly productive workers. Since the berdaches are very good providers, a Crow traditionalist pointed out to me, and give many gifts to their boyfriends, the man could get a reputation for being lazy. One of the common taunts that Plains Indians might aim at the husband of the berdache is that he wants a wife who not only keeps house but hunts for him as well.

Why would a man go against all this teasing and marry a berdache anyway? Most of the early ethnographers who interviewed berdaches never asked this question. When I have asked Indians this, I get a mere shrug of the shoulders and a vague statement like "I don't know, he just wants to do it." Mohaves attribute the ability of an *alyha* to attract a man to their shamanistic powers of love magic. More concretely, they consider *alyha* to be lucky, and their luck extends to their husband. Such beliefs can predispose some men to marry berdaches.

This belief is realistic, in the sense that a husband benefits from the much-publicized prosperity of a berdache household. Among the Hidatsa, for example, berdaches did all the work that women did for their husbands. Yet beyond this, they were noted as being stronger than women, and never burdened with pregnancy or nursing an infant. Hidatsa statements from the 1930s tell of berdaches working harder than the average wife and exceeding the usual productivity of women in many activities. This was the reason given for chiefs and other prominent men among the California Mission Indians wanting to marry *cuit, uluqui,* or *coia.* A *lhamana* that Matilda Coxe Stevenson knew at Zuni was one of the richest persons of the pueblo. In the 1880s he "allied himself to a man" and until the time when Stevenson left the pueblo in 1897 "this couple were living together, and they were two of the hardest workers in the pueblo and among the most prosperous."

Another reason for a man to be attracted to marriage with a berdache has to do with marital stability. In contrast to Western notions of feminine "nest building" and masculine promiscuity, among the Mohaves the stereotypes are reversed. Young women are known for their licentious habits and their disinclination to stick with one man for long. Men, who more likely crave a stable home, will often turn to an older woman or an *alyha*. . . .

Traditionally, Lakota culture accepted the *winkte* only as a secondary spouse, to be married after a man already had a female wife and children. Since Lakotas no longer have plural marriages, if a man takes a *winkte* for a spouse that means there would be no heterosexual marriage and progeny. A way to discourage this exclusive homosexuality on the part of men is to make them an object of laughter. The berdache is exempt from the kidding because he is not seen as a man. The culture, after all, is not objecting to the homosexual behavior. If a man wishes to have sexual relations with a berdache, there is no objection among the Lakotas as long as he does not settle into a permanent relationship. What society objects to is behavior that might prevent reproduction. Still, despite this discouragement, some men will go against the norm and marry a berdache.

The laughter among the Mohaves is a case in point. Any kind of sexual matter is an occasion for humor among them, but the jokes about the husband of the *alyha* fly so thick around him that many of the men will eventually leave the berdache. Despite the fact that the berdache provides a stable home and is more likely to be faithful than a female wife, such marriages are not stable. Rather than see the laughter as a condemnation of homosexuality, we should understand it as a balancing mechanism. With all the advantages that marriage with an *alyha* offers for Mohave men (prosperity, stability, luck, sex), if there were not some disadvantages then too many men might marry berdaches and the population growth might be threatened. But by keeping the majority of male marriages short-term, the joking ensures that most men mate with women at some point and have children.

Other cultures accomplish this same goal by restricting male marriages to those men who have already had children. Thus, it is only acceptable for a berdache to become a second or third wife in a polygynous family where the female wife has already reproduced. Among the Hidatsas, berdaches usually marry older men who are beyond their childbearing years. None of these patterns of marriage threatens the reproduction of the population.

The Zapotecs are typical of a culture in which men customarily marry a berdache only after they have married women and produced children. While boys may participate in homosexual behavior before their marriage, by the time Zapotec men are thirty years old almost all of them (not including berdaches, of course) marry women and have children. Yet it is not uncommon for men to leave a heterosexual marriage after a time. According to ethnographer Beverly Chiñas, "A middle-aged man with a grown family may leave his wife and move in with a male lover and generally this scarcely raises an eyebrow. Over the nearly two decades since my fieldwork began several prominent citizens with grown children have left their heterosexual mates to live with same-sex lovers." One case involved a former mayor of the town. People might talk about this for a little while, but they soon adapt to the change in the same way they would to a new heterosexual pairing after a divorce. There is no ostracism of a same-sex couple.

In the case of a wife's death, berdaches will be praised for stepping in to rescue a family. Among the Zapotecs a famous case occurred when a man's wife died while their several children were still young. The man married a *muxe* who became a substitute mother. The berdache cooked, laundered clothes, and did the shopping for the family. Other Zapotecs admired the *muxe* greatly for the sacrifices he made, saying "every one of those children got an education and was sent to school clean and well-fed." He and the widower lived together as a respected couple, until the *muxe*'s death many years later. Zapotecs judged him by his sacrifices for the children, rather than by his sexual behavior. . . .

A Comparative Analysis of Same-Sex Partnership Protections

DEBORAH M. HENSON

From the International Journal of Law and the Family 7 *(1993), 282–313*

Nowhere in the world is same-sex marriage legal. Here's a description of the closest approximations yet: in Denmark and Sweden.

On 7 June 1989, the Danish Parliament passed a bill entitled the Act of Registration of Partnership legalizing homosexual relationships with a 71–47 (and five abstentions) vote in the Danish Folketing after forty years of campaigning by gay rights advocates. This legislation is the first of its kind to grant homosexual couples the legal status comparable to married couples—with the exception of adoption and custody rights. The new law provides for "registered partnerships" which give each partner the same rights to inheritance, tax deductions, social service entitlements as married partners have, in addition to mandating similar obligations as well: tax liabilities and partner support upon separation. Although the statute does not call the partnership a marriage, and gay couples cannot marry in the Danish People's Church (Evangelical Lutheran), partners who choose to dissolve their relationships must undertake divorce proceedings. Some gay rights advocates, particularly lesbians, are not completely satisfied with the new law because it precludes registered partners from adopting a child or obtaining joint custody in the event of divorce.

This legislation followed the work of a Commission, mandated by Parliament in 1984, to study the situation of homosexuals in Denmark. The scope of the study was delineated by Parliament as follows:

> As it is recognized that homosexuals ought to be able to live and participate in society according to their identity, and that this opportunity is not sufficiently open to homosexuals at present, the Commission will assemble and present scientific documentation regarding the life of homosexuals and sponsor research designed to produce evidence regarding the juridical, social and cultural situation of homosexuals. In furtherance of these objectives, the Commission will put forward proposals for measures for removing existing discrimination against homosexuals within all sectors of society and also for improving their position, including proposals regarding conditions relevant to their permanent cohabitation.

The Parliament also instructed the Commission to consider the proposals regarding unmarried heterosexual cohabitants made by the Matrimonial Law Reform Commission, as well as current developments in other Scandinavian countries.

The Commission released its report in 1988 and recommended the current bill for registering homosexual partnerships. The debate in Parliament over the proposed measure was "extensive and passionate," but the bill passed and became effective on 1 October 1989. The Commission's primary goal was to investigate the status of homosexuals in Denmark and to remove discrimination against them. In addition to granting that the registration of partnerships provides for the same legal consequences as marriage, except where otherwise specified, the Act also allows registered partners to be included whenever Danish law refers to "marriage" or "spouse." If the terms in a given statute are "husband" or "wife," however, registered partners are not included in the coverage. And international treaties' provisions for spouses will not apply to registered partners unless the contracting parties agree to such an inclusion.

This vanguard legislation was an evolutionary outgrowth of many years of tolerance for unmarried cohabitation in Denmark and in the Scandinavian countries in general. In 1988, heterosexual cohabitation comprised approximately twenty percent of all couples. The Matrimonial Law Reform Commission of 1969 issued its report in 1983 and characterized marriage as "the best juridical frame for the family and the best security, socially, emotionally, and economically for individual members of the family." . . .

At present, Sweden is the only other country which has some form of protective national legislation for lesbian and gay couples. Theirs is not the marriage-like institution, but rather the establishment of a property regime and some limited inheritance provisions for same-sex couples on par with other unmarried heterosexual cohabitants. The history of the legislation demonstrates the typical process of balancing political agendas. About a decade ago, the Swedish Government appointed a Commission which in 1984 recommended that homosexual cohabitees be granted the same status as unmarried heterosexual cohabitants. The Commission noted that the reason for not recommending that homosexuals have the right to marry was a concession to public opinion. The Commission's report also recommended that the Swedish Instrument of Government, which protects fundamental rights, should be amended to prohibit discrimination against homosexuals. That recommendation also was not adopted.

Although the Swedish Parliament could not go as far as the Commission recommended, it did enact comprehensive legislation for heterosexual and homosexual cohabitants. With its passage in 1987, the Cohabitees (Joint Homes) Act extended the legal rights of heterosexual partners, thereby narrowing the gap between married and unmarried couples. During the same session, the Homosexual Cohabitees Act was enacted which expressly applies the Cohabitees (Joint Homes) Act, as well as certain other statutes, to lesbian and gay couples.

This legislation provides for *inter vivos* or *mortis causa* distribution of a joint home and to household goods and furnishings, as long as both have been acquired for joint use by the couple. Additionally, the Act restricts alienation, lease, sale, and mortgage of the property to joint consent, or if that consent is not possible, then by court order. The inheritance aspects of this law operate essentially to create a forced portion for the surviving cohabitant, but concern only the joint dwelling and household goods. Couples may opt out of the provisions of the Act by written contract. Thus, in Sweden, somewhat differently than in Denmark, homosexual couples' protections mirrored the expanded legal protections granted to heterosexual cohabitants. Egalitarianism and general moral tolerance are important principles in this Social Democratic country, as evidenced, in part, by the Swedish Parliament's recognition of homosexuality in 1973: "[H]omosexuality is from society's point of view a fully acceptable way of living together."

CHAPTER TWO

In God's Name?
THE RELIGIOUS WAR CONTINUES

Although much of the current debate about same-sex marriage concerns the civil and secular, it cannot help but invoke the religious and the sacred. By far the most powerful organization involved in the same-sex marriage fight is the Christian Coalition, which bases its opposition primarily on religious and scriptural grounds. Presented here are those very biblical injunctions—from Genesis, Leviticus, and Paul—and the Catholic bishops' defense of traditional notions of the meaning of marriage and family. Here, too, are modern, secular defenses of the Scriptures and the position of the church, from Dennis Prager's account of the Judeo-Christian prohibitions on homosexuality to Jean Bethke Elshtain's natural law–based concerns about same-sex marriage.

Much has now also been written from an explicitly Christian and Jewish perspective in defense of same-sex marriages: Bishop

John Shelby Spong's and Rabbi Yoel Kahn's are among the most powerful arguments that now exist. And the refusal of many lesbian and gay people of faith to acquiesce in being excluded from their religious traditions is one of the more remarkable phenomena now driving the debate forward. This chapter can provide, alas, only a flavor of the thinking and praying that is now taking place in congregations across the West.

The Holy Bible
The King James Version

Translations, interpretations, and inferences disagree about the meanings of these passages. Note, for example, how the prohibition against homosexual intercourse in Leviticus is in the same chapter as prohibitions on incest and failing to keep kosher dietary laws. But here are the biblical texts at the center of the controversy, in the most gripping English translation ever printed. Judge for yourself.

GENESIS 2: 18–24

And the LORD God said, *It is* not good that the man should be alone; I will make him an help meet for him.

And out of the ground the LORD God formed every beast of the field, and every fowl of the air; and brought *them* unto Adam to see what he would call them: and whatsoever Adam called every living creature, that *was* the name thereof.

And Adam gave names to all cattle, and to the fowl of the air, and to every beast of the field; but for Adam there was not found an help meet for him.

And the LORD God caused a deep sleep to fall upon Adam, and he slept: and he took one of his ribs, and closed up the flesh instead thereof;

And the rib, which the LORD God had taken from man, made he a woman, and brought her unto the man.

And Adam said, This *is* now bone of my bones, and flesh of my flesh: she shall be called Woman, because she was taken out of Man.

Therefore shall a man leave his father and his mother, and shall cleave unto his wife: and they shall be one flesh.

LEVITICUS 20: 7–16; 22–27

Sanctify yourselves therefore, and be ye holy: for I *am* the LORD your God.

And ye shall keep my statutes, and do them: I *am* the LORD which sanctify you.

For every one that curseth his father or his mother shall be surely put to death: he hath cursed his father or his mother; his blood *shall be* upon him.

And the man that committeth adultery with *another* man's wife, *even he* that committeth adultery with his neighbour's wife, the adulterer and the adulteress shall surely be put to death.

And the man that lieth with his father's wife hath uncovered his father's nakedness: both of them shall surely be put to death; their blood *shall be* upon them.

And if a man lie with his daughter in law, both of them shall surely be put to death: they have wrought confusion; their blood *shall be* upon them.

If a man also lie with mankind, as he lieth with a woman, both of them have committed an abomination: they shall surely be put to death; their blood *shall be* upon them.

And if a man take a wife and her mother, it *is* wickedness: they shall be burnt with fire, both he and they; that there be no wickedness among you.

And if a man lie with a beast, he shall surely be put to death: and ye shall slay the beast.

And if a woman approach unto any beast, and lie down thereto, thou shalt kill the woman, and the beast: they shall surely be put to death; their blood *shall be* upon them. . . .

Ye shall therefore keep all my statutes, and all my judgments, and do them: that the land, whither I bring you to dwell therein, spue you not out.

And ye shall not walk in the manners of the nation, which I cast out before you: for they committed all these things, and therefore I abhorred them.

But I have said unto you, Ye shall inherit their land, and I will give it unto you to possess it, a land that floweth with milk and honey: I *am* the LORD your God, which have separated you from *other* people.

Ye shall therefore put difference between clean beasts and unclean, and between unclean fowls and clean: and ye shall not make your souls abominable by beast, or by fowl, or by any manner of living thing that creepeth on the ground, which I have separated from you as unclean.

And ye shall be holy unto me: for I the LORD *am* holy, and have severed you from *other* people, that ye should be mine.

A man also or woman that hath a familiar spirit, or that is a wizard, shall surely be put to death: they shall stone them with stones: their blood *shall be* upon them.

THE EPISTLE OF PAUL THE APOSTLE TO THE ROMANS 1: 18–19; 22–32

For the wrath of God is revealed from heaven against all ungodliness and unrighteousness of men, who hold the truth in unrighteousness;

Because that which may be known of God is manifest in them; for Goth hath shewed *it* unto them. . . .

Professing themselves to be wise, they became fools,

And changed the glory of the uncorruptible God into an image made like to corruptible man, and to birds, and four-footed beasts, and creeping things.

Wherefore God also gave them up to uncleanness through the lusts of their own hearts, to dishonour their own bodies between themselves:

Who changed the truth of God into a lie, and worshipped and served the creature more than the Creator, who is blessed for ever. Ă-mĕn.

For this cause God gave them up unto vile affections: for even their women did change the natural use into that which is against nature:

And likewise also the men, leaving the natural use of the woman, burned in their lust one toward another; men with men working that which is unseemly, and receiving in themselves that recompence of their error which was meet.

And even as they did not like to retain God in *their* knowledge, God gave them over to a reprobate mind, to do those things which are not convenient;

Being filled with all unrighteousness, fornication, wickedness, covetousness, maliciousness; full of envy, murder, debate, deceit, malignity; whisperers,

Backbiters, haters of God, despiteful, proud, boasters, inventors of evil things, disobedient to parents,

Without understanding, convenantbreakers, without natural affection, implacable, unmerciful;

Who knowing the judgment of God, that they which commit such things are worthy of death, not only do the same, but have pleasure in them that do them.

1 CORINTHIANS 6: 1–3; 7–11

Dare any of you, having a matter against another, go to law before the unjust, and not before the saints?

Do ye not know that the saints shall judge the world? and if the world shall be judged by you, are ye unworthy to judge the smallest matters?

Know ye not that we shall judge angels? how much more things that pertain to this life? . . .

Now therefore there is utterly a fault among you, because ye go to law one with another. Why do ye not rather take wrong? why do ye not rather *suffer yourselves to* be defrauded?

Nay, ye do wrong, and defraud, and that *your* brethren.

Know ye not that the unrighteousness shall not inherit the kingdom of God? Be not deceived neither fornicators, nor idolators, nor adulterers, nor effeminate, nor abusers of themselves with mankind,

Nor thieves, nor covetous, nor drunkards, nor revilers, nor extortioners, shall inherit the kingdom of God.

And such were some of you: but ye are washed, but ye are sanctified, but ye are justified in the name of the Lord Jesus, and by the Spirit of our God. . . .

Statement on Same-Sex Marriage

REV. JOSEPH L. CHARRON AND REV. WILLIAM S. SKYLSTAD

for the National Conference of Catholic Bishops, July 19, 1996

The essential Roman Catholic position.

The Roman Catholic Church believes that marriage is a faithful, exclusive, and lifelong union between one man and one woman, joined as husband and wife in an intimate partnership of life and love. This union was established by God with its own proper laws. By reason of its very nature, therefore, marriage exists for the mutual love and support of the spouses and for the procreation and education of children. These two purposes, the unitive and the procreative, are equal and inseparable. The institution of marriage has a very important relationship to the continuation of the human race, to the total development of the human person, and to the dignity, stability, peace, and prosperity of the family and of society.

Furthermore, we believe the natural institution of marriage has been blessed and elevated by Christ to the dignity of a sacrament. This means that Christian marriage is more than a contract. Because they are married in the Lord, the spouses acquire a special relationship to each other and to society. Their love becomes a living image of the manner in which the Lord personally loves his people and is united with them. Living a Christian sacramental marriage becomes their fundamental way of attaining salvation.

Because the marital relationship offers benefits, unlike any other, to persons, to society, and to the church, we wish to make it clear that the institution of marriage, as the union of one man and one woman, must be preserved, protected, and promoted in both private and public realms. At a time when family life is under significant stress, the principled defense of marriage is an urgent necessity for the wellbeing of children and families, and for the common good of society.

Thus, we oppose attempts to grant the legal status of marriage to a relationship between persons of the same sex. No same-sex union can realize the unique and full potential which the marital relationship expresses. For this reason, our opposition to "same-sex marriage" is not an instance of unjust discrimination or animosity toward homosexual persons. In fact, the Catholic Church teaches emphatically that individuals and society must respect the basic human dignity of all persons, including those with a homosexual orientation. Homosexual persons have a right to and deserve our respect, compassion, understanding, and defense against bigotry, attacks, and abuse.

We therefore urge Catholics and all our fellow citizens to

commit themselves both to upholding the human dignity of every person and to upholding the distinct and irreplaceable community of marriage.

Marriage's True Ends
THE EDITORS

From Commonweal *May 17, 1996*

Against Gay Marriage
JEAN BETHKE ELSHTAIN

From Commonweal, *October 22, 1991*

Why, for Catholics, procreation cannot be completely divorced from the true meaning of marriage—and why same-sex marriage is therefore unacceptable. Two complementary pieces from the generally liberal American Catholic magazine Commonweal.

MARRIAGE'S TRUE ENDS

Should marriage be essentially a contractual arrangement between two individuals to be defined as they see fit? Or does marriage recognize and embody larger shared meanings that cannot be lightly divorced from history, society, and nature—shared meanings and social forms that create the conditions in which individuals can achieve their own fulfillment? Popular acceptance of premarital sex and cohabitation gives us some sense of the moral and social trajectory involved. Both developments were welcomed as expressions of greater honesty and even better preparations for marriage. Yet considerable evidence now suggests that these newfound "freedoms" have contributed to the instability and trivialization of marriage itself, and have not borne the promises once made for them of happier lives. Similarly, elevating same-sex unions to the same moral and legal status as marriage will further throw into doubt marriage's fundamental purposes and put at risk a social practice and moral ideal vital to all.

The heterosexual exclusivity of marriage can be defended in the same way social policy rightly shows a preference for the formation of intact two-parent families. In both cases, a normative definition of family life is indispensable to any coherent and effective public action. Certainly mutual love and care are to be encouraged wherever possible. But the justification and rationale for marriage as a social institution cannot rest on the goods of companionship alone. Resisting such a reductionist understanding is not merely in the interests of heterosexuals. There are profound social goods at stake in holding together the biological, relational, and procreative dimensions of human love.

"There are countless ways to 'have' a child," writes theologian Gilbert Meilaender of the social consequences and human meaning of procreation (*Body, Soul, & Bioethics,* University of Notre Dame Press, 1996). "Not all of them amount to doing the same thing. Not all of them will teach us to discern the equal humanity of the child as one who is not our product but, rather, the natural development of shared love, like to us in dignity. . . . To conceive, bear, give birth to, and rear a child ought to be an affirmation and a recognition: affirmation of the good of life that we ourselves were given; recognition that this life bears its own creative power to which we should be faithful."

Is there really any doubt that in tying sexual attraction to love and love to children and the creation of families, marriage fundamentally shapes our ideas of human dignity and the nature of society? Same-sex marriage, whatever its virtues, would narrow that frame and foreshorten our perspective. Marriage, at its best, tutors us as no other experience can in the given nature of human life and the acceptance of responsibilities we have not willed or chosen. Indeed, it should tutor us in respect for the given nature of homosexuality and the dignity of homosexual persons. With this respect comes a recognition of difference—a difference with real consequences.

Still, it is frequently objected that if the state does not deny sterile or older heterosexual couples the right to marry, how can it deny that right to homosexual couples, many of whom are already rearing children?

Exceptions do not invalidate a norm or the necessity of norms. How some individuals make use of marriage, either volitionally or as the result of some incapacity, does not determine the purpose of that institution. In that context, heterosexual sterility does not contradict the meaning of marriage in the way same-sex unions would. If marriage as a social form is first a procreative bond in the sense that Meilaender outlines, then marriage necessarily presupposes sexual differentiation, for human procreation itself presupposes sexual differentiation. We are all the offspring of a man and a woman, and marriage is the necessary moral and social response to that natural human condition. Consequently, sexual differentiation, even in the absence of the capacity to procreate, conforms to marriage's larger design in a way same-sex unions cannot. For this reason sexual differentiation is marriage's defining boundary, for it is the precondition of marriage's true ends.

AGAINST GAY MARRIAGE

Every society embraces an image of a body politic. This complex symbolism incorporates visions and reflections on who is inside and who is outside; on what counts as order and disorder; on what is cherished and what is despised. This imagery is fluid but not, I will argue, entirely up for grabs. For without some continuity in our imagery and concern, we confront a deepening nihilism. In a world of ever-more transgressive enthusiasms, the individual—the self—is more, not less, in thrall to whatever may be the reigning ethos. Ours is a culture whose reigning ethic is surely individualism and freedom. Great and good things have come from this stress on freedom and from the insistence that there are things that cannot and must not be done for me and to me in the name of some overarching collective. It is, therefore, unsurprising that anything that comes before us in the name of "rights" and "freedom" enjoys a *prima facie* power, something akin to political grace.

But perhaps we have reached the breaking point. When Madonna proclaims, in all sincerity, that mock masturbation before tens of thousands is "freedom of expression" on a par, presumably, with the right to petition, assemble, and protest, something seems a bit out of whack—distorted, quirky, not-quite-right. I thought about this sort of thing a lot when I listened to the stories of the "Mothers of the Disappeared" in Argentina and to their invocation of the language of "human rights" as a fundamental immunity—the right not to be tortured and "disappeared." I don't believe there is a slippery slope from queasiness at, if not repudiation of, public sexual acts for profit, orchestrated masturbation, say, and putting free speech as a fundamental right of free citizens in peril. I don't think the body politic has to be nude and sexually voracious—getting, consuming, demanding pleasure. That is a symbolism that courts nihilism and privatism (however publicly it may be trumpeted) because it repudiates intergenerational, familial, and communal contexts and believes history and tradition are useful only to be trashed. Our culture panders to what social critic John O'Neill calls the "libidinal body," the body that titillates and ravishes and is best embodied as young, thin, antimaternal, calculating, and disconnected. Make no mistake about it: much of the move to imagery of the entitled self and the aspirations to which it gives rise are specifically, deeply, and troublingly antinatal—hostile to the regenerative female body and to the symbolism of social regeneration to which this body is necessarily linked and has, historically, given rise.

Don't get me wrong: not every female body must be a regenerative body. At stake here is not mandating and coercing the lives of individuals but pondering the fate of a society that, more and more, repudiates generativity as an animating image in favor of aspiration without limit of the contractual and "wanting" self. One symbol and reality of the latter is the search for intrusive intervention in human reproducing coming from those able to command the resources of genetic engineers and medical reproduction experts, also, therefore, those who have more clout over what gets lifted up as our culture's dominant sense of itself. One finds more and more the demand that babies can and must be made whenever the want is there. This demandingness, this transformation of human procreation into a technical operation, promotes a project Oliver O'Donovan calls "scientific self-transcendence." The technologizing of birth is antiregenerative, linked as it is to a refusal to accept any natural limits. What technology "can do," and the law permits, we seem ready to embrace. Our ethics rushes to catch up with the rampant rush of our forged and incited desires.

These brief reflections are needed to frame my equally brief comments on the legality, or not, of homosexual marriage. I have long favored domestic partnership possibilities—ways to regularize and stabilize commitments and relationships. But marriage is not, and never has been, primarily about two people—it is and always has been about the possibility of generativity. Although in any given instance, a marriage might not have led to the raising of a family, whether through choice or often unhappy recognition of, and final reconciliation to, the infertility of one or another spouse, the symbolism of marriage-family as social regenesis is fused in our centuries-old experience with marriage ritual, regulation, and persistence.

The point of criticism and contentions runs: in defending the family as framed within a horizon of intergenerationality, one privileges a restrictive ideal of sexual and intimate relations. There are within our society, as I already noted, those who believe this society can and should stay equally open to all alternative arrangements, treating "life-styles" as so many identical peas in a pod. To be sure, families in modernity coexist with those who live another way, whether heterosexual and homosexual unions that are by choice or by definition childless; communalists who diminish individual parental authority in favor of the preeminence of the group; and so on.

But the recognition and acceptance of plural possibilities does not mean each alternative is equal to every other with reference to specific social goods. No social order has ever existed that did not endorse certain activities and practices as preferable to others. Ethically responsible challenges to our terms of exclusion and inclusion push toward a loosening but not a wholesale negation in our normative endorsement of intergenerational family life. Those excluded by, or who exclude themselves from, the familial intergenerational ideal, should not be denied social space for their own practices. And it is possible that if what were at stake were, say, seeking out and identifying those creations of self that enhance an aesthetic construction of life and sensibility, the romantic bohemian or rebel would get higher marks than the Smith family of Remont, Nebraska. Nevertheless, we should be cautious about going too far in the direction of a wholly untrammeled pluralism lest we become so vapid that we are no longer capable of distinguishing between the moral weightiness of, say, polishing one's Porsche and sitting up all night with an ill child. The intergenerational family, as symbolism of social regenesis, as tough and compelling reality, as defining moral norm, remains central and critical in nurturing recognitions of human frailty, mortality, and finitude and in inculcating moral limits and constraints. To resolve the untidiness of our public and private relations by either reaffirming and unambiguously a set of unitary, authoritative norms or eliminating all such norms as arbitrary is to jeopardize the social goods that democratic and familial authority, paradoxical in relation to one another, promise—to men and women as parents and citizens and to their children.

Homosexuality, the Bible, and Us—
A Jewish Perspective

DENNIS PRAGER

From Volume 6, no. 2 of Ultimate Issues
April–June, 1990

*A conservative talk-show host and popular Jewish intellectual
wrestles with why modern Jews should not dispense with ancient injunctions—in a leading neoconservative journal.*

... The Hebrew Bible, in particular the Torah (the first five
books of the Bible), has done more to civilize the world than any
other book or idea in history. It is the Hebrew Bible that gave
humanity such ideas as a universal, moral, loving God; ethical
obligations to this God; the need for history to move forward to
moral and spiritual redemption; the belief that history has meaning; and the notion that human freedom and social justice are
the divinely desired states for all people. It gave the world the
Ten Commandments and ethical monotheism.

Therefore, when this Bible makes strong moral procla-
mations, I listen with great respect. And regarding male homosexuality—female homosexuality is not mentioned—this Bible
speaks in such clear and direct language that one does not have
to be a religious fundamentalist in order to be influenced by its
views. All that is necessary is to consider oneself a serious Jew or
Christian.

Jews or Christians who take the Bible's views on homosexuality seriously are not obligated to prove that they are not funda-
mentalists or literalists, let alone bigots (though people have

used the Bible to defend bigotry). The onus is on those who view homosexuality as compatible with Judaism or Christianity to reconcile this view with their Bible.

Given the unambiguous nature of the biblical attitude toward homosexuality, however, such a reconciliation is not possible. All that is possible is to declare: "I am aware that the Bible condemns homosexuality, and I consider the Bible wrong." That would be an intellectually honest approach.

But this approach leads to another problem. If one chooses which of the Bible's moral values to take seriously (and the Bible states its prohibition of homosexuality not only as a law, but as a value—"it is an abomination"), of what moral use is the Bible?

Advocates of religious acceptance of homosexuality respond that while the Bible is morally advanced in some areas, it is morally regressive in others. Its condemnation of homosexuality is cited as one example, and the Torah's acceptance of slavery as another.

Far from being immoral, however, the Torah's prohibition of homosexuality was a major part of its liberation of the human being from the bonds of unrestrained sexuality and of women from being peripheral to men's lives.

As for slavery, while the Bible declares homosexuality wrong, it never declares slavery good. If it did, I would have to reject the Bible as a document with moral relevance to our times. With its notion of every human being created in God's image and with its central event being liberation from slavery, it was the Torah which first taught humanity that slavery is wrong. The Torah's laws regarding slavery exist not to perpetuate it, but to humanize it. And within Jewish life, these laws worked. Furthermore, the slavery that is discussed in the Torah bears no resemblance to black slavery or other instances with which we are familiar. Such slavery, which includes the kidnapping of utterly innocent people, was prohibited by the Torah.

Another argument advanced by advocates of religious acceptance of homosexuality is that the Bible prescribes the death penalty for a multitude of sins, including such seemingly inconsequential acts as gathering wood on the Sabbath. Since we no longer condemn people who violate the Sabbath, why continue to condemn people who engage in homosexual acts?

The answer is that we do not derive our approach toward homosexuality only from the fact that the Torah made it a capital offense. We learn it from the fact that the Bible *makes a moral statement* about homosexuality. It makes no such statement about gathering wood on the Sabbath. The Torah uses its strongest term of disapprobation, "abomination," to describe homosexuality. It is the Bible's moral evaluation of homosexuality that distinguishes homosexuality from other offenses, capital or otherwise. As Professor Greenberg, who betrays no inclination toward religious belief, writes, "When the word *toevah* ("abomination") does appear in the Hebrew Bible, it is sometimes applied to idolatry, cult prostitution, magic, or divination, and is sometimes used more generally. *It always conveys great repugnance"* [emphasis added].

Moreover, it lists homosexuality together with child sacrifice among the "abominations" practiced by the peoples living in the land about to be conquered by the Jews. The two are certainly not morally equatable, but they both characterized the morally primitive world that Judaism opposed. They both characterized a way of life opposite to the one that God demanded of Jews (and even of non-Jews—homosexuality is among the sexual offenses that is covered by one of the "seven laws of the children of Noah" which Judaism holds all people must observe).

Finally, the Bible adds a unique threat to the Jews if they engage in homosexuality and the other offenses of the Canaanites: "You will be vomited out of the land" just as the non-Jews who practice these things were vomited out of the land. Again, as

Greenberg notes, this threat "suggests that the offenses were considered serious indeed."

It is impossible for Judaism to make peace with homosexuality, because homosexuality denies many of Judaism's most fundamental values. It denies life; it denies God's expressed desire that men and women cohabit; and it denies the root structure that the Bible prescribes for all mankind, the family.

If one can speak of Judaism's essence, it is contained in the Torah statement, "I have set before you life and death, the blessing and the curse, and you shall choose life." Judaism affirms whatever enhances life, and it opposes or separates whatever represents death. Thus, meat (death) is separated from milk (life); menstruation (death) is separated from sexual intercourse (life); carnivorous animals (death) are separated from vegetarian, kosher animals (life). This is probably why the Torah juxtaposes child sacrifice with male homosexuality. Though they are not morally analogous, both represent death: One deprives children of life, the other prevents their having life.

God's first declaration about man (the human being generally, and the male specifically) is, "It is not good for man to be alone." Now, presumably, in order to solve the problem of man's aloneness, God could have made another man, or even a community of men. However, God solved man's aloneness by creating one other person, a woman—not a man, not a few women, not a community of men and women. Man's solitude was not a function of his not being with other people; it was a function of his being without a woman.

Of course, Judaism also holds that women need men. But both the Torah statement and Jewish law have been more adamant about men marrying than about women marrying. Judaism is worried about what happens to men and to society when men do not channel their drives into marriage. In this regard, the Torah and Judaism were highly prescient: The overwhelming majority of violent crimes are committed by unmarried men.

In order to become fully human, male and female must join. In the words of Genesis, "God created the human . . . male and female He created them." The union of male and female is not merely some lovely ideal; it is the essence of the biblical outlook on becoming human. To deny it is tantamount to denying a primary purpose of life. . . .

Judaism has a sexual ideal—marital sex. All other forms of sexual behavior, though not equally wrong, deviate from that ideal. The further they deviate, the stronger Judaism's antipathy. Thus there are varying degrees of sexual wrongs. There is, one could say, a continuum of wrong which goes from premarital sex, to adultery, and on to homosexuality, incest, and bestiality.

We can better understand why Judaism rejects homosexuality by understanding its attitudes toward these other unacceptable practices. For example, if a Jew were to argue that never marrying is as equally valid a lifestyle as marrying, normative Judaism would forcefully reject this claim. Judaism states that a life without marrying is a less holy, less complete, and a less Jewish life. Thus, only married men were allowed to be high priests, and only men who had children could sit as judges on the Jewish supreme court, the Sanhedrin.

To put it in modern terms, while an unmarried rabbi can be the spiritual leader of a congregation, he would be dismissed by almost any congregation if he publicly argued that remaining single is as Jewishly valid a way of life as married life.

Despite all this, no Jew could argue that single Jews must be ostracized from Jewish communal life. Single Jews are to be loved and included in Jewish family, social, and religious life.

These attitudes toward not marrying should help clarify Judaism's attitude toward homosexuality. First, it contradicts the Jewish ideal. Second, it cannot be held to be equally valid.

Third, those publicly committed to it may not serve as public Jewish role models. But fourth, homosexuals must be included in Jewish communal life and loved as fellow human beings and as Jews. . . .

Accepting homosexuality as the social, moral, or religious equivalent of heterosexuality would constitute the first modern assault on the extremely hard-won, millenia-old battle for a family-based, sexually monogamous society. While it is labeled as progress, the acceptance of homosexuality would not be new at all. . . .

Gay activists and some liberal groups such as the ACLU argue for the right of homosexuals to marry. Generally, two arguments are advanced—that society should not deny anyone the right to marry, and that if male homosexuals were given the right to marry, they would be considerably less likely to cruise.

The first argument is specious because there is no "right to marry." There is no right to marry more than one partner at a time, or to marry an immediate member of one's family. Society does not allow either practice. Though the ACLU and others believe that society has no rights, only individuals do, most Americans feel otherwise. Whether this will continue to be so, as Judaism and Christianity lose their influence, remains to be seen.

The second argument may have some merit, and insofar as homosexual marriages would decrease promiscuity among gay men, it would be a very positive development for both gays and society. But homosexual marriage would be unlikely to have such an effect. The male propensity to promiscuity would simply overwhelm most homosexual males' marriage vows. It is women who keep most heterosexual men monogamous, or at least far less likely to cruise, but gay men have no such brake on their cruising natures. Male nature, not the inability to marry, compels gay men to wander from man to man. This is proven by the behavior of lesbians, who, though also prevented from marrying each other, are not promiscuous. . . .

Blessing Gay and Lesbian Commitments
BISHOP JOHN SHELBY SPONG

From Living in Sin?, *1990*

An Episcopalian bishop details his own coming to terms with the reality of homosexual partnerships—and why he believes gay men and women deserve the church's blessing.

Everything I now know about homosexuality, through conversations with gay and lesbian people, the books I have read, and the experts with whom I have talked, has led me to the conclusion that a homosexual orientation is a minority but perfectly natural characteristic on the human spectrum of sexuality. It is not something one chooses, it is something one is. . . .

Gays and lesbians, like all people, have unique gifts and contributions to offer the human family, some of which might well be present in them because of, not in spite of, their sexual orientation. But it is hard to discover gifts that celebrate one's being when the atmosphere in which one lives is laced with a murderous, oppressive hostility toward who one is. . . .

If my conclusions about gay and lesbian people are valid, then the whole of society must be seen as guilty of a cruel oppression of this courageous minority. The time has surely come

not just to tolerate, or even to accept, but to celebrate and welcome the presence among us of our gay and lesbian fellow
human beings.

One way to do that is for the church to admit publicly its
own complicity in their oppression, based on its vast ignorance
and prejudice. It is time to overcome that dark chapter of
church history by living new chapters with an attitude that embraces yesterday's exile, practices the inclusiveness of God's love,
and celebrates the unique gifts of all of God's diverse children.
The one act that above all others will best show a serious intention to change the church's attitude will be for the church to
state its willingness and eager desire to bless and affirm the love
that binds two persons of the same gender into a life-giving relationship of mutual commitment. That ritual act alone will an-
nounce to the homosexual world and to ourselves a shift that will
be believed. No matter how that liturgy is discussed or defined,
the media, the critics, and the world at large will hear it and talk
about it as the marriage of homosexuals. But before we decide
what to call this service, we need to understand what it is and
what it is not. The central clue to this is to discover what the
church does and does not do in marriage.

The church does not, in fact, marry anyone. People marry
each other. The state, not the church, defines the nature of legal
marriage. It does so by giving to married couples the right of
joint property ownership. It is not within the power of the
church to change this legal fact, though its implications need to
be addressed. What the church does in holy matrimony is hear
people's public vows to love each other, to live in a faithful relationship, and to be mutually supportive and caring in all of life's
vicissitudes. Then the church adds to that vow of commitment
its blessing. That blessing is really the church's only contribu-
tion. The church blesses the commitment to be a couple that issues from the vows of the two people who stand before "God

and this company." That blessing conveys ecclesiastical sanction on the relationship and the official willingness of the church and, through the church, of society to support, undergird, and stabilize in every way possible the life of the newly formed couple. The hope of the church is that this sanction and the resultant public support might enable the vows exchanged in good faith before the altar to have an increased chance of being kept.

If the conveying of blessing and official approval is the church's gift to give, then surely that can be given to any relationship of love, fidelity, commitment, and trust that issues in life for the two people involved. We have not in the past as a church withheld blessing from many things. We have blessed fields when crops were planted, houses when newly occupied, pets in honor of Saint Francis, and even the hounds at a Virginia fox hunt. We have blessed MX missiles called "Peacemakers" and warships whose sole purpose was to kill and destroy, calling them, in at least one instance, *Corpus Christi*—the Body of Christ. Why would it occur to us to withhold our blessing from a human relationship that produces a more complete person in each of the partners, because of their life together? Surely the only possible answer to that question is that the church has shared in the habitual prejudice of the ages. Now I call on the church to step out of this prejudice and bless relationships between human beings that are marked by love, fidelity, and the hope of a lifetime of mutual responsibility. What this service is called can then be left to the people involved, and they can then urge the state to accord such relationships the legal benefits of marriage. . . .

The heterosexual community needs to see and experience homosexual unions that are marked by integrity and caring and are filled with grace and beauty. The heterosexual majority seems to assume that the only form homosexual lovemaking takes is the promiscuous life of gay bars, pornography, and one-night stands. They are ever ready to condemn that behavior pattern as morally unacceptable—and so it is. But two things seem to have been overlooked by those who make these judgments. First, promiscuity, pick-up bars, pornography, and one-night stands are not unknown in the heterosexual world. That kind of behavior is destructive no matter what the sexual orientation of those who live out that style of life. Second, heterosexual people have the publicly accepted, blessed, and affirmed alternative of marriage that has as yet not been available to the homosexual population. If there is no such positive alternative for homosexual persons, then what is the church's expectation for them? If the church or society refuses to recognize or promote any positive alternative in which love and intimacy can sustain a gay or lesbian couple, then those institutions are guilty of contributing to the very promiscuity that they condemn. . . .

The fact is that the homosexual population has recognized and supported committed couples, long ahead of the church. In numbers far greater than the "straight" majority suspects, gay people have forged this alternative for themselves with no official help or sanction from anyone. Though those homosexual persons alienated from the church might not welcome the church's Johnny-come-lately arrival on this scene, I believe that the vast majority who crave a sign of society's acceptance of their existence would, if not for themselves then for others. But whether welcomed or not, this is a step the church must take *for the church's sake*. We need to be cleansed from our sin. . . .

People do change, and the knowledge explosion continues each day. I am a living example of these facts. Ten years ago I would have been shocked and aghast at the things I am writing at this moment. Five years ago I still had to be pushed to take an inclusive position. However, scientific data that made me aware that my prejudice grew out of ignorance combined with the witness of gay and lesbian people, some of whom were clergy, to educate me. When I became open to new possibilities, then the humanity of representatives of the homosexual world was able to touch my humanity. They loved me and they invited me into the integrity and life-giving power present in their relationships. It was my recognition of the meaning and validity at work in their mutually committed lives that enabled me to accept the new data and to walk slowly but surely away from the prejudice of a lifetime. . . .

The *Kedushah* of Homosexual Relationships

RABBI YOEL H. KAHN

From the Central Conference of American Rabbis Yearbook, *XCIV, 1989*

> *If God made some people homosexual, a rabbi at the Congregation Sha'ar Zahav in San Francisco argues, why would He not want them brought fully into the Jewish community of faith and custom?*

If the goal of Jewish life is to live in *kedushah* (sanctity), can we sanctify and bless homosexual relationships without compromising the integrity of our tradition? If we do wish to bless these relationships, can we reconcile this new stand with the historical

Jewish teaching in favor of heterosexual, procreative marriage as the normative and ideal form of Jewish family life? . . . We will examine this question in relation to God, Torah and Israel.

I begin with the most fundamental yet unanswerable question: What does God want of us? As a liberal Jew, I am usually reluctant to assert that I know precisely what "God wants." For me to begin by stating that "God calls us to affirm the sanctity of homosexual relationships" (a statement I believe to be true) would be to assert a privileged claim as little open to dispute as the counter-assertion by Rabbi David Bleich that these relationships today remain *"to'evah"* (an abomination). How would one respond to such an argument?

Thus, although our assertion of what God wants properly begins our debate, in fact it cannot. Our conclusions about God's expectations of us in a particular matter develop against the background of our unfolding, wider understanding of what God summons us to do—rooted in what we know about God and God's nature. In the foreground is all that we have learned from the scientific disciplines, from universal ethics, from Jewish tradition, and from our own prayerful conscience. It is when they touch, where the background of what we have already learned of God's expectations of us and God's nature meets foreground of knowledge, prayer, and conscientious reflection about a subject, that we may discern God's will.

My teacher Eugene Borowitz writes that he does not hear a clear message from God about homosexuality, as he has in other areas. I differ from Rabbi Borowitz. I believe that we can hear and affirm what God expects of us in this matter. My understanding of what God wants emerges from the background of God's justice and compassion, and is shaped in the foreground by religious interpretation of the insights of modern science. It is this foreground which has changed in recent years and leads me to dissent from the teachings of our received tradition.

The overwhelming consensus of modern science—in every discipline—is that homosexual relations are as "natural" to us as heterosexuality is. Now, to call something "natural" is a descriptive act; what occurs in nature is not inherently good or bad. Assigning of meaning is a religious act. I, along with many others, have come to recognize sexual orientation as a primary, deep part of the human personality, inseparably bound up with the self. Science does not know what creates homosexual attraction in some people, heterosexual attraction in others; yet today we recognize that some people can only be fulfilled in relationships with people of the same sex. What do we say to them? What does God expect of them and of us?

I do not believe that God creates in vain. Deep, heartfelt yearning for companionship and intimacy is not an abomination before God. God does not want us to send the gays and lesbians among us into exile—either cut off from the Jewish community or into internal exile, living a lie for a lifetime. I believe that the time has come, I believe that God summons us to affirm the proper and rightful place of the homosexual Jew—and her or his family—in the synagogue and in the Jewish people. . . .

When we confront the text [of the Bible] honestly, we face a twofold challenge: first, we must dissent from an explicit Biblical injunction which has been in force until modern times. Now, dissenting from Leviticus has not been an obstacle for us before; Reform Judaism has long abandoned the Biblical and rabbinic proscriptions in the area of ritual purity in marriage. Robert Kirschner . . . argues convincingly that the Biblical and rabbinic injunctions forbidding male homosexual acts are no longer applicable to the situation of homosexuals today. It is important for us to realize that the Biblical authors proscribed particular sexual acts, the motivation for which they could only understand as sinful.

We begin from an entirely different perspective than our

ancestors did. If we grant that homosexual acts are not inherently sinful, then can a homosexual relationship be sanctified? When two Jews, graduates of our schools, alumni of our camps and youth movements, members of our synagogues, promise to establish a Jewish home, pledge to live together in faithfulness and integrity, and ask for God's blessing and our own on their union, is this *to'evah* or is it *kedushah?*

Do we look at this committed and loving couple from an I–It perspective, which sees a particular act and condemns it, or with I–Thou understanding, which affirms the propriety of sexual intimacy in the context of holistic and enduring relationship? Let me be clear: I do not propose merely that we politely overlook the historical Jewish teaching condemning homosexual behavior but that we explicitly affirm its opposite: the movement from *to'evah* to *kedushah*. This transformation in our Jewish standard, from a specific act to the evaluation of the context in which acts occur, seems to me entirely consistent with Reform Jewish thought and practice.

Many are prepared to affirm that for some Jews homosexuality is the proper expression of the human need for intimacy and fulfillment. Still, I know that some are reluctant to endorse *kiddushin* (sanctified covenantal union, usually translated "marriage") for same-sex couples because these relationships apparently disregard the historical and continuing Jewish preference for what Eugene Borowitz and others have called "the procreative family." How can we grant Jewish sanctity, they ask, to a form of family which by its essence precludes procreation, a primary purpose of *kiddushin?*

My reply has three parts. First, we cannot hold homosexual families to a higher standard than we do heterosexual ones. We do not require proof of fertility or even an intention to become parents before we are willing to marry a heterosexual couple. Is the homosexual couple who uses adoption, artificial insemination, or other means to fulfill the Jewish responsibility to parent so different from the heterosexual family who does the same?

Second, does *kiddushin* require procreation? While Judaism has always had a preference for procreative marriage, our tradition has also validated the possibility that some unions will not produce children. *Halachah* states that a woman who does not bear children after ten years can be divorced by her husband. But the evidence that this law was reluctantly or negligibly enforced is precisely the type of historical example Reform responsa often cite to support the explicit expansion of a value we find implicit in our historical tradition. The Jewish tradition has never insisted that the sole purpose of sexual expression is procreation, as evidenced by the numerous rabbinic discussions on the *mitzvah* of sexual intimacy and pleasure.

Third, the situation of the gay and lesbian Jews among us points out the need for new categories in our thinking. Reform Judaism is committed to affirming the responsibility of the individual. Can we not teach that a heterosexual relationship is the proper form of *kedushah* for many and a homosexual relationship may be a proper form for others? Can we not create a plurality of expressions of convenantal responsibility and fulfillment and teach that different Jews will properly fulfill their Jewish communal and religious responsibilities in different ways?

Finally, I would like to introduce into this discussion of Torah a different text than those which have shaped our debate so far. Mine is a classic Jewish text, the record of a uniquely Jewish form of revelation—the text of our history. The history of our people, writ large, has been a continuing source of revelation. For our own generation the recollection of events that we witnessed has assumed the force of Torah, and makes demands upon us as a people and as individual Jews. But our history is not only writ large—history is also written in the small, daily events of our lives. . . .

When I arrived to assume my pulpit in San Francisco four years ago, deep down I still believed that gay and lesbian relationships and families were, somehow, not as real, not as stable, not as committed as heterosexual marriages. I could tell many stories of what I have learned since. There are the two women who have lived together for many years without familial or communal support, who have endured long distances and job transfers, because employers thought them both single and admitting their homosexuality would have endangered their livelihoods, women who have cared for each other without benefit of insurance coverage or health benefits or any legal protection. They came to me one Friday night and simply asked: "Rabbi, this is our twenty-fifth anniversary, will you say a blessing?"

Mine is a synagogue living with AIDS. I have been humbled by the unquestioning devotion of the man who, for more than two years, went to work each morning, calling intermittently throughout the day to check in on his partner, and spent each night comforting, talking, preparing meals, and waking in the middle of the night to carry his loved one to the bathroom. Who would have imagined, when they first chatted twelve years before, that their life together would take this path? The loving caregiver stayed at his partner's side throughout the period of his illness and until his death.

These many lives have taught me about the possibility of enduring loyalty, the meaning of commitment, and the discovery of reservoirs of strength in the face of unimaginable pain and suffering. If the covenant people are summoned to be God-like, then these Jews live their lives *b'tzelem Elohim* and these relationships are surely of true covenantal worth. *Kiddushin* is, in Eugene Borowitz's words, "Judaism's preferred condition in which to work out one's destiny. . . . Because it is a unique fusion of love and demand, of understanding and judgment, of personal giving and receiving, nothing else can teach us so well the meaning of covenant." If "[i]t is the situation where we are most thoroughly challenged to be a Jew and where . . . we may personally exemplify what it means to be allied with God in holiness," then the Torah scroll of lived history records the *kedushah* of these relationships.

I would like to conclude with a word about *kiddushin* and the Jewish people. I have been repeatedly asked, If we elevate homosexual families to an equal status with heterosexual families, will we not undermine the already precarious place of the traditional family? I do not believe that encouraging commitment, stability, and openness undermines the institution of family—it enhances it. At present, many gay and lesbian Jews are estranged from the synagogue, the Jewish community, and their families of origin because of continued fear, stigma, and oppression. Welcoming gay and lesbian families into the synagogue will strengthen all our families by bringing the exiles home and by reuniting children, parents, and siblings who have been forced to keep their partners and innermost lives hidden. *K'lal yisrael* (the community and unity of the Jewish people) is strengthened when we affirm that there can be more than one way to participate in the Covenant.

Creation and Natural Law

JEFFREY JOHN

From Permanent, Faithful, Stable: Christian
Same-Sex Partnerships, 1993

*John argues from an Anglican standpoint that fidelity should
be a more central issue for Christian marriage than procreation, and that homosexuals can pass that test, if they would
only be allowed to.*

Some will still argue that even a relationship of this quality
must be condemned on the ground of Paul's so-called natural
law objection that it is against the God-given pattern of creation.
In an article defending this position one writer sums up such an
argument with the comment that "to accept homosexual acts by
inverts would be to deny the doctrine of creation . . . the whole
biblical teaching on creation, sex, marriage, forgiveness and redemption will be fundamentally altered" (G. Wenham).

So let's consider the biblical argument from creation. What,
scripturally speaking, is the purpose of sex? What was God's will
in creating male and female? One might have assumed childbirth, but, surprisingly perhaps, in Genesis itself the primary
reason that God created a companion for Adam is not said to be
procreation, but because "God said, 'It is not good for man to be
alone'" (2:18). Complementarity and companionship are at least
as much a part of God's plan in creation as childbirth. Indeed it
is remarkable that in the Genesis account childbirth emerges
only as an afterthought, and in the rather negative context of

God's punishment of Eve (3:16). It is highly significant that Jesus and Paul, while both referring to the creation story, never once mention procreation or physical sexual difference in their teaching about marriage. On the contrary, their stress is entirely on the quality of the relationship, and in particular that it should be a covenant of total sexual fidelity and indissoluble union. Furthermore, the insistence on fidelity is never explained, as we might expect, with reference to practical reasons of childbearing or domestic stability, but always with reference to the personal and spiritual implications of sexual union.

For Paul, sexual union *always* has spiritual consequences, whether for good or ill. Promiscuous sexual activity involves desecration of the body, which is a temple of the Spirit and itself a member of the Body of Christ (1 Corinthians 6: 15–20). But where sexual union expresses mutual love and commitment, that relationship becomes a μυστήριον (Ephesians 5: 32), a holy mystery or sacrament which reflects the covenant union of the faithful love between Christ and the Church, and which itself becomes a channel of love and grace in the world. For each human being to make such a covenant is for him or her to realize an important part of what it means to be made in God's image. It means to further his primary and ultimate purpose in creation by reproducing the kind of creative (but not necessarily procreative) self-giving love that is basic to God's own nature. Accepting homosexual relationships does not mean jettisoning this fundamental biblical teaching about the sacramental character of human sexuality.

Those who continue to cling to a natural law argument against homosexuality on the basis of Romans 1 should also be reminded that Paul appeals more frequently and clearly to natural law and the creation story in order to justify his now abandoned teachings about the veiling and silencing of women. Paul said that women must be veiled because man was created first and it is primarily man who is the image of God (1 Corinthians 11: 7–8). It is shameful for a man to wear long hair and a woman to wear short hair because "nature itself teaches us so" (1 Corinthians 11: 14; a much clearer expression of "natural law" than anything in Romans 1). No woman is permitted to teach or to hold authority over men, and women are commanded to be silent "because Adam was formed first, then Eve; and Adam was not deceived, but the woman was deceived and became a transgressor" (1 Timothy 2: 12–14). These are theological arguments which appeal to God's plan in creation no less than Romans 1: 18ff., and indeed Paul is much clearer about their authoritative status and the practical rules he intends to deduce from them, even to the point of saying the silencing of women is a command of the Lord, and if anyone disputes it he is to be rejected (1 Corinthians 14: 33–38). It is obvious that Paul lays far more weight of doctrine and authority on this teaching about women than on his passing references to homosexuality. Yet the fact that today it is consistently ignored, even in the most traditional churches, is not felt to "deny the doctrine of creation" or "to alter fundamentally the whole biblical teaching on creation, sex, marriage, forgiveness and redemption."

I remarked that the original biblical prohibition of homosexuality was probably written in the situation of the Babylonian exile, as a mark of Jewish separateness from the surrounding culture. Babylon remains a powerful symbol for modern secular society, and in one sense it might fairly be argued that the situation of Christians has *not* changed. As "aliens and exiles" Christians still understand themselves to be called, no less than the Jews in Babylon, to a distinctive morality and a distinctive holiness which will challenge the world in sexual matters as in all else (1 Peter 2: 3). This is not to be denied. The point is that the most distinctive and constructive witness that homosexual Christians can offer, both to "Babylon" in the shape of the secular gay scene and to the Church itself, is the witness of relationships marked by the same quality of holy and faithful love to which heterosexual Christians are called in marriage. . . .

What You Do
ANDREW SULLIVAN

From The New Republic, *March 3, 1996*

> *If procreation is essential to marriage, then why doesn't Patrick Buchanan have any children?*

ndrew, it's not who you are. It is what you do!" Buchanan yelled across the table. We were engaged in a typically subtle "Crossfire" debate on same-gender marriage. I'd expected the explosion, but it nevertheless surprised me. Only minutes before, off the air, Buchanan had been cooing over my new haircut. But at least he could distinguish, like any good Jesuit, between the sin and the sinner. It was when his mind drifted to thoughts of homosexual copulation that his mood violently swung.

Okay, Pat, let's talk copulation. It isn't only me that has a problem here.

Buchanan's fundamental issue with "what homosexuals do"

is that it's what he calls a "vice." (I'll leave aside the demeaning reduction of "what homosexuals do" to a sexual act.) Now, there's a clear meaning for a vice: it's something bad that a person freely chooses to do, like, say, steal. But Buchanan concedes that gay relations aren't quite like that; they are related to a deeper, "very powerful impulse," (his words) to commit them. So a homosexual is like a kleptomaniac who decides to steal. Kleptomania is itself an involuntary, blameless condition, hard to resist, but still repressible. Kleptomaniacs, in Buchanan's words, "have the capacity not to engage in those acts. They have free will."

So far, so persuasive. The question begged, of course, is why same-gender sexual acts are wrong in the first place. In the case of kleptomania it's a no-brainer: someone else is injured directly by your actions; they're robbed. But, in the case of homosexual acts, where two consenting adults are engaged in a private activity, it's not at all clear who the injured party is. Buchanan's concern with homosexual acts derives, of course, from the Roman Catholic Church. And the Church's teaching about homosexual sex is closely related to its teaching about the sinfulness of all sexual activity outside a loving, procreative Church marriage.

The sexual act, the Church affirms, must have two core elements: a "procreative" element, the willingness to be open to the creation of new life; and a "unitive" element, the intent to affirm a loving, faithful union. In this, the Church doesn't single out homosexuals for condemnation. The sin of gay sex is no more and no less sinful on these grounds than masturbation, extramarital sex, marital sex with contraception, heterosexual oral sex or, indeed, marital sex without love.

In some ways, of course, homosexual sex is *less* sinful. The heterosexual who chooses in marriage to use contraception, or who masturbates, is turning away from a viable alternative: a unitive, procreative sexual life. The homosexual has no such option; she is denied, because of something she cannot change, a sexual act which is both unitive and procreative. If a lesbian had sexual relations with a man, she could be procreative but not unitive, because she couldn't fully love him. And if she had sex with another woman, she could be unitive in her emotions but, because of biology, not procreative. So the lesbian is trapped by the Church's teaching, excluded from a loving relationship for no fault of her own; and doomed to a loveless life as a result.

The Church urges compassion for such people (a teaching which, somewhere along the way, seems to have escaped Buchanan). But the Church's real compassion is reserved for another group of people who, like homosexuals, are unable, through no fault of their own, to have unitive and procreative sex: infertile heterosexuals. The Church expresses its compassion not by excluding these couples from the sacrament of marriage, but by including them. Sterile couples are allowed to marry in church and to have sex; so are couples in which the wife is post-menopausal. It's understood that such people have no choice in the matter; they may indeed long to have unitive and procreative sex; and to have children. They are just tragically unable, as the Church sees it, to experience the joy of a procreative married life.

The question, of course, is Why doesn't this apply to homosexuals? In official teaching, the Church has conceded (Buchanan hedges on this point) that some homosexuals "are definitively such because of some kind of innate instinct or a pathological constitution judged to be incurable." They may want, with all the will in the world, to have a unitive and procreative relationship; they can even intend to be straight. But they can't and they aren't. So why aren't they allowed to express their love as humanely as they possibly can, along with the infertile and the elderly?

The theologians' best answer to this is simply circular. Marriage, they assert, is by definition between a man and a woman. When pressed further, they venture: well, sexual relations between two infertile heterosexuals could, by a miracle, yield a child. But, if it's a miracle you're counting on, why couldn't it happen to two gay people? Who is to put a limit on the power of God? Well, the Church counters, homosexuality isn't natural, it's an "objective disorder." But what is infertility if it isn't a disorder? The truth is, as the current doctrine now stands, the infertile are defined by love and compassion, while homosexuals are defined by loneliness and sin. The Church has no good case why this should be so.

I harp on this issue of the infertile for one delicate reason: Patrick and Shelley Buchanan do not have kids. Why not? Generally, I wouldn't dream of bringing up such a question, but I am merely adhering to the same rules Buchanan has laid out for me. From the public absence of his children, as from the public statement of my homosexuality, I can infer certain things about Buchanan's "lifestyle." Either Buchanan is using contraception, in which case he is a hypocrite; or he or his wife is infertile, and he is, one assumes, engaging in non-procreative sex. Either way, I can see no good reason why his sexual life is any more sinful than mine.

Of course, by merely bringing up Buchanan's childlessness, I will be judged to have exceeded the bounds of legitimate debate. But why doesn't the same outrage attach to Buchanan for his fulminations against others whose inability to lead a procreative married life is equally involuntary? Of course, Buchanan goes even further: because of what he infers about my private sexual life, he would celebrate discrimination against me and use the bully pulpit of a campaign to defame me. Why is it unthinkable that someone should apply the same standards to him?

I'll tell you why it's unthinkable. No one should be singled out and stigmatized for something he cannot change, especially if that something is already a source of pain and struggle. Indeed, I would regard anyone's inability to have children, if he wanted to, to be a sadness I should privately sympathize with and publicly say nothing about. Why, I wonder, cannot Buchanan express the same compassion and fairness for me?

CHAPTER THREE

It Is So Ordered?
THE PATH OF THE COURTS

The United States Supreme Court has not yet come close to ruling on the issue of same-sex marriage—and it is unlikely to do so for years. But the Court hovers in the background of the debate as an ominous presence, because it has played such a decisive role in civil rights and cultural battles of the recent past. The circumstances of its future rulings are as opaque as their possible results—but that does not mean that there is no way to understand its predicament better.

The extracts that follow trace the arguments in the Court's rulings on marriage and homosexuality in the recent past—which, until now, have remained entirely separate issues. They also detail the key arguments in legal rulings by other courts in many states, rulings in cases that have tried to find a place for same-sex marriage within the myriad legal precedents on homosexuality, sodomy, privacy, and marriage itself. The body of literature in this area is immense and complex. These extracts represent a mere shard of the existing rulings, so the reader should peruse them with care and then consult the full documents for a proper understanding of the legal precedents they contain.

Taken together, these diverse fragments show the wrestling of the legal mind with the issues raised by same-sex marriage. Can marriage be simply redefined in the law? Should an institution that is available for deadbeat dads and convicted felons be denied law-abiding lesbian mothers of young children? Can a fundamental right to marry be unequally dispensed? Is homosexuality a private or a public matter? The rulings appear in chronological order, with the more recent Supreme Court rulings extracted at greater length. The implications of these legal arguments for the broader political debate are discussed further in Chapters 6 and 10.

Marriage and the Right to Privacy
GRISWOLD V. CONNECTICUT

From Justice Douglas's ruling for the majority, U.S. Supreme Court, June 1965

In protecting the use of contraception as falling under an individual's right to privacy, the Court elaborates on how seriously
it takes the right to marry, which predates, Justice Douglas
argues, the Bill of Rights.

The present case, then, concerns a relationship lying within the zone of privacy created by several fundamental constitutional guarantees. And it concerns a law which, in forbidding the *use of* contraceptives rather than regulating their manufacture or sale, seeks to achieve its goals by means having a maximum destructive impact upon that relationship. Such a law cannot stand in light of the familiar principle, so often applied by this Court, that a "governmental purpose to control or prevent activities constitutionally subject to state regulation may not be achieved by means which sweep unnecessarily broadly and thereby invade the area of protected freedoms" (*NAACP* v. *Alabama*) . . . Would we allow the police to search the sacred precincts of marital bedrooms for telltale signs of the use of contraceptives? The very idea is repulsive to the notions of privacy surrounding the marriage relationship.

We deal with a right of privacy older than the Bill of Rights—older than our political parties, older than our school system. Marriage is a coming together for better or for worse, hopefully enduring, and intimate to the degree of being sacred. It is an association that promotes a way of life, not causes; a harmony in living, not political faiths; a bilateral loyalty, not commercial or social projects. Yet it is an association for as noble a purpose as any involved in our prior decisions. . . .

Race and the Right to Marry
LOVING V. VIRGINIA

From Justice Warren's ruling for the U.S. Supreme Court, June 1967

> *This is the finding of the famous interracial marriage case that struck down antimiscegenation laws on the grounds that they violated equal protection. Again, notice how strongly the*

Court defends the freedom to marry: "one of the vital personal rights essential to the orderly pursuit of happiness by free men."

The two statutes under which appellants were convicted and sentenced are part of a comprehensive statutory scheme aimed at prohibiting and punishing interracial marriages. The Lovings were convicted of violating § 20–58 of the Virginia Code:

"Leaving State to evade law.—If any white person and colored person shall go out of this State, for the purpose of being married, and with the intention of returning, and be married out of it, and afterwards return to and reside in it, cohabiting as man and wife, they shall be punished as provided in § 20–59, and the marriage shall be governed by the same law as if it had been solemnized in this State. The fact of their cohabitation here as man and wife shall be evidence of their marriage.". . .

There can be no question but that Virginia's miscegenation statutes rest solely upon distinctions drawn according to race. The statutes proscribe generally accepted conduct if engaged in by members of different races. Over the years, this Court has consistently repudiated "[d]istinctions between citizens solely because of their ancestry" as being "odious to a free people whose institutions are founded upon the doctrine of equality.". . .

At the very least, the Equal Protection Clause demands that racial classifications, especially suspect in criminal statutes, be subjected to the "most rigid scrutiny,". . . and if they are ever to be upheld, they must be shown to be necessary to the accomplishment of some permissible state objective, independent of the racial discrimination which it was the object of the Fourteenth Amendment to eliminate. Indeed, two members of this Court have already stated that they "cannot conceive of a valid legislative purpose . . . which makes the color of a person's skin the test of whether his conduct is a criminal offense.". . . .

There is patently no legitimate overriding purpose independent of invidious racial discrimination which justifies this classification. The fact that Virginia prohibits only interracial marriages involving white persons demonstrates that the racial classifications must stand on their own justification, as measures designed to maintain White Supremacy. We have consistently denied the constitutionality of measures which restrict the rights of citizens on account of race. There can be no doubt that restricting the freedom to marry solely because of racial classifications violates the central meaning of the Equal Protection Clause. . . .

These statues also deprive the Lovings of liberty without due process of law in violation of the Due Process Clause of the Fourteenth Amendment. The freedom to marry has long been recognized as one of the vital personal rights essential to the orderly pursuit of happiness by free men. . . .

Marriage is one of the "basic civil rights of man," fundamental to our very existence and survival. . . .

To deny this fundamental freedom on so unsupportable a basis as the racial classifications embodied in these statutes, classifications so directly subversive of the principle of equality at the heart of the Fourteenth Amendment, is surely to deprive all the State's citizens of liberty without due process of law. The Fourteenth Amendment requires that the freedom of choice to marry not be restricted by invidious racial discriminations. Under our Constitution, the freedom to marry, or not marry, a person of another race resides with the individual and cannot be infringed by the State. . . .

These convictions must be reversed.

It is so ordered.

Same-Sex Marriage and the Right to Privacy

BAKER V. NELSON

*From the ruling of the Supreme Court of Minnesota,
October 1971*

> *The attempt to argue that the right to same-sex marriage is in-
> cluded within the right to privacy established by* Griswold v.
> Connecticut *began early, but it has never been upheld. Here's
> a segment of an early ruling against it in Minnesota in 1971.
> The Court based much of its argument against this applica-
> tion on the link between procreation and marriage. There's
> even a reference to Genesis.*

Statute governing marriage does not authorize marriage between persons of same sex, and such marriages are accordingly prohibited. . . .

Statute prohibiting marriage of persons of the same sex does
not offend First, Eighth, Ninth or Fourteenth Amendments to
the United States Constitution. . . .

Petitioners contend, first, that the absence of an express
statutory prohibition against same-sex marriages evinces a legislative intent to authorize such marriages. We think, however,
that a sensible reading of the statute discloses a contrary intent.

Minn.St. c. 517, which governs "marriage," employs that
term as one of common usage, meaning the state of union between persons of the opposite sex. It is unrealistic to think that
the original draftsmen of our marriage statutes, which date from

territorial days, would have used the term in any different sense. The term is of contemporary significance as well, for the present statute is replete with words of heterosexual import such as "husband and wife" and "bride and groom.". . .

Petitioners contend, second, that Minn.St. c. 517, so interpreted, is unconstitutional. There is a dual aspect to this contention: The prohibition of a same-sex marriage denies petitioners a fundamental right guaranteed by the Ninth Amendment to the United States Constitution, arguably made applicable to the states by the Fourteenth Amendment, and petitioners are deprived of liberty and property without due process and are denied the equal protection of the laws, both guaranteed by the Fourteenth Amendment.

These constitutional challenges have in common the assertion that the right to marry without regard to the sex of the parties is a fundamental right of all persons and that restricting marriage to only couples of the opposite sex is irrational and invidiously discriminatory. We are not independently persuaded by these contentions and do not find support for them in any decisions of the United States Supreme Court.

The institution of marriage as a union of man and woman, uniquely involving the procreation and rearing of children within a family, is as old as the book of Genesis. *Skinner v. Oklahoma* . . . which invalidated Oklahoma's Habitual Criminal Sterilization Act on equal protection grounds, stated in part: "Marriage and procreation are fundamental to the very existence and survival of the race." This historic institution manifestly is more deeply founded than the asserted contemporary concept of marriage and societal interests for which petitioners contend. The due process clause of the Fourteenth Amendment is not a charter for restructuring it by judicial legislation.

Griswold v. Connecticut. . ., upon which petitioners rely, does not support a contrary conclusion. A Connecticut criminal statute prohibiting the use of contraceptives by married couples was held invalid, as violating the due process clause of the Fourteenth Amendment. The basic premise of that decision, however, was that the state, having authorized marriage, was without power to intrude upon the right of privacy inherent in the marital relationship. Mr. Justice Douglas, author of the majority opinion, wrote that this criminal statute "operates directly on an intimate relation of husband and wife,". . . and that the very idea of its enforcement by police search of "the sacred precincts of marital bedrooms for telltale signs of the use of contraceptives is repulsive to the notions of privacy surrounding the marriage relationship.". . . In a separate opinion for three justices, Mr. Justice Goldberg similarly abhorred this state disruption of "the traditional relation of the family—a relation as old and as fundamental as our entire civilization.". . .

The equal protection clause of the Fourteenth Amendment, like the due process clause, is not offended by the state's classification of persons authorized to marry. There is no irrational or invidious discrimination. Petitioners note that the state does not impose upon heterosexual married couples a condition that they have a proved capacity or declared willingness to procreate, posing a rhetorical demand that this court must read such condition into the statute if same-sex marriages are to be prohibited. Even assuming that such a condition would be neither unrealistic nor offensive under the Griswold rationale, the classification is no more than theoretically imperfect. We are reminded, however, that "abstract symmetry" is not demanded by the Fourteenth Amendment.

Loving v. Virginia . . . does indicate that not all state restrictions upon the right to marry are beyond reach of the Fourteenth Amendment. But in common sense and in a constitutional sense, there is a clear distinction between a marital restriction based merely upon race and one based upon the fundamental difference in sex. . . .

The Definitional Argument
JONES V. HALLAHAN

From the ruling of the Court of Appeals of Kentucky, November 1973

The Court of Appeals of Kentucky sets out the classic legal argument: marriage by definition involves a man and a woman. End of discussion.

The sections of Kentucky statutes relating to marriage do not include a definition of that term. It must therefore be defined according to common usage.

Webster's New International Dictionary, second edition, defines marriage as follows:

A state of being married, or being united to a person or persons of the opposite sex as husband or wife; also, the mutual relation of husband and wife; wedlock; abstractly, the institution whereby men and women are joined in a special kind of social and legal dependence, for the purpose of founding and maintaining a family.

The *Century Dictionary and Encyclopedia* defines marriage as

> The legal union of a man with a woman for life; the state or condition of being married; the legal relation of spouses to each other; wedlock; the formal declaration or contract by which a man and a woman join in wedlock.

Black's Law Dictionary, fourth edition, defines marriage as:

> The civil status, condition or relation of one man and one woman united in law for life, for the discharge to each other and the community of the duties legally incumbent upon those whose association is founded on the distinction of sex.

Kentucky statutes do not specifically prohibit marriage between persons of the same sex nor do they authorize the issuance of a marriage license to such persons.

Marriage was a custom long before the state commenced to issue licenses for that purpose. For a time the records of marriage were kept by the church. Some states even now recognize a common-law marriage which has neither the benefit of license nor clergy. In all cases, however, marriage has always been considered as the union of a man and a woman and we have been presented with no authority to the contrary.

It appears to us that appellants are prevented from marrying, not by the statutes of Kentucky or the refusal of the County Court Clerk of Jefferson County to issue them a license, but rather by their own incapability of entering into a marriage as that term is defined.

A license to enter into a status or a relationship which the parties are incapable of achieving is a nullity. If the appellants had concealed from the clerk the fact that they were of the same sex and he had issued a license to them and a ceremony had been performed, the resulting relationship would not constitute a marriage . . .

The Sex Discrimination Point: Refuted
SINGER V. HARA

*From the ruling of the Court of Appeals
of Washington, Division 1, May 1974*

The winning argument in Baehr v. Lewin *in Hawaii—that denying same-sex marriage constitutes a form of sex discrimination—had been tried before but had always failed. Here's an early failure, again based on the notion that child rearing is essential to marriage rights.*

We are of the opinion that a common-sense reading of the language of the ERA indicates that an individual is afforded no protection under the ERA unless he or she first demonstrates that a right or responsibility has been denied solely because of that individual's sex. Appellants are unable to make such a showing because the right or responsibility they seek does not exist. The ERA does not create any new rights or responsibilities, such as the conceivable right of persons of the same sex to marry one another; rather, it merely insures that existing rights and responsibilities, or such rights and responsibilities as may be created in the future, which previously might have been wholly or partially denied to one sex or to the other, will be equally available to members of either sex. The form of discrimination or difference in legal treatment which comes within the prohibition of the ERA necessarily is of an invidious character because it is discrimination based upon the fortuitous circumstance of one's membership in a particular sex per se. This is not to say, however, that the ERA prohibits all legal differentiations which might be made among males and females. A generally recognized "corollary" or exception to even an "absolute" interpretation of the ERA is the proposition that laws which differentiate between the sexes are permissible so long as they are based upon the unique physical characteristics of a particular sex, rather than upon a person's membership in a particular sex per se. . . .

In the instant case, it is apparent that the state's refusal to grant a license allowing the appellants to marry one another is not based upon appellant's status as males, but rather it is based upon the state's recognition that our society as a whole views marriage as the appropriate and desirable forum for procreation and the rearing of children. . . .

Not So Fundamental A Right
ZABLOCKI V. REDHAIL

From Justice Powell's concurring opinion for the U.S. Supreme Court, January 1978

A Wisconsin statute had tried to enforce child support by denying a marriage license to fathers who were delinquent. The Supreme Court found such a statute unconstitutional. A

worried Justice Powell, however, expressed his view that the
state could nevertheless put some limits on the right to marry,
in particular with regard to homosexuality.

On several occasions, the Court has acknowledged the importance of the marriage relationship to the maintenance of values essential to organized society. "This Court has long recognized that freedom of personal choice in matters of marriage and family life is one of the liberties protected by the Due Process Clause of the Fourteenth Amendment.". . .Our decisions indicate that the guarantee of personal privacy or autonomy secured against unjustified governmental interference by the Due Process Clause "has some extension to activities relating to marriage" *Loving v. Virginia*. . . . "While the outer limits of this aspect of privacy have not been marked by the Court, it is clear that among the decisions that an individual may make without unjustified government interference are personal decisions 'relating to marriage'" *Carey v. Population Services International*. . . .

Thus it is fair to say that there is a right of marital and familial privacy which places some substantive limits on the regulatory power of government. But the Court has yet to hold that all regulation touching upon marriage implicates a "fundamental right" triggering the most exacting judicial scrutiny. . . . *Loving* involved a denial of a "fundamental freedom" on a wholly unsupportable basis—the use of classifications "directly subversive of the principle of equality at the heart of the Fourteenth Amendment. . . ." It does not speak to the level of judicial scrutiny of, or governmental justification for, "supportable" restrictions on the "fundamental freedom" of individuals to marry or divorce.

In my view, analysis must start from the recognition of domestic relations as "an area that has long been regarded as a virtually exclusive province of the States." . . . The marriage relation traditionally has been subject to regulation, initially by the ecclesiastical authorities, and later by the secular state. As early as *Pennoyer v. Neff* . . . (1878) this Court noted that a State "has absolute right to prescribe the conditions upon which the marriage relation between its own citizens shall be created, and the causes for which it may be dissolved." The State, representing the collective expression of moral aspirations, has an undeniable interest in ensuring that its rules of domestic relations reflect the widely held values of its people.

> Marriage, as creating the most important relation in life, as having more to do with the morals and civilization of a people than any other institution, has always been subject to the control of the legislature. That body prescribes the age at which parties may contract to marry, the procedure or form essential to constitute marriage, the duties and obligations it creates, its effects upon the property rights of both, present and prospective, and the acts which may constitute grounds for its dissolution. (*Maynard v. Hill* [1888].)

State regulation has included bans on incest, bigamy, and homosexuality, as well as various preconditions to marriage, such as blood tests. Likewise, a showing of fault on the part of one of the partners traditionally has been a prerequisite to the dissolution of an unsuccessful union. A "compelling state purpose" inquiry would cast doubt on the network of restrictions that the States have fashioned to govern marriage and divorce. . . .

No Right to Sodomy

BOWERS V. HARDWICK

From Justice White's and Justice Blackmun's opinions
for the U.S. Supreme Court, June 1986

> *Here's the now-famous ruling upholding Georgia's ban on*
> *sodomy. But notice the beginnings of a rift on the morality or*
> *otherwise of private homosexual conduct. Within a decade,*
> *the tone of the Court would be drastically different (see* Romer
> v. Evans *below).*

Justice White

... After being charged with violating the Georgia statute
criminalizing sodomy by committing that act with another adult
male in the bedroom of his home, respondent Hardwick (respondent) brought suit in Federal District Court, challenging
the constitutionality of the statute insofar as it criminalized consensual sodomy. The court granted the defendants' motion to
dismiss for failure to state a claim. The Court of Appeals reversed and remanded, holding that the Georgia statute violated
respondent's fundamental rights.

Held: The Georgia statute is constitutional. ...

The Constitution does not confer a fundamental right upon
homosexuals to engage in sodomy. None of the fundamental
rights announced in this Court's prior cases involving family relationships, marriage, or procreation bear any resemblance to
the right asserted in this case. And any claim that those cases
stand for the proposition that any kind of private sexual conduct

between consenting adults is constitutionally insulated from state proscription is unsupportable. . . .

Against a background in which many States have criminalized sodomy and still do, to claim that a right to engage in such conduct is "deeply rooted in this Nation's history and tradition" or "implicit in the concept of ordered liberty" is, at best, facetious. . . .

There should be great resistance to expand the reach of the Due Process Clauses to cover new fundamental rights. Otherwise, the Judiciary necessarily would take upon itself further authority to govern the country without constitutional authority. The claimed right in this case falls far short of overcoming this resistance. . . .

The fact that homosexual conduct occurs in the privacy of the home does not affect the result. . . .

Sodomy laws should not be invalidated on the asserted basis that majority belief that sodomy is immoral is an inadequate rationale to support the laws. . . .

Justice Blackmun

. . . This case is no more about "a fundamental right to engage in homosexual sodomy," as the Court purports to declare . . . than *Stanley v. Georgia* . . . was about a fundamental right to watch obscene movies, or *Katz v. United States* . . . was about a fundamental right to place interstate bets from a telephone booth. Rather, this case is about "the most comprehensive of rights and the right most valued by civilized men," namely "the right to be let alone" *Olmstead v. United States.*

Like Justice Holmes, I believe that "[i]t is revolting to have no better reason for a rule of law than that so it was laid down in the time of Henry IV. It is still more revolting if the grounds upon which it was laid down have vanished long since, and the rule simply persists from blind imitation of the past.". . . A State can no more punish private behavior because of religious intolerance than it can punish such behavior because of racial animus. "The Constitution cannot control such prejudices, but neither can it tolerate them. Private biases may be outside the reach of the law, but the law cannot, directly or indirectly, give them effect" *Palmore v. Sidoti.*

Even Prisoners Can Marry
TURNER V. SAFELY

*From Justice O'Connor's ruling for the majority,
U.S. Supreme Court, June 1987*

Justice Sandra Day O'Connor explains why many aspects of marriage can apply even to prison inmates. The right of convicted murderers to marry is inviolable, yet the right of homosexuals is not.

We disagree with petitioners that Zablocki does not apply to prison inmates. It is settled that a prison inmate "retains those [constitutional] rights that are not inconsistent with his status as a prisoner or with the legitimate penological objectives of the corrections system.". . .

The right to marry, like many other rights, is subject to substantial restrictions as a result of incarceration. Many important attributes of marriage remain, however, after taking into account the limitations imposed by prison life. First, inmate marriages, like others, are expressions of emotional support and public commitment. These elements are an important and significant aspect of the marital relationship. In addition, many religions recognize marriage as having spiritual significance; for some inmates and their spouses, therefore, the commitment of marriage may be an exercise of religious faith as well as an expression of personal dedication. Third, most inmates eventually will be released by parole or commutation, and therefore most inmate marriages are formed in the expectation that they ultimately will be fully consummated. Finally, marital status often is a precondition to the receipt of government benefits (e.g., Social Security benefits), property rights (e.g., tenancy by the entirety, inheritance rights), and other, less tangible benefits (e.g., legitimation of children born out of wedlock). These incidents of marriage, like the religious and personal aspects of the marriage commitment, are unaffected by the fact of confinement or the pursuit of legitimate corrections goals. Taken together, we conclude that these remaining elements are sufficient to form a constitutionally protected marital relationship in the prison context. . . .

The Sex Discrimination Point: Upheld

BAEHR V. LEWIN

From the Supreme Court's ruling,
Supreme Court of Hawaii, May 1993

Here's the ruling that roiled America. The Hawaii court's deci-
sion that banning same-sex marriage violated the Hawaii
Constitution's equal rights clause put the ruling on very firm
legal ground. Notice how carefully the Court bases its inter-
pretation of this clause on both Hawaiian and federal rulings.
And notice how it dismisses same-sex marriage rights as an ex-
tension of a right to privacy. It is a ruling as dramatic in its
implications as it is conservative in its methodology.

The precise question facing this court is whether we will extend
the *present* boundaries of the fundamental right of marriage
to include same-sex couples, or, put another way, whether we
will hold that same-sex couples possess a fundamental right to
marry. In effect, as the applicant couples frankly admit, we are
being asked to recognize a new fundamental right. There is no
doubt that "[a]s the ultimate judicial tribunal with final, unre-
viewable authority to interpret and enforce the Hawaii Constitution, we are free to give broader privacy protection . . . than that
given by the federal constitution."... However, we have also
held that the privacy right found in article I, section 6 is similar
to the federal right and that no "purpose to lend talismanic effect" to abstract phrases such as "intimate decision" or "personal
autonomy" can "be inferred from [article I, section 6], any more
than . . . from the federal decisions."...

In the case that first recognized a fundamental right to privacy, *Griswold v. Connecticut*, . . . the Court declared that it was "deal[ing] with a right . . . older than the Bill of Rights[.]". . . And in a concurring opinion, Justice Goldberg observed that judges "determining which rights are fundamental" must look not to "personal and private notions," but

> to the "traditions and [collective] conscience of our people" to determine whether a principle is "so rooted [there] . . . as to be ranked as fundamental.". . . The inquiry is whether a right involved "is of such a character that it cannot be denied without violating those 'fundamental principles of liberty and justice which lie at the base of all our civil and political institutions.'". . .

Applying the foregoing standards to the present case, we do not believe that a right to same-sex marriage is so rooted in the traditions and collective conscience of our people that failure to recognize it would violate the fundamental principles of liberty and justice that lie at the base of all our civil and political institutions. Neither do we believe that a right to same-sex marriage is implicit in the concept of ordered liberty, such that neither liberty nor justice would exist if it were sacrificed. Accordingly, we hold that the applicant couples do not have a fundamental constitutional right to same-sex marriage arising out of the right to privacy or otherwise. . . .

Marriage is a state-conferred legal status, the existence of which gives rise to rights and benefits reserved exclusively to that particular relationship. This court construes marriage as "'a partnership to which both partners bring their financial resources as well as their individual energies and efforts.'". . . So zealously has this court guarded the state's role as the exclusive progenitor of the marital partnership that it declared, over seventy years ago, that "common law" marriages—*i.e.*, "marital" unions existing in the absence of a state-issued license and not performed by a person or society possessing governmental authority to solemnize marriages—would no longer be recognized in the Territory of Hawaii. . . .

The applicant couples correctly contend that the [Department of Health's] refusal to allow them to marry on the basis that they are members of the same sex deprives them of access to a multiplicity of rights and benefits that are contingent upon that status. Although it is unnecessary in this opinion to engage in an encyclopedic recitation of all of them, a number of the most salient marital rights and benefits are worthy of note. They include: (1) a variety of state income tax advantages, including deductions, credits, rates, exemptions, and estimates . . . (2) public assistance from and exemptions relating to the Department of Human Services . . . (3) control, division, acquisition, and disposition of community property . . . (4) rights relating to dower, curtesy, and inheritance . . . (5) rights to notice, protection, benefits, and inheritance . . . (6) award of child custody and support payments in divorce proceedings . . . (7) the right to spousal support . . . (8) the right to enter into premarital agreements . . . (9) the right to change of name . . . (10) the right to file a nonsupport action . . . (11) post-divorce rights relating to support and property division . . . (12) the benefit of the spousal privilege and confidential marital communications . . . (13) the benefit of the exemption or real property from attachment or execution . . . and (14) the right to bring a wrongful death action. . . .

The equal protection clauses of the United States and Hawaii Constitutions are not mirror images of one another. The fourteenth amendment to the United States Constitution somewhat concisely provides, in relevant part, that a state may not "deny to any person within its jurisdiction the equal protection of the laws." Hawaii's counterpart is more elaborate. Article I, section 5 of the Hawaii Constitution provides in relevant part that "[n]o person shall . . . be denied the equal protection of the laws, *nor be denied the enjoyment of the person's civil rights or be discriminated against in the exercise thereof because of* race, religion, *sex,* or ancestry" (emphasis added). Thus, by its plain language, the Hawaii Constitution prohibits state-sanctioned discrimination against any person in the exercise of his or her civil rights on the basis of sex. . . . Rudimentary principles of statutory construction render manifest the fact that, by its plain language, HRS § 572-1 restricts the marital relation to a male and a female. "'[T]he fundamental starting point for statutory interpretation is the language of the statute itself. . . . [W]here the statutory language is plain and unambiguous,'" we construe it according "'to its plain and obvious meaning.'" . . . Accordingly, on its face and (as Lewin admits) as applied, HRS § 572-1 denies same-sex couples access to the marital status and its concomitant rights and benefits. . . .

Relying primarily on four decisions construing the law of other jurisdictions, Lewin contends that "the fact that homosexual [sic—actually, same-sex] partners cannot form a state-licensed marriage is not the product of impermissible discrimination" implicating equal protection considerations, but rather "a function of their biologic inability as a couple to satisfy the definition of the status to which they aspire.". . . Put differently, Lewin proposes that "the right of persons of the same sex to marry one another does not exist because marriage, by definition and usage, means a special relationship between a man and a woman.". . .

We believe Lewin's argument to be circular and unpersuasive. . . .

The facts in *Loving* and the respective reasoning of the Virginia courts, on the one hand, and the United States Supreme Court, on the other, both discredit the reasoning . . . and unmask the tautological and circular nature of Lewin's argument that HRS § 572-1 does not implicate article I, section 5 of the Hawaii Constitution because same-sex marriage is an innate impossibility. Analogously to Lewin's argument and the rationale of the *Jones* court, the Virginia courts declared that interracial marriage simply could not exist because the Deity had deemed such a union intrinsically unnatural . . . , and, in effect, because it had theretofore never been the "custom" of the state to recognize mixed marriages, marriage "always" having been construed to presuppose a different configuration. With all due respect to the Virginia courts of a bygone era, we do not believe that trial judges are the ultimate authorities on the subject of Divine Will, and, as *Loving* amply demonstrates, constitutional law may mandate, like it or not, that customs change with an evolving social order. . . .

"Whenever a denial of equal protection of the laws is alleged, as a rule our initial inquiry has been whether the legislation in question should be subjected to 'strict scrutiny' or to a 'rational basis' test.". . .

Our decision in *Holdman* is key to the present case in several respects. First, we clearly and unequivocally established, for purposes of equal protection analysis under the Hawaii Constitution, that sex-based classifications are subject, as a *per se* matter, to some form of "heightened" scrutiny, be it "strict" or "intermediate," rather than mere "rational basis" analysis. Second, we assumed, *arguendo,* that such sex-based classifications were subject to "strict scrutiny." Third, we reaffirmed the longstanding principle that this court is free to accord greater protections to Hawaii's citizens under the state constitution than are recognized under the United States Constitution. And fourth, we looked to the *then current* case law of the United States Supreme Court for guidance.

Of the decisions of the United States Supreme Court cited in *Holdman, Frontiero v. Richardson, supra,* was by far the most significant. . . .

The disagreement among the eight-justice majority lay in the level of judicial scrutiny applicable to instances of statutory sex-based discrimination. The Brennan plurality agreed with the Frontieros' contention that "classifications based upon sex, like classifications based upon race, alienage, and national origin, are inherently suspect and must therefore be subjected to close judicial scrutiny.". . . Thus, the Brennan plurality applied the "strict scrutiny" standard to its review of the illegal statutes. Justice Stewart concurred in the judgment, "agreeing that the statutes . . . work[ed] an invidious discrimination in violation of the Constitution.". . .

Particularly noteworthy in *Frontiero,* however, was the concurring opinion of Justice Powell, joined by the Chief Justice and Justice Blackmun (the Powell group). The Powell group agreed that "the challenged statutes constitute[d] an unconstitutional discrimination against servicewomen," but deemed it "unnecessary for the Court *in this case* to characterize sex as a suspect classification, with all of the far-reaching implications of such a holding.". . .

Central to the Powell group's thinking was the following explanation:

> There is another . . . reason for deferring a general categorizing of sex classifications as invoking the strictest test of judicial scrutiny. *The Equal Rights Amendment, which if adopted will resolve the substance of this precise question,* has been

approved by Congress and submitted for ratification by the States. If this Amendment is duly adopted, it will represent the will of the people accomplished in the manner prescribed by the Constitution. By acting prematurely and unnecessarily, . . . the Court has assumed a decisional responsibility at the very time when state legislatures, functioning within the traditional democratic process, are debating the proposed Amendment. It seems . . . that this reaching out to pre-empt by judicial action a major political decision which is currently in process of resolution does not reflect appropriate respect for duly prescribed legislative processes. . . .

The Powell group's concurring opinion therefore permits but one inference: had the Equal Rights Amendment been incorporated into the United States Constitution, at least seven members (and probably eight) of the *Frontiero* Court would have subjected statutory sex-based classifications to "strict" judicial scrutiny.

In light of the interrelationship between the reasoning of the Brennan plurality and the Powell group in *Frontiero*, on the one hand, and the presence of article I, section 3—the Equal Rights Amendment—in the Hawaii Constitution, on the other, it is time to resolve once and for all the question left dangling in *Holdman*. Accordingly, we hold that sex is a "suspect category" for purposes of equal protection analysis under article I, section 5 of the Hawaii Constitution and that HRS § 572-1 is subject to the "strict scrutiny" test. It therefore follows, and we so hold, that (1) HRS § 572-1 is presumed to be unconstitutional (2) unless Lewin, as an agent of the State of Hawaii, can show that (a) the statute's sex-based classification is justified by compelling state interests and (b) the statute is narrowly drawn to avoid unnecessary abridgements of the applicant couples' constitutional rights. . . .

As a final matter, we are compelled to respond to Judge Heen's suggestion that denying the appellants access to the multitude of statutory benefits "conferred upon spouses in a legal marriage . . . is a matter for the legislature, which can express the will of the populace in deciding whether such benefits should be extended to persons in [the applicant couples'] circumstances.". . . In effect, we are being accused of engaging in judicial legislation. We are not. The result we reach today is in complete harmony with the *Loving* Court's observation that any state's powers to regulate marriage are subject to the constraints imposed by the constitutional right to the equal protection of the laws. . . .

If it should ultimately be determined that the marriage laws of Hawaii impermissibly discriminate against the appellants, based on the suspect category of sex, then that would be the result of the interrelation of existing legislation.

[W]hether the legislation under review is wise or unwise is a matter with which we have nothing to do. Whether it . . . work[s] well or work[s] ill presents a question entirely irrelevant to the issue. The only legitimate inquiry we can make is whether it is constitutional. If it is not, its virtues, if it have any, cannot save it; if it is, its faults cannot be invoked to accomplish its destruction. If the provisions of the Constitution be not upheld when they pinch as well as when they comfort, they may as well be abandoned. . . .

Homosexuals and Equal Protection

ROMER V. EVANS

*From Justice Kennedy's majority ruling and Justice
Scalia's dissent, U.S. Supreme Court, May 1996*

*In the middle of the marriage wars came this decision in the
summer of 1996: that Colorado's Amendment 2 unconstitu-
tionally singled out homosexuals as a class by deeming them
ineligible for protective legislation. The implications of this
decision for marriage rights could be minimal or enormous.
But the sweep of Justice Kennedy's language suggests a Rubi-
con has been crossed—as does the sharpness of Justice Scalia's
dissent.*

Justice Kennedy

One century ago, the first Justice Harlan admonished this
Court that the Constitution "neither knows nor tolerates classes
among citizens" *Plessy v. Ferguson* (1896) (dissenting opinion).
Unheeded then, those words now are understood to state a commitment to the law's neutrality where the rights of persons are at
stake. The Equal Protection Clause enforces this principle and
today requires us to hold invalid a provision of Colorado's Constitution.

The enactment challenged in this case is an amendment to
the Constitution of the State of Colorado, adopted in a 1992
statewide referendum. The parties and the state courts refer to
it as "Amendment 2," its designation when submitted to the vot-
ers. The impetus for the amendment and the contentious cam-

paign that preceded its adoption came in large part from ordinances that had been passed in various Colorado municipalities. . . . What gave rise to that statewide controversy was the protection the ordinances afforded to persons discriminated against by reason of their sexual orientation. Amendment 2 repeals these ordinances to the extent they prohibit discrimination on the basis of "homosexual, lesbian or bisexual orientation, conduct, practices or relationships."

Yet Amendment 2, in explicit terms, does more than repeal or rescind these provisions. It prohibits all legislative, executive or judicial action at any level of state or local government designed to protect the named class. . . .

The state's principle argument in defense of Amendment 2 is that it puts gays and lesbians in the same position as all other persons. So, the state says, the measure does no more than deny homosexuals special rights. This reading of the amendment's language is implausible. . . .

Sweeping and comprehensive is the change in legal status effected by this law. So much is evident from the ordinances that the Colorado Supreme Court declared would be void by operation of Amendment 2. Homosexuals, by state decree, are put in a solitary class with respect to transactions and relations in both the private and governmental spheres. The amendment withdraws from homosexuals, but no others, specific legal protection from the injuries caused by discrimination, and it forbids reinstatement of these laws and policies. . . .

We cannot accept the view that Amendment 2's prohibition on specific legal protections does no more than deprive homosexuals of special rights. To the contrary, the amendment imposes a special disability upon those persons alone. Homosexuals are forbidden the safeguards that others enjoy or may seek without constraint. . . . We find nothing special in the protections Amendment 2 withholds. These are protections taken for granted by most people either because they already have them or do not need them. . . .

Central to the idea of the rule of law and to our own Constitution's guarantee of equal protection is the principle that government and each of its parts remain open on impartial terms to all who seek its assistance. Respect for this principle explains why laws singling out a certain class of citizens for disfavored legal status or general hardships are rare. A law declaring that in general it shall be more difficult for one group of citizens than for all others to seek aid from the government is itself a denial of equal protection of the laws in the most literal sense. "The guaranty of 'equal protection of the laws is a pledge of the protection of equal laws.'" . . .

The primary rationale the state offers for Amendment 2 is respect for other citizens' freedom of association, and in particular the liberties of landlords or employers who have personal or religious objections to homosexuality.

Colorado also cites its interest in conserving resources to fight discrimination against other groups. The breadth of the amendment is so far removed from these particular justifications that we find it impossible to credit them. . . .

We must conclude that Amendment 2 classifies homosexuals not to further a proper legislative end but to make them unequal to everyone else. This Colorado cannot do. A state cannot so deem a class of persons a stranger to its laws. . . .

Justice Scalia

The court has mistaken a Kulturkampf for a fit of spite. . . .

No principle set forth in the Constitution . . . prohibits what Colorado has done here. But the case for Colorado is much stronger than that. What it has done is not only unprohibited, but eminently reasonable. . . .

The Court's opinion contains grim, disapproving hints that Coloradans have been guilty of "animus" or "animosity" toward homosexuality. . . . Of course it is our moral heritage that one should not hate any human being or class of human beings. But I had thought that one could consider certain conduct reprehensible—murder, for example, or polygamy, or cruelty to animals—and could exhibit even "animus" toward such conduct. . . . The Colorado amendment does not, to speak entirely precisely, prohibit giving favored status to people who are homosexuals; they can be favored for many reasons—for example, because they are senior citizens or members of racial minorities. But it prohibits giving them favored status because of their homosexual conduct. . . .

There is a problem, however, which arises when criminal sanction of homosexuality is eliminated but moral and social disapprobation of homosexuality is meant to be retained. . . . Because those who engage in homosexual conduct tend to reside in disproportionate numbers in certain communities, have high disposable income and of course care about homosexual-rights issues much more ardently than the public at large, they possess political power much greater than their numbers, both locally and statewide. Quite understandably, they devote this political power to achieving not merely a grudging social toleration, but full social acceptance, of homosexuality. . . .

Today's opinion has no foundation in American constitutional law, and barely pretends to. The people of Colorado have adopted an entirely reasonable provision which does not even disfavor homosexuals in any substantive sense, but merely denies them preferential treatment. Amendment 2 is designed to prevent piecemeal deterioration of the sexual morality favored by a majority of Coloradans, and is not only an appropriate means to that legitimate end, but a means that Americans have employed before. Striking it down is an act not of judicial judgment, but of political will.

CHAPTER FOUR

Why Marry?

THE DEBATE ON THE LEFT

For decades, the issue of same-sex marriage has been anything but noncontroversial among gay men and lesbians. Although the idea of marriage rights goes back centuries, the American gay rights movement, in its post-1969 incarnation, eschewed it. Marriage, the argument ran, was an oppressive, sexist, and inherently heterosexual institution. The movement's goal was to weaken the institution as a whole, to subvert and undermine it, and to create alternative structures within which to explore homosexual desire, love, and family. Even now, many gay rights organizations devote almost no energy or resources to the issue, considering it unnecessarily emotive and irrelevant. And academic "queer theorists" remain deeply suspicious of marriage. But in the last decade advocates who see marriage as the linchpin of gay civil rights have grown in strength and numbers. Intellectuals and activists have generated a structure of support and arguments for the many lesbian and gay couples who have sought the right to marry. And the Hawaii case, together with the subsequent congressional debate, has raised the issue to a new level among gay men and lesbians.

What follows are among the most eloquent and cogent of the arguments that have emerged over the years—from Paula Ettelbrick's early worries to Evan Wolfson's growing confidence and conviction. Mary Dunlap's poem "Choosing" expresses the acute emotional conflicts many homosexuals feel about the institution as a whole. Lesbian writer E. J. Graff argues that equality in marriage is a deeply radicalizing move; Frank Browning laments its normalizing effect on gay life. Finally, Hannah Arendt—the only heterosexual writer in this chapter—asserts the centrality of marriage to any civil equality.

Since When Is Marriage a Path to Liberation?

PAULA ETTELBRICK

From OUT/LOOK National Gay and Lesbian Quarterly, *no. 6, Fall 1989*

A traditional leftist worries about what same-sex marriage would do to the radical agenda.

M arriage is a great institution . . . if you like living in institutions," according to a bit of T-shirt philosophy I saw recently. Certainly, marriage is an institution. It is one of the most venerable, impenetrable institutions in modern society. Marriage provides the ultimate form of acceptance for personal, intimate relationships in our society, and gives those who marry an insider status of the most powerful kind.

Steeped in a patriarchal system that looks to ownership, property, and dominance of men over women as its basis, the institution of marriage has long been the focus of radical-feminist revulsion. Marriage defines certain relationships as more valid than all others. Lesbian and gay relationships, being neither legally sanctioned nor commingled by blood, are always at the bottom of the heap of social acceptance and importance.

Given the imprimatur of social and personal approval that marriage provides, it is not surprising that some lesbians and gay men among us would look to legal marriage for self-affirmation. After all, those who marry can be instantaneously transformed from "outsiders" to "insiders," and we have a desperate need to become insiders.

It could make us feel okay about ourselves, perhaps even relieve some of the internalized homophobia that we all know so well. Society will then celebrate the birth of our children and mourn the death of our spouses. It would be easier to get health insurance for our spouses, family memberships to the local museum, and a right to inherit our spouse's cherished collection of lesbian mystery novels even if she failed to draft a will. Never again would we have to go to a family reunion and debate about the correct term for introducing our lover/partner/significant other to Aunt Flora. Everything would be quite easy and very nice.

So why does this unlikely event so deeply disturb me? For two major reasons. First, marriage will not liberate us as lesbians and gay men. In fact, it will constrain us, make us more invisible, force our assimilation into the mainstream, and undermine the goals of gay liberation. Second, attaining the right to marry will not transform our society from one that makes narrow, but dramatic, distinctions between those who are married and those who are not married to one that respects and encourages choice of relationships and family diversity. Marriage runs contrary to two of the primary goals of the lesbian and gay movement: the affirmation of gay identity and culture and the validation of many forms of relationships.

When analyzed from the standpoint of civil rights, certainly lesbians and gay men should have a right to marry. But obtaining a right does not always result in justice. White male firefighters in Birmingham, Alabama, have been fighting for their "rights" to retain their jobs by overturning the city's affirmative-action guidelines. If their "rights" prevail, the courts will have failed in rendering justice. The "right" fought for by the white male fire-fighters, as well as those who advocate strongly for the "rights" to legal marriage for gay people, will result, at best, in limited or narrowed "justice" for those closest to power at the expense of those who have been historically marginalized. . . .

Justice for gay men and lesbians will be achieved only when we are accepted and supported in this society despite our differences from the dominant culture and the choices we make regarding our relationships. Being queer is more than setting up house, sleeping with a person of the same gender, and seeking state approval for doing so. It is an identity, a culture with many variations. It is a way of dealing with the world by diminishing the constraints of gender roles that have for so long kept women and gay people oppressed and invisible. Being queer means pushing the parameters of sex, sexuality, and family, and in the process transforming the very fabric of society. Gay liberation is inexorably linked to women's liberation. Each is essential to the other.

The moment we argue, as some among us insist on doing, that we should be treated as equals because we are really just like married couples and hold the same values to be true, we undermine the very purpose of our movement and begin the dangerous process of silencing our different voices. As a lesbian, I am fundamentally different from nonlesbian women. That's the point. Marriage, as it exists today, is antithetical to my liberation as a lesbian and as a woman because it mainstreams my life and voice. I do not want to be known as "Mrs. Attached-To-Somebody-Else." Nor do I want to give the state the power to regulate my primary relationship. . . .

By looking to our sameness and de-emphasizing our differences, we do not even place ourselves in a position of power that would allow us to transform marriage from an institution that emphasizes property and state regulation of relationships to an institution that recognizes one of many types of valid and respected relationships. Until the Constitution is interpreted to respect and encourage differences, pursuing the legalization of same-sex marriage would be leading our movement into a trap; we would be demanding access to the very institution that, in its current form, would undermine our movement to recognize many different kinds of relationships. We would be perpetuating the elevation of married relationships and of "couples" in general, and further eclipsing other relationships of choice.

Ironically, gay marriage, instead of liberating gay sex and sexuality, would further outlaw all gay and lesbian sex that is not performed in a marital context. Just as sexually active nonmarried women face stigma and double standards around sex and sexual activity, so too would nonmarried gay people. The only legitimate gay sex would be that which is cloaked in and regulated by marriage. Its legitimacy would stem not from an acceptance of gay sexuality, but because the Supreme Court and society in general fiercely protect the privacy of marital relationships. Lesbians and gay men who do not seek the state's stamp of approval would clearly face increased sexual oppression.

Undoubtedly, whether we admit it or not, we all need to be

accepted by the broader society. That motivation fuels our work to eliminate discrimination in the workplace and elsewhere, fight for custody of our children, create our own families, and so on. The growing discussion about the right to marry may be explained in part by this need for acceptance. Those closer to the norm or to power in this country are more likely to see marriage as a principle of freedom and equality. Those who are acceptable to the mainstream because of race, gender, and economic status are more likely to want the right to marry. It is the final acceptance, the ultimate affirmation of identity.

On the other hand, more marginal members of the lesbian and gay community (women, people of color, working class, and poor) are less likely to see marriage as having relevance to our struggles for survival. After all, what good is the affirmation of our relationships (that is, marital relationships) if we are rejected as women, people of color, or working class?

The path to acceptance is much more complicated for many of us. For instance, if we choose legal marriage, we may enjoy the right to add our spouse to our health insurance policy at work, since most employment policies are defined by one's marital status, not family relationship. However, that choice assumes that we have a job and that our employer provides us with health benefits. For women, particularly women of color who tend to occupy the low-paying jobs that do not provide health-care benefits at all, it will not matter one bit if they are able to marry their women partners. The opportunity to marry will neither get them the health benefits nor transform them from outsider to insider.

Of course, a white man who marries another white man who has a full-time job with benefits will certainly be able to share in those benefits and overcome the only obstacle left to full societal assimilation—the goal of many in his class. In other words, gay marriage will not topple the system that allows only the privileged few to obtain decent health care. Nor will it close the privilege gap between those who are married and those who are not.

Marriage creates a two-tier system that allows the state to regulate relationships. It has become a facile mechanism for employers to dole out benefits, for businesses to provide special deals and incentives, and for the law to make distinctions in distributing meager public funds. None of these entities bothers to consider the relationship among people; the love, respect, and need to protect that exists among all kinds of family members. Rather, a simple certificate of the state, regardless of whether the spouses love, respect, or even see each other on a regular basis, dominates and is supported. None of this dynamic will change if gay men and lesbians are given the option of marriage. . . .

If the laws changed tomorrow and lesbians and gay men were allowed to marry, where would we find the incentive to continue the progressive movement we have started that is pushing for societal and legal recognition of all kinds of family relationships? To create other options and alternatives? To find a place in the law for the elderly couple who, for companionship and economic reasons, live together but do not marry? To recognize the right of a longtime, but unmarried, gay partner to stay in his rent-controlled apartment after the death of his lover, the only named tenant on the lease? To recognize the family relationship of the lesbian couple and the two gay men who are jointly sharing child-raising responsibilities? To get the law to acknowledge that we may have more than one relationship worthy of legal protection?

The lesbian and gay community has laid the groundwork for revolutionizing society's views of family. The domestic-partnership movement has been an important part of this progress insofar as it validates nonmarital relationships. Because it is not limited to sexual or romantic relationships, domestic partnership provides an important opportunity for many who are not related by blood or marriage to claim certain minimal protections.

It is crucial, though, that we avoid the pitfall of framing the push for legal recognition of domestic partners (those who share a primary residence and financial responsibilities for each other) as a stepping-stone to marriage. We must keep our eyes on the goals of providing true alternatives to marriage and of radically reordering society's view of family. . . . We must not fool ourselves into believing that marriage will make it acceptable to be gay or lesbian. We will be liberated only when we are respected and accepted for our differences and the diversity we provide to this society. Marriage is not a path to that liberation.

Choosing
MARY C. DUNLAP

From Law and Sexuality: A Review of Lesbian and Gay Legal Issues *1 (1991)*

In a poetic footnote to a legal article, Mary Dunlap confronts her own conflicts about marriage as an instrument of her oppression—and liberation.

The girls I watched so closely and adoringly
in fifth grade, then young women in eighth,
eleventh, college, law school, life after
At first, they varied so, a bright rainbow
I cherished

The Debate on the Left

But revolved more and more, faster and faster
Around a common, central myth
Of devastating, even deadly, force:

To marry
Would give life, value to the life,
Identity to each female
Lucky enough, attractive enough
To draw a man
To vows.

This myth, this centrifuge of sexist conformity,
Built on a vicious cycle of female inferiority
Tossed, cajoled and ultimately smashed these beings
into a sameness: increasingly fearful deference
To the male.

Meanwhile, my sister scolded me, "you'll never say, 'yes,'
in a wedding, the most you'd yield is
'Maybe.'"

"Or, maybe not," I answered.

Proud and hurt, and very deeply blessed
by my belief, defiant, resilient
That I am valuable in my self,
I escaped
The centrifuge of marriage.

And now I see
The vows they took have turned to blows
Too often, and jokes, and infidelities

SAME-SEX MARRIAGE: PRO AND CON

Celebrated as "romance," culminating in
divorce, or worse, routine denial
Understood as normal, modern, mundane
Entertainment

Disguising the essential horror
Distracting from the pain, breath-taking

Of the basic whirlpool drowning tragedy:
That anyone should ever have to wait for
That anyone should ever choose to look to
Another
For her own (for his own)
Boundless, immutable, miraculous personal worth. . . .

After my father died, December 1984,
my mother took me aside, not in sheer grief,
But in a statement of abiding and lifelong belief,
Said:
I WAS NOTHING
TILL I MARRIED YOUR FATHER.

I rage and bawl and struggle to this moment
Against the awful truth and the awful lie
of this statement in Mother's life,
in so many women's lives.
I WAS NOTHING
TILL I MARRIED YOUR FATHER.

So, given the extreme force of the circular saw lie
That a woman is only as good as her marriage
This lie that worked to separate
Mother from her own life

(And how many millions of others, I wonder)
Is it possible
Can it ever conceivably be

That the dreadful institution of marriage
that has broken all those girlchildren's souls
this idea that invalidates women, that
corrupts female identity into a product for men to buy

This monstrosity, marriage,

Could ever be tamed, changed, moved,
Transmogrified
By the love between two women
By the love between two men

Into a place of nurturing and shelter
For this most illegitimate of relationships
the lesbian couple
the gay partnership

this relationship so homeless and beaten down

Lifted into a place of succor and respect
For both, for each
Marriage without regard to gender
   by Church or State
   ("gender" saved for one's own appreciate regard
   and the lover's, total and tender)

Can we these most unwelcome outsiders
We these gay and lesbian lovers
Be let in?
And want to, choose to
Go?

Without destruction of all we have learned
Outside, feminist, hetero-
dox lessons
About the centrifuge's crush
and the untolled cost of the awful lie
For the question is not, finally,
   May we *marry*?

It is

   Can *we* marry? . . .

Why We Should Fight for the Freedom to Marry

EVAN WOLFSON

From the Journal of Gay, Lesbian, and Bisexual
Identity *1, no. 1 (1996)*

Evan Wolfson was among the first advocates of same-sex mar-
riage, and he is now the most tireless advocate on the issue.
Here's a recent broadside against his fair-weather friends in
the lesbian and gay leadership.

Imagine if tomorrow, by act of law, lesbians and gay men were
denied the right to raise children together in a protected relationship or to have their committed relationships recognized

and given benefits such as annuities, pension plans, Social Security, and Medicare. Or if by act of law, same-sex couples who have lived together for the longest time were not allowed joint filing of tax returns, joint insurance policies for home, auto, and health, or access during dissolution or divorce to protections such as community property and child support.

Imagine how you would feel if you and your partner were told that, because of that act of law, you had to choose between love and country because your same-sex relationship was not respected for immigration and residency. Or that the act of law meant that your partner's death left you without rights of inheritance, protection against eviction from the home you had shared, exemption from oppressive taxation, or even bereavement leave. Imagine that the act of law stamped you as unqualified to make decisions about your partner's health or medical treatment, or even her or his funeral arrangements. Or that the act of law branded you as permanent sexual outlaws, unequal citizens, and even not fully human—because of the gender of the person you love.

In fact, that act of law has already happened; it's called "same-sex couples can't get married." All this unequal treatment and more is already there, because in all 50 states, lesbians and gay men are denied the basic human right, the constitutional freedom, to marry.

Because literally hundreds of important legal, economic, practical, and social benefits and protections flow directly from marriage, the exclusion from this central social institution wreaks real harm on real-life same-sex couples every day. From lesbian mothers denied custody of their children or the right to adopt their partner's children (case after case), to gay men literally separated at the INS office because they could not find a country that would allow them to live together (case after case), to gay people out in the cold when a relationship ended, or unable to get an order of protection against domestic violence when the relationship went sour—the denial of marriage rights has been a stone wall against which we have run up again and again. . . .

Although no discrimination is exactly the same, and there is no reason to get into an argument over some "hierarchy of oppression" there are many analogies to be drawn from this nation's previous experience in excluding people from the institution of marriage. For example, Stephanie Smith of the National Center for Lesbian Rights/Lesbians of Color Project has spoken eloquently of the parallels between the "different-sex restriction" still in force against gay and lesbian people's choice of a marital partner and the "same-race restriction" that less than 30 years ago prevented interracial couples from marrying.

Consider this law imposing a "same-race restriction" on marriage struck down (only twenty-seven years ago!) by the U.S. Supreme Court in *Loving v. Virginia.* "All marriages between a white person and a colored person shall be absolutely *void* without any decree of divorce or other legal process." Notice how closely it resembles the equally offensive and unconstitutional bill imposing a "different-sex restriction" on marriage, recently proposed in South Dakota: "Any marriage between persons of the same gender is null and *void* from the beginning."

In *Loving,* a black woman and a white man were criminally convicted for violating Virginia's miscegenation law, which imposed a "same-race restriction" on marriage. Exiling (!) the Lovings from their home state for 25 years and declaring their marriage "void," the trial judge stated,

> Almighty God created the races white, black, yellow, malay, and red, and he placed them on separate continents. . . . The fact that he separated the races shows that he did not intend for the races to mix.

The Supreme Court struck down this "same-race restriction" on marital choice as a "measure . . . designed to maintain White Supremacy." In much the same way, the "different-sex restriction" deprives gay and lesbian people of a basic human right and brands us as inferior, second-class citizens, thus justifying and reinforcing stereotypes and prejudice as well as other discrimination.

People today forget how the language now being used against same-sex couples' equal marriage rights not so long ago was used against interracial couples—denying people's equal human dignity and freedom to share in the rights and responsibilities of marriage. Today, you even hear some *gay* and *lesbian* people saying that the fact that marriage is today denied to same-sex couples shows that it is intrinsically heterosexual, ignoring the fact that marriage (like other social institutions we are part of or seek to make our own choices whether or not to be part of) has changed throughout history to meet the needs and values of real people.

Now imagine if the Lovings had been told that instead of challenging this discrimination and fighting for their right to marry, they should instead devote their limited resources solely to unhooking benefits and protections from marriage. Or if the lawyers working on their case from the ACLU and the Japanese-American Citizens League both of which have endorsed Lambda's Marriage Resolution calling for equal marriage rights for gay people had said that we should not work on ending the ban on interracial marriage until we achieve universal health care.

Would anyone say that people in love should accept discrimination based on their race or religion until other injustices are rectified? Or would we say that *both* the discrimination and the other injustices should be combatted and that those like the Lovings are right to challenge their exclusion from a central social institution? Would we counsel the Lovings to accept un-equal treatment, or even "separate-but-equal"? And if we wouldn't, why should people facing discrimination based on their gender or sexual orientation, or the gender or sexual orientation of the person they love most, have to accept it either? . . .

Why Marry?

FRANK BROWNING

From The New York Times, *April 17, 1996*

Browning, a leftist writer and National Public Radio contrib-
utor, prefers more diverse relationship models to marriage.

Thursday morning, and it's my turn to move our cars for street cleaning. Gene has already bribed the cats into silence with food.

So begins the day here in Windsor Terrace, a quiet Brooklyn neighborhood populated by many kinds of families: a lesbian couple next door—and beyond them an Italian widow who rents out rooms, an Irish-American grandmother who shares her house with her daughter's family, the multigenerational Korean family that owns the corner grocery.

We gay couples, of course, are not considered families under the law, a fact that the bishops and Buchananites insist will never change and that many gay activists have identified as

America's next great civil rights struggle. Indeed, a court case in Hawaii may soon lead to that state's recognition of same-sex marriage.

I suppose it's a good thing for gay adults to be offered the basic nuptial rights afforded to others. We call that equal treatment before the law. But I'm not sure the marriage contract is such a good plan for us.

The trouble with gay marriage is not its recognition of our "unnatural unions." The problem is with the shape of marriage itself. What we might be better off seeking is civic and legal support for different kinds of families that can address the emotional, physical and financial obligations of contemporary life. By rushing to embrace the standard marriage contract, we could stifle one of the richest and most creative laboratories of family experience.

We gay folk tend to organize our lives more like extended families than nuclear ones. We may love our mates one at a time, but our "primary families" are often our ex-lovers and our ex-lovers' ex-lovers.

The writer Edmund White noticed this about gay male life 20 years ago; he called it the "banyan tree" phenomenon, after the tree whose branches send off shoots that take root to form new trunks. Nowhere has the banyan-tree family proved stronger than in AIDS care, where often a large group of people—ex-mates and their friends and lovers—tend the sick and maintain the final watch.

Modern marriage, by comparison, tends to isolate couples from their larger families and sometimes from friends—especially if they are ex-lovers. And a nuclear family with working parents has often proved less than ideal in coping with daily stresses or serious illness.

The marriage model could prove especially problematic for

rearing children. In a gay family, there are often three parents—a lesbian couple, say, and the biological father. Sometimes, four or five adults are committed to nurturing the children. In such cases, a marriage between two might bring second-class status to the rest of the extended family and diminish their parental roles.

(Those who think that only a father and mother can successfully raise a child should visit Italy, Japan, Greece, Thailand or American family archives, which show that before World War II, grandparents, aunts, uncles and older siblings had vital child-rearing roles.)

Precisely because homosexuals have resided outside the law, they have invented family forms that respond to late twentieth-century needs, while formulating social and moral codes that provide love, freedom and fidelity (if not always monogamy).

All I need do is look up and down Windsor Terrace to see that the family includes all sorts of relationships and obligations.

Each of us, hetero or homo, has a stake in nurturing a diverse landscape of families. Only a minority of us have marriages like Donna Reed's or Harriet Nelson's. Even Pat Buchanan knows that.

Retying the Knot
E. J. GRAFF

From the Nation, *June 24, 1996*

Lesbian intellectual E. J. Graff believes that same-sex marriage represents the most radical step of all—a way to transform one of the most powerful institutions in society.

The right wing gets it: Same-sex marriage is a breathtakingly subversive idea. So it's weirdly dissonant when gay neocons and feminist lesbians publicly insist—the former with enthusiasm, the latter with distaste—that same-sex marriage would be a conservative move, confining sexual free radicals inside some legal cellblock. It's almost as odd (although more understandable) when pro-marriage liberals ply the rhetoric of fairness and love, as if no one will notice that for thousands of years marriage has meant Boy+Girl=Babies. But same-sex marriage seems fair only if you accept a philosophy of marriage that, although it's gained ground in the past several centuries, still strikes many as radical: the idea that marriage (and therefore sex) is justified not by reproduction but by love.

Sound like old news? Not if you're the Christian Coalition, the Pope or the Orthodox rabbinate, or if you simply live in one of many pre-industrial countries. Same-sex marriage will be a direct hit against the religious right's goal of re-enshrining biology as destiny. Marriage is an institution that towers on our social horizon, defining how we think about one another, formalizing contact with our families, neighborhoods, employers, insurers, hospitals, governments. Allowing two people of the same sex to marry shifts that institution's message.

That's why the family-values crowd has trained its guns on us, from a new hate video called *The Ultimate Target of the Gay Agenda: Same-Sex Marriages* to the apocalyptically named Defense of Marriage Act. The right wing would much rather see outré urban queers throwing drunken kisses off bar floats than have two nice married girls move in next door, with or without papoose, demonstrating to every neighborhood kid that a good marriage is defined from the inside out, that sodomy is a sin only in the mind of the beholder.

Chilled by that coming shift, antimarriage conservatives have also been disingenuous in their arguments, which basically come down to crying "tradition!" like a Tevye chorus. Even a quick glance at social history shows what conservatives pretend isn't so: Very little about marriage is historically consistent enough to be "traditional." That it involves two people? Then forget the patriarch Jacob, whose two wives and two concubines produced the head of the twelve tribes. That it involves a religious blessing? Not early Christian marriages, before marriage was a sacrament. That it is recognized by law? Forget centuries of European prole "marriages" conducted outside the law, in which no property was involved. That it's about love, not money? So much for centuries of negotiation about medieval estates, bride-price, morning gift and dowry (not to mention brideburnings in today's India). Those who tsk away such variety, insisting that everyone knows what marriage *really* is, miss the point. Marriage is—marriage always has been—variations on a theme. Each era's marriage institutionalizes the sexual bond in a way that makes sense for that society, that economy, that class.

So what makes sense in ours? Or, to put it another way, what is contemporary marriage for? That's the question underlying the debate as right-wing and gay activists prepare for Hawaii's aftermath. Its answer has to fit our economic lives. In a GNP based on how well each of us plumbs our talents and desires in deciding what to make, buy or sell, we can hardly instruct those same innards to shut up about our sexual lives—as people could in a pre-industrial society where job, home and religion were all dictated by history. The right wants it both ways: Adam Smith's economy *and* feudal sexual codes. If same-sex marriage becomes legal, that venerable institution will ever after stand for sexual choice, for cutting the link between sex and diapers.

Ah, but it already does. Formally, U.S. marriage hasn't been justified solely by reproduction since 1965, when the Supreme

Court batted down the last laws forbidding birth control's sale to married couples. In Margaret Sanger's era, contraception was charged with "perversion of natural functions," "immorality" and "fostering egotism and enervating self-indulgence." Dire diseases were predicated for those who indulged. Those are, almost word for word, the charges hurled by every critic of homosexuality—and for the same reasons. Once their ideologies are economically outdated, what can conservatives invoke except the threat of divine judgment?

All of which is why same-sex marriage is being considered in every postindustrial country, and why it seems simply "fair" to so many, including Hawaii's Supreme Court. That sense of fairness also draws on the liberal idea that a pluralist democracy's institutions should be capacious, that civic marriage should be one-size-fits-all. But same-sex marriage does more than just fit; it announces that marriage has changed shape.

As with any social change, there will be more consequences, which look pretty progressive to me. There are practical benefits: the ability to share insurance and pension benefits, care for our ill partners, inherit automatically, protect our children from desperate custody battles. And marriage will end a negative: Our sexual lives can no longer be considered felonious, which stings us in fights ranging from child custody to civil rights.

A more notable progressive shift is that, since same-sex couples will enter the existing institution, not some back-of-the-bus version called "domestic partnership" or "queer marriage," marriage law will have to become gender-blind. Once we can marry, jurists will have to decide every marriage, divorce and custody question (theoretically at least) for equal partners, neither having more historical authority. Our entrance might thus rock marriage more toward its egalitarian shore.

Some progressives, feminists and queer nationalists

nevertheless complain that instead of demanding access to the institution as it is, we should be dismantling marriage entirely. But lasting social change evolves within and alters society's existing institutions. No one will force same-sex couples to darken the institution's doors: we'll merely gain the choices available to heterosexual pairs. None of this will alter a hard fact of contemporary life: Every commitment—to job, spouse, community, religion—must be invented from the inside out. Making lesbians and gay men more visible legally will insist that there is no traditional escape: that our society survives not by rote but by heart.

Connubial Personae
CAMILLE PAGLIA

From 10 Percent *magazine, May–June* 1995

An interview with Camille Paglia, a writer who defies categorization. So, it seems, does her argument about same-sex marriage.

10 Percent: What's your position on same-sex marriage?

Paglia: I think that it's a flash point for antigay backlash. It's the word *marriage*, coming out of the Judeo-Christian tradition, that has caused so much resistance. My problem is that I'm not so sure that Judeo-Christianity could or should honor or legitimize gay marriages. If there are going to be unions between gays, they should be outside the orthodox religious line—maybe pagan in some way. I do feel that some sort of commitment ceremony or union is in the best interest of the whole society as a way to strengthen gay relationships.

10 Percent: So what sort of alternative marriage ceremony are you envisioning for gay people?

Paglia: The truly radical position would be that there should be a separate ceremony, not just for gay marriages, but for all marriages. Gay activism has been stupid in demanding that marriages be performed in churches and synagogues. The truly radical argument would have been for us to appeal to progressive straights and say to them, *Renounce* the marriage ceremony. If you are really progressive, don't pay lip service to gay rights. Do what people did in the '6os: Don't get married! It's in our interest as gays to want to strengthen relationships, so we do want to return to the idea of ceremony and ritual again, but let's find something that's gender and sexual-orientation neutral. And we should invite all progressive straight people to join us in this new kind of ceremony—whatever it is.

10 Percent: What would a ceremony with you and Alison Maddex be like?

Paglia: If Hawaii does legalize gay marriage, Alison and I would certainly be going. The idea of travelling to a Pacific Island to have a wedding ceremony is wonderful. I love it. Pele the Volcano Goddess, presumably, would be the presiding deity of such a ceremony. I love the idea of making a voyage back to nature.

10 Percent: Would other lesbian and gay couples follow suit?

Paglia: I think there will be a stampede of major proportions, but it may cause a backlash. That's the problem: calling it a *marriage*. If you say to some working-class guy on the street, "Do you believe in gay *marriages*?" it makes him have an absolute convulsion of revulsion. Marriage was traditionally meant for male and female. It was a bond for the raising of children, so it always had a procreative meaning. It has a long, sacred tradition behind it. I hate any time that gay causes get mixed up with seeming to profane other people's sacred traditions. The gay activist leadership has been totally clumsy about that. Rather than treating religion in a serious way and saying, "We respect the tradition of marriage," gay activism is associated with throwing balloons full of blood at the steps of St. Patrick's Cathedral.

10 Percent: Will the lesbian and gay divorce rate resemble the straight one?

Paglia: Who knows? My experience is that gay men's idea of marriage or any kind of relationship is rather open. That's why a lot of people are a little skeptical. Gay men—they're "together for 30 years": what does that mean? That means they go out and pick up strangers every two weeks. That's a very sophisticated view of marriage. Lesbians aren't like that. Lesbians *nest* in one big cinnamon bun where they fuse and it's all very sweet and nice. I like the idea of marriage, but I'm not sure that gay relationships have been tested over time. If we can't convince each other about it, I don't know how we're going to convince the greater world.

Crossing the Threshold
EVAN WOLFSON

From the Review of Law and Social Change *no. 3*
(1994–1995)

Why, against conventional wisdom, the right to marry is widely popular among lesbians and gay men.

In an argument typical of many intra-community critics of marriage challenges, Nancy Polikoff contends: "[T]he desire to marry in the lesbian and gay community is an attempt to mimic the worst of mainstream society, an effort to fit into an inherently problematic institution that betrays the promise of both lesbian and gay liberation and radical feminism."

There are at least two disturbing premises embedded in this argument. . . .

First, why is a lesbian's aspiration to marry "an attempt to mimic," rather than a genuine expression of her desires? Professor Mary C. Dunlap quotes one lesbian's observation:

> [I]t was strange to me when people in our community talked about commitment ceremonies as mocking heterosexual experience, because for me the creation of our Brit Ahavah [Jewish wedding ritual] was so different from a heterosexual wedding. The fact that gays and lesbians do this against all odds makes the whole process completely different.

Nor is this woman's desire to get married unusual. In the words of one gay man, "if it is freely chosen, a marriage license is as fine an option as sexual license. All I ask is the right to choose for myself, but that is exactly the right that society has never granted. . . ." One historian generalizes that "[g]ays and lesbians are raised in the same culture as everyone else. When they settle down they want gold bands, they want legal documents, they want kids." Even though equal marriage rights, until recently, seemed a dream, all available evidence suggests that the vast majority of gay and non-gay people alike share such sentiments.

In a 1994 survey by *The Advocate,* the largest existing poll of gay men on the subject, nearly two-thirds of the respondents stated unequivocally that they would marry a man if they were legally able to; 85 percent responded "yes" or "maybe"; only 15 percent said they would not marry. A significantly smaller, earlier poll by another journal presented similar results: 83 percent of lesbians and gay men in the study said they would "definitely" get married if they could. . . .

Like non-gay people, many lesbians and gay men offer less romantic explanations of their desire for equal marriage rights. For instance, noting the difficulties that gay people experience in terminating relationships and securing legal assistance, one attorney remarks: "I used to say, 'Why do we want to get married? It doesn't work for straight people.'. . . But now I say we should care: They have the privilege of divorce and we don't. We're left out there to twirl around in pain.". . .

For several years now, Lambda's intake has reflected a constant, high level of interest in marriage within our communities. During the 1987 March on Washington, thousands of lesbians and gay men participated in an event pointedly billed "The Wedding," in which they celebrated their relationships by exchanging personal vows before an officiant in front of the Internal Revenue Service Building. In his travels across the United

States and again around the world, Neil Miller chronicled gay person after person either seeking marriage or indeed, as far as possible, actually wedding their partners.

Consider, for example, the experience of one couple that Miller encountered:

> Des was reluctant. She didn't believe in marriage and was opposed to imitating what she viewed as the heterosexual model. "I had a women's studies point of view," she noted. But gradually Trinity convinced her that marriage simply represented an expression of love and commitment that was neither intrinsically heterosexual nor homosexual. . . .

The suggestion that lesbians and gay men who want equal marriage rights do not know what is best for them as gay people is not uncommon in the intra-community arguments against pursuing marriage. In the charge that the demand for equal marriage rights is insufficiently radical or liberationist, a contemnable desire to "mimic" or "emulate" the non-gay world, or a sell-out of less "assimilationist" or less "privileged" gay people, there is an inescapable whiff of imputed false consciousness. However, given the diversity and number of women and men within our communities who strongly want the equal right to marry, the imputation seems wrong, as well as unfair. . . .

What many gay people do not want is an all-or-nothing model imposed on their lesbian or gay identity; they want both to be gay *and* married, to be gay *and* part of the larger society. For these lesbians and gay men, being gay is not just about being different, it is also about being equal. Their deeply held convictions about how they want to live their lives and liberation are not mere mimicry. They are entitled to respect within our community as well as by the state. . . .

Reflections on Little Rock

HANNAH ARENDT

From Dissent *6, no. 1 (Winter 1959)*

This may seem a quirky choice, but this short statement shows how marriage rights were also controversial within another civil rights movement—in the 1950s and 1960s. Here Arendt argues that ending antimiscegenation laws was more important than desegregating public schools.

The right to marry whoever one wishes is an elementary human right compared to which "the right to attend an integrated school, the right to sit where one pleases on a bus, the right to go into any hotel or recreation area or place of amusement, regardless of one's skin or color or race" are minor indeed. Even political rights, like the right to vote, and nearly all other rights enumerated in the Constitution, are secondary to the inalienable human rights to "life, liberty and the pursuit of happiness" proclaimed in the Declaration of Independence; and to this category the right to home and marriage unquestionably belongs.

CHAPTER FIVE

How Conservative a Project?

THE DEBATE ON THE RIGHT

One of the earliest twists of the same-sex marriage debate was the argument that it was a conservative reform: it would promote stability and monogamy among homosexuals and responsibility in the society as a whole. One of the clearest statements of this argument was contained in an article I wrote in 1989 in The New Republic, *entitled "Here Comes the Groom: A Conservative Case for Gay Marriage." It subsequently formed a part of the third chapter of my book,* Virtually Normal. *I should apologize, perhaps, for including my own work at length, but it is, I think, still the most cited argument of its type, so it is a natural place to start.*

The arguments against this position were almost immediate, specifically from Hadley Arkes in the National Review *and later from James Q. Wilson in* Commentary. *While ceding some ground to my position, both nevertheless argued that putting an end to an exclusively heterosexual definition of marriage would have radically unconservative ramifications.*

Subsequently, the debate took off with Jonathan Rauch's elegant 1996 essay, also published in The New Republic, *and the* Economist *editorial, which echoes Rauch's arguments. Two of the smartest conservative writers around have also chimed in—Richard Posner and William Safire. Both oppose same-sex marriage for quirkily different reasons. Finally, Amy Schwartz and Katha Pollitt observe this debate from outside the conservative fold—one criticizing the conservative rush toward equality between gays and straights, and another celebrating it.*

The Conservative Case
ANDREW SULLIVAN

From Virtually Normal: An Argument About Homosexuality, 1995

In this excerpt from my book I try to show how every conservative argument against same-sex marriage collapses upon close examination. This passage concentrates on the conservative notion that legalizing same-sex marriage would undermine traditional heterosexual marriage.

The most common conservative argument against same-sex marriage is that the public acceptance of homosexuality subverts the stability and self-understanding of the heterosexual family. But here the conservative position undermines itself somewhat. Since most conservatives concede the presence of a number of involuntarily homosexual persons, they must also concede that these persons are already part of "heterosexual" families. They are sons and daughters, brothers and sisters, even mothers and fathers, of heterosexuals. The distinction between "families" and "homosexuals" is, to begin with, empirically false; and the stability of existing families is closely linked to how homosexuals are treated within them. Presumably, it is against the interest of heterosexual families to force homosexuals into roles they are not equipped to play and may disastrously perform. This is not an abstract matter. It is quite common that homosexual fathers and mothers who are encouraged into heterosexual marriages subsequently find the charade and dishonesty too great to bear: spouses are betrayed, children are abandoned, families are broken, and lives are ruined. It is also common that homosexual sons and daughters who are denied the love and support of their families are liable to turn against the institution of the family, to wound and destroy it, out of hurt and rejection. And that parents, inculcated in the kind of disdain of homosexuality conservatives claim is necessary to protect the family, react to the existence of gay children with unconscionable anger and pain, and actually help destroy loving families.

Still, conservatives may concede this and still say that it's worth it. The threat to the stability of the family posed by public disapproval of homosexuality is not as great as the threat posed by public approval. How does this argument work? Largely by saying that the lives saved by preventing wavering straights from becoming gay are more numerous than the lives saved by keeping gay people out of heterosexual relationships and allowing greater tolerance of gay members of families themselves; that the stability of the society is better served by the former than by the latter. Now, recall that conservatives are not attempting to assert absolute moral truths here. They are making an argument about social goods, in this case, social and familial stability. They are saying that a homosexual life is, on the face of it, worse than a heterosexual life, as far as society is concerned. In Harvard psychologist E. L. Pattullo's words,

> Though we acknowledge some influences—social and biological—beyond their control, we do not accept the idea that people of bad character had no choice. Further, we are concerned to maintain a social climate that will steer them in the direction of the good.

The issue here is bad character and the implied association of bad character with the life of homosexuals. Although many conservatives feel loath to articulate what they mean by this life, it's clear what lies behind it. So if they won't articulate it, allow me. They mean by "a homosexual life" one in which emotional commitments are fleeting, promiscuous sex is common, disease is rampant, social ostracism is common, and standards of public decency, propriety, and self-restraint are flaunted. They mean a way of life that deliberately subverts gender norms in order to unsettle the virtues that make family life possible, ridicules heterosexual life, and commits itself to an ethic of hedonism, loneliness, and deceit. They mean by all this "the other," against which any norm has to be defended and any cohesive society protected. So it is clear that whatever good might be served by preventing gay people from becoming parents or healing internal wounds within existing families, it is greatly outweighed by the dangers of unleashing this kind of ethic upon the society as a whole.

But the argument, of course, begs a question. Is this kind of life, according to conservatives, what a homosexual life *necessarily* is? Surely not. If homosexuality is often indeed involuntary, as conservatives believe, then homosexuals are not automatically the "other"; they are sprinkled randomly throughout society, into families that are very much like anybody else's, with characters and bodies and minds as varied as the rest of humanity. If all human beings are, as conservatives believe, subject to social inducements to lead better or worse lives, then there is nothing inevitable at all about a homosexual leading a depraved life. In some cases, he might even be a paragon of virtue. Why then is the choice of a waverer to live a homosexual rather than a heterosexual life necessarily a bad one, from the point of view of society? Why does it lead to any necessary social harm at all?

Of course, if you simply define "homosexual" as "depraved," you have an answer; but it's essentially a tautologous one. And if you argue that in our society at this time, homosexual lives simply *are* more depraved, you are also begging a question. There are very few social incentives of the kind conservatives like for homosexuals *not* to be depraved: there's little social or familial support, no institution to encourage fidelity or monogamy, precious little religious or moral outreach to guide homosexuals into more virtuous living. This is not to say that homosexuals are not responsible for their actions, merely that in a large part of homosexual subculture there is much a conservative would predict, when human beings are abandoned with extremely few social incentives for good or socially responsible behavior. But the proper conservative response to this is surely not to infer that this behavior is inevitable, or to use it as a reason to deter others from engaging in a responsible homosexual existence, if that is what they want; but rather to construct social institutions and guidelines to modify and change that behavior for the better. But that is what conservatives resolutely refuse to do.

Why? Maybe for conservatives, there is something inherent even in the most virtuous homosexual life that renders it less desirable than the virtuous heterosexual life, and therefore merits social discouragement to deter the waverers. Let's assume, from a conservative perspective, the best-case scenario for such a waverer: he can choose between a loving, stable, and responsible same-sex relationship and a loving, stable, and responsible opposite-sex relationship. Why should society preference the latter?

The most common response is along the lines of Hadley Arkes, the conservative commentator, who has written on this subject on occasion. It is that the heterosexual relationship is good for men not simply because it forces them to cooperate and share with other human beings on a daily basis but because it forces them into daily contact and partnership with *women:*

> It is not marriage that domesticates men; it is women. Left to themselves, these forked creatures follow a way of life that George Gilder once recounted in its precise, chilling measures: bachelors were twenty-two times more likely than married men to be committed to hospital for mental disease (and ten times more likely to suffer chronic diseases of all kinds). Single men had nearly double the mortality rate of married men and three times the mortality rate of single women. Divorced men were three times more likely than divorced women to commit suicide or die by murder, and they were six times more likely to die of heart disease.

I will leave aside the statistical difficulties here: it's perfectly possible that many of the problems Arkes recounts were reasons why the men didn't get married, rather than consequences of their failing to do so. Let's assume, for the sake of argument, that Arkes is right: that marriage to a woman is clearly preferable to being single for an adult man; that such a man is more likely to be emotionally stable, physically healthy, psychologically in balance; and that this is good for the society as a whole. There is in this argument a belief that women are naturally more prone to be stable, nurturing, supportive of stability, fiscally prudent, and family-oriented than men, and that their connection to as many men as possible is therefore clearly a social good. Let's assume also, for the sake of argument, that Arkes is right about that too. It's obvious, according to conservatives, that society should encourage a stable opposite-sex relationship over a stable same-sex relationship.

But the waverer has another option: *he can remain single.* Should society actually encourage him to do this rather than involve himself in a stable, loving same-sex relationship? Surely, even conservatives who think women are essential to the successful socialization of men would not deny that the discipline of domesticity, of shared duties and lives, of the inevitable give-and-take of cohabitation and love with anyone, even of the same sex, tends to benefit men more than the option of constant, freewheeling, etiolating bachelorhood. But this would mean creating a public moral and social climate which preferred stable gay relationships to gay or straight bachelorhood. And it would require generating a notion of homosexual responsibility that would destroy the delicately balanced conservative politics of private discretion and undiscriminating public disapproval. So conservatives are stuck again: their refusal to embrace responsible public support for virtuous homosexuals runs counter to their entire social agenda.

Arkes's argument also leads to another (however ironic) possibility destabilizing to conservatism's delicate contemporary compromise on the homosexual question: that for a wavering woman, a lesbian relationship might actually be socially *preferable* to a heterosexual relationship. If the issue is not mere domesticity but the presence of women, why would two women not be better than one, for the sake of children's development and social stability? Since lesbianism seems to be more amenable to choice than male homosexuality in most studies and surveys, conservatism's emphasis on social encouragement of certain behaviors over others might be seen as even more relevant here. If conservatism is about the social benefits of feminizing society, there is no reason why it should not be an integral part of the movement for women to liberate themselves completely from men. Of course, I'm being facetious; conservatives would be terrified by all the single males such a society would leave rampaging around. But it's not inconceivable at all from conservative premises that, solely from the point of view of the wavering woman, the ascending priorities would be: remaining single, having a stable, loving opposite-sex relationship, and having a stable, loving same-sex relationship. And there is something deliciously ironic about the sensibility of Hadley Arkes and E. L. Pattullo finding its full fruition in a lesbian collective.

Still, the conservative has another option. He might argue that removing the taboo on homosexuality would unravel an entire fabric of self-understanding in the society at large that could potentially destabilize the whole system of incentives for stable family relationships. He might argue that now, of all times, when families are in an unprecedented state of collapse, is not the occasion for further tinkering with this system; that the pride of heterosexual men and women is at stake; that their self-esteem and self-understanding would be undermined if society saw them as equivalent to homosexuals. In this view, the stigmatization of homosexuals is the necessary corollary to the celebration of traditional family life.

Does this ring true? To begin with, it's not at all clear why, if public disapproval of homosexuals is indeed necessary to keep families together, homosexuals of all people should bear the primary brunt of the task. But it's also not clear why the corollary really works to start with. Those homosexuals who have no choice at all to be homosexual, whom conservatives do not want to be in a heterosexual family in the first place, are clearly no threat to the heterosexual family. Why would accepting that such people exist, encouraging them to live virtuous lives, incorporating their difference into society as a whole, necessarily devalue the traditional family? It is not a zero-sum game. Because they have no choice but to be homosexual, they are not choosing that option over heterosexual marriage; and so they are not sending any social signals that heterosexual family life should be denigrated.

The more difficult case, of course, pertains to Arkes's "waverers." Would allowing them the option of a stable same-sex relationship as a preferable social option to being single really undermine the institution of the family? Is it inconceivable that a society can be subtle in its public indications of what is and what is not socially preferable? Surely, society can offer a hierarchy of choices, which, while preferencing one, does not necessarily denigrate the others, but accords them some degree of calibrated respect. It does this in many other areas. Why not in sexual arrangements?

You see this already in many families with homosexual members. While some parents are disappointed that their son or daughter will not marry someone of the opposite sex, provide grandchildren and sustain the family line for another generation, they still prefer to see that child find someone to love and live with and share his or her life with. That child's siblings, who may be heterosexual, need feel no disapproval attached to their own marriage by the simple fact of their sibling's difference. Why should society as a whole find it an impossible task to share in the same maturity? Even in the most homosexualized culture, conservatives would still expect over eighty percent of couples to be heterosexual: why is their self-esteem likely to be threatened by a paltry twenty percent—especially when, according to conservatives, the homosexual life is so self-evidently inferior?

In fact, it's perfectly possible to combine a celebration of the traditional family with the celebration of a stable homosexual relationship. The one, after all, is modeled on the other. If constructed carefully as a conservative social ideology, the notion of stable gay relationships might even serve to buttress the ethic of heterosexual marriage, by showing how even those excluded from it can wish to model themselves on its shape and structure. This very truth, of course, is why liberationists are so hostile to the entire notion. Rather than liberating society from asphyxiating conventions it actually harnesses one minority group—homosexuals—and enlists them in the conservative structures that liberationists find so inimical. One can indeed see the liberationists' reasons for opposing such a move. But why should conservatives oppose it?

The Closet Straight
HADLEY ARKES

From National Review, *July 5, 1993*

This early response to the arguments outlined in "The Politics of Homosexuality," an essay I wrote for The New Republic *in May 1993 and elaborated in* Virtually Normal, *hit on several subsequent conservative themes. But the most important is the inherently heterosexual nature of the marriage bond. Arkes believes that homosexuals who want the right to marry essentially want the right to be straight.*

What Andrew Sullivan wants, most of all, is marriage. And he wants it for reasons that could not have been stated more powerfully by any heterosexual who had been raised, as Sullivan was, in the Catholic tradition and schooled in political philosophy. "The apex of emotional life," says Sullivan, "is found in the marital bond." The erotic interest may seek out copulation, but the fulfillment of eros depends on the integrity of a bond woven of sentiment and confirmed by law. Marriage is more than a private contract; it is "the highest public recognition of our personal integrity." Its equivalent will not be supplied by a string of sensual nights, accumulated over many years of "living together." The very existence of marriage "premises the core of our emotional development. It is the architectonic institution that frames our emotional life."

No one could doubt for a moment: as much as any of the "guys" in the Damon Runyon stories, the man who wrote those lines is headed, irresistibly, for marriage. What he craves—homosexual marriage—would indeed require the approval conferred by law. It would also require a benediction conferred by straight people, who would have to consent to that vast, new modeling of our laws. That project will not be undertaken readily, and it may not be undertaken at all. Still, there is something, rooted in the nature of Andrew Sullivan, that must needs marriage.

But as Mona Charen pointed out, in an encounter with Sullivan at the National Review Institute conference this winter (*NR*, March 29), it is not marriage that domesticates men; it is women.

I had the chance to see my own younger son, settled with three of his closest friends in a townhouse in Georgetown during his college years. The labors of the kitchen and the household were divided with a concern for domestic order, and the abrasions of living together were softened by the ties of friendship. And yet, no one, entering that house, could doubt for a moment that he was in a camp occupied for a while by young males, with their hormones flowing.

This is not to deny, of course, that men may truly love men, or commit themselves to a life of steady friendship. But many of us have continued to wonder just why any of these relations would be enhanced in any way by adding to them the ingredients of penetration—or marriage. The purpose of this alliance, after all, could not be the generation of children, and a marriage would not be needed then as the stable framework for welcoming and sheltering children. For gays, the ceremony of marriage could have the function of proclaiming to the world an exclusive love, a special dedication, which comes along with a solemn promise to forgo all other, competing loves. In short, it would draw its power from the romance of monogamy. But is that the vision that drives the movement for "gay rights"? An excruciating yearning for monogamy?

That may indeed be Andrew Sullivan's own yearning, but his position is already marking him as a curious figure in the camp of gay activists. When Sullivan commends the ideal of marriage for gays, he would seem to be pleading merely for the inclusion of gay "couples" in an institution that is indeed confined to pairs, of adults, in monogamous unions. But that is not exactly the vision of gay sex.

For many activists and connoisseurs, Sullivan would represent a rather wimpish, constricted view of the world they would open to themselves through sexual liberation. After all, the permissions for this new sexual freedom have been cast to that amorphous formula of "sexual orientation": the demand of gay rights is that we should recede from casting moral judgments on the way that people find their pleasure in engagements they regard as "sexual." In its strange abstraction, "sexual orientation" could take in sex with animals or the steamier versions of sadomasochism. The devotees of S&M were much in evidence during the recent march in Washington, but we may put aside for a moment these interests, to consider others which are even more exotic yet. There is, for example, the North American Man-Boy

Love Association, a contingent of gay activists who identify themselves, unashamedly, as pedophiles. They insist that nothing in their "sexual orientation" should disqualify them to work as professional counselors, say, in the schools of New York, and to counsel young boys. And since they respect themselves, they will not hold back from commending their own way of life to their young charges. If there is to be gay marriage, would it be confined then only to adults? And if men are inclined to a life of multiple partners, why should marriage be confined to two persons? Why indeed should the notion of gay marriage be scaled down to fit the notions held by Andrew Sullivan?

The sources of anguish run even deeper here than Sullivan may suspect, for his dilemma may be crystallized in this way: If he would preserve the traditional understanding of marriage and monogamy, he would not speak for much of a constituency among gays. But if the notion of "marriage" were enlarged and redefined—if it could take in a plurality of people and shifting combinations—it could hardly be the kind of marriage that Sullivan devoutly wishes as "the apex of emotional life" and "the highest public recognition of our personal integrity."

In traditional marriage, the understanding of monogamy was originally tied to the "natural teleology" of the body—to the recognition that only two people, no more and no fewer, can generate children. To that understanding of a union, or a "marriage," the alliance of two men would offer such an implausible want of resemblance that it would appear almost as a mocking burlesque. It would be rather like confounding, as Lincoln used to say, a "horse chestnut" and a "chestnut horse." The mockery would be avoided if the notion of marriage could be opened, or broadened, to accommodate the varieties of sexual experience. The most notable accommodation would be the acceptance of several partners, and the change could be readily reckoned precisely because it would hardly be novel: the proposal for gay marriage would compel us to look again—to look anew with eyes unclouded by prejudice—to the ancient appeal of polygamy. After all, there would be an Equal Protection problem now: we could scarcely confine this new "marital" arrangement only to members of one gender. But then, once the arrangement is opened simply to "consenting adults," on what ground would we object to the mature couplings of aunts and nephews, or even fathers and daughters—couplings that show a remarkable persistence in our own age, even against the barriers of law and sentiment that have been cast up over centuries? All kinds of questions, once placed in a merciful repose, may reasonably be opened again. They become live issues once we are willing to ponder that simple question, Why should marriage be confined, after all, to couples, and to pairs drawn from different sexes?

That question, if it comes to be treated as open and problematic, will not readily be closed, or not at least on the terms that Andrew Sullivan seeks. The melancholy news then is this: We cannot deliver to him what he wants without introducing, into our laws, notions that must surely undercut the rationale and the justification for marriage. The marriage that he wants, he cannot practicably have; but in seeking it, he runs the risk of weakening even further the opinion that sustains marriage as "the architectonic institution that frames our emotional life." . . .

Against Homosexual Marriage

JAMES Q. WILSON

From Commentary, *March 1996*

In a rigorous point-by-point engagement with the arguments
of Virtually Normal, *James Q. Wilson expresses the conserva-*
tive desire not to impose change against the moral sensibilities
of a heterosexual majority.

Sullivan recounts three main arguments concerning homosexual marriage, two against and one for. He labels them prohibitionist, conservative, and liberal. I think it easier to grasp the
origins of the three main arguments by referring to the principles on which they are based.

The prohibitionist argument is in fact a biblical one; the
heart of it was stated by Dennis Prager in an essay reprinted in
the *Public Interest* ("Homosexuality, the Bible, and Us," Summer 1993). When the first books of the Bible were written, and
for a long time thereafter, heterosexual love is what seemed at
risk. In many cultures—not only in Egypt or among the Canaan-
ite tribes surrounding ancient Israel but later in Greece, Rome,
and the Arab world, to say nothing of large parts of China, Japan,
and elsewhere—homosexual practices were common and widely
tolerated or even exalted. The Torah reversed this, making the
family the central unit of life, the obligation to marry one of the
first responsibilities of man, and the linkage of sex to procreation
the highest standard by which to judge sexual relations. Leviticus puts the matter sharply and apparently beyond quibble.

Thou shalt not live with mankind as with womankind; it is an abomination. . . . If a man also lie with mankind, as he lieth with a woman, both of them have committed an abomination; they shall surely be put to death; their blood shall be upon them.

Sullivan acknowledges the power of Leviticus but deals with it by placing it in a relative context. What is the nature of this "abomination"? Is it like killing your mother or stealing a neighbor's bread, or is it more like refusing to eat shellfish or having sex during menstruation? Sullivan suggests that all of these injunctions were written on the same moral level and hence can be accepted or ignored *as a whole.* He does not fully sustain this view, and in fact a refutation of it can be found in Prager's essay. In Prager's opinion and mine, people at the time of Moses, and for centuries before him, understood that there was a fundamental difference between whom you killed and what you ate, and in all likelihood people then and for centuries earlier linked whom you could marry closer to the principles that defined life than they did to the rules that defined diets.

The New Testament contains an equally vigorous attack on homosexuality by St. Paul. Sullivan partially deflects it by noting Paul's conviction that the earth was about to end and the Second Coming was near; under these conditions, all forms of sex were suspect. But Sullivan cannot deny that Paul singled out homosexuality as deserving of special criticism. He seems to pass over this obstacle without effective retort.

Instead, he takes up a different theme, namely, that on grounds of consistency many heterosexual practices—adultery, sodomy, premarital sex, and divorce, among others—should be outlawed equally with homosexual acts of the same character. The difficulty with this is that it mistakes the distinction alive in most people's minds between marriage as an institution and marriage as a practice. As an institution, it deserves unqualified support; as a practice, we recognize that married people are as imperfect as anyone else. Sullivan's understanding of the prohibitionist argument suffers from his unwillingness to acknowledge this distinction.

The second argument against homosexual marriage—Sullivan's conservative category—is based on natural law as originally set forth by Aristotle and Thomas Aquinas and more recently restated by Hadley Arkes, John Finnis, Robert George, Harry V. Jaffa, and others. How it is phrased varies a bit, but in general its advocates support a position like the following: man cannot live without the care and support of other people; natural law is the distillation of what thoughtful people have learned about the conditions of that care. The first thing they have learned is the supreme importance of marriage, for without it the newborn infant is unlikely to survive or, if he survives, to prosper. The necessary conditions of a decent family life are the acknowledgment by its members that a man will not sleep with his daughter or a woman with her son and that neither will openly choose sex outside marriage.

Now, some of these conditions are violated, but there is a penalty in each case that is supported by the moral convictions of almost all who witness the violation. On simple utilitarian grounds it may be hard to object to incest or adultery; if both parties to such an act welcome it and if it is secret, what differences does it make? But very few people, and then only ones among the overeducated, seem to care much about mounting a utilitarian assault on the family. To this assault, natural-law theorists respond much as would the average citizen—never mind "utility," what counts is what is right. In particular, homosexual uses of the reproductive organs violate the condition that sex serve solely as the basis of heterosexual marriage.

To Sullivan, what is defective about the natural-law thesis is that it assumes different purposes in heterosexual and homosexual love: moral consummation in the first case and pure utility or pleasure alone in the second. But in fact, Sullivan suggests, homosexual love can be as consummatory as heterosexual. He notes that as the Roman Catholic Church has deepened its understanding of the involuntary—that is, in some sense genetic—basis of homosexuality, it has attempted to keep homosexuals in the church as objects of affection and nurture, while banning homosexual acts as perverse.

But this, though better than nothing, will not work, Sullivan writes. To show why, he adduces an analogy to a sterile person. Such a person is permitted to serve in the military or enter an unproductive marriage; why not homosexuals? If homosexuals marry without procreation, they are no different (he suggests) from a sterile man or woman who marries without hope of procreation. Yet people, I think, want the form observed even when the practice varies; a sterile marriage, whether from choice or necessity, remains a marriage of a man and a woman. To this Sullivan offers essentially an aesthetic response. Just as albinos remind us of the brilliance of color and genius teaches us about moderation, homosexuals are a "natural foil" to the heterosexual union, "a variation that does not eclipse the theme." Moreover, the threat posed by the foil to the theme is slight as compared to the threats posed by adultery, divorce, and prostitution. To be consistent, Sullivan once again reminds us, society would have to ban adulterers from the military as it now bans confessed homosexuals.

But again this misses the point. It would make more sense to ask why an alternative to marriage should be invented and praised when we are having enough trouble maintaining the institution at all. Suppose that gay or lesbian marriage were authorized; rather than producing a "natural foil" that would "not eclipse the theme," I suspect such a move would call even more seriously into question the role of marriage at a time when the threats to it, ranging from single-parent families to common divorces, have hit record highs. Kenneth Minogue recently wrote of Sullivan's book that support for homosexual marriage would strike most people as "mere parody," one that could further weaken an already strained institution.

To me, the chief limitation of Sullivan's view is that it presupposes that marriage would have the same, domesticating, effect on homosexual members as it has on heterosexuals, while leaving the latter largely unaffected. Those are very large assumptions that no modern society has ever tested.

Nor does it seem plausible to me that a modern society resists homosexual marriages entirely out of irrational prejudice. Marriage is a union, sacred to most, that unites a man and woman together for life. It is a sacrament of the Catholic Church and central to every other faith. Is it out of misinformation that every modern society has embraced this view and rejected the alternative? Societies differ greatly in their attitude toward the income people may have, the relations among their various races, and the distribution of political power. But they differ scarcely at all over the distinctions between heterosexual and homosexual couples. The former are overwhelmingly preferred over the latter. The reason, I believe, is that these distinctions involve the nature of marriage and thus the very meaning—even more, the very possibility—of society.

The final argument over homosexual marriage is the liberal one, based on civil rights.

As we have seen, the Hawaiian Supreme Court ruled that any state-imposed sexual distinction would have to meet the test of strict scrutiny, a term used by the U.S. Supreme Court only for racial and similar classifications. In doing this, the Hawaiian court distanced itself from every other state court decision— there are several—in this area so far. A variant of the suspect-class argument, though, has been suggested by some scholars who contend that denying access to a marriage license by two people of the same sex is no different from denying access to two people of different sexes but also different races. The Hawaiian Supreme Court embraced this argument as well, explicitly comparing its decision to that of the U.S. Supreme Court when it overturned state laws banning marriages involving miscegenation.

But the comparison with black-white marriages is itself suspect. Beginning around 1964, and no doubt powerfully affected by the passage of the Civil Rights Act of that year, public attitudes toward race began to change dramatically. Even allowing for exaggerated statements to pollsters, there is little doubt that people in fact acquired a new view of blacks. Not so with homosexuals. Though the campaign to aid them has been going on vigorously for about a quarter of a century, it has produced few, if any, gains in public acceptance, and the greatest resistance, I think, has been with respect to homosexual marriages.

Consider the difference. What has been at issue in race relations is not marriage among blacks (for over a century, that right has been universally granted) or even miscegenation (long before the civil-rights movement, many Southern states had repealed such laws). Rather, it has been the routine contact between the races in schools, jobs, and neighborhoods. Our own history, in other words, has long made it clear that marriage is a different issue from the issue of social integration.

There is another way, too, in which the comparison with race is less than helpful, as Sullivan himself points out. Thanks to the changes in public attitudes I mentioned a moment ago, gradually race was held to be not central to decisions about hiring, firing, promoting, and schooling, and blacks began to make extraordinary advances in society. But then, in an effort to enforce this new view, liberals came to embrace affirmative action, a policy that said that race *was* central to just such issues, in order to ensure that *real* mixing occurred. This move created a crisis, for liberalism had always been based on the proposition that a liberal political system should encourage, as John Stuart Mill put it, "experiments in living" free of religious or political direction. To contemporary liberals, however, being neutral about race was tantamount to being neutral about a set of human preferences that in such matters as neighborhood and schooling left groups largely (but not entirely) separate.

Sullivan, who wisely sees that hardly anybody is really prepared to ignore a political opportunity to change lives, is not disposed to have much of this either in the area of race or in that of sex. And he points out with great clarity that popular attitudes toward sexuality are anyway quite different from those about race, as is evident from the fact that wherever sexual orientation is subject to local regulations, such regulations are rarely invoked. Why? Because homosexuals can "pass" or not, as they wish; they can and do accumulate education and wealth; they exercise political power. The two things a homosexual cannot do are join the military as an avowed homosexual or marry another homosexual.

The result, Sullivan asserts, is a wrenching paradox. On the one hand, society has historically tolerated the brutalization inflicted on people because of the color of their skin, but freely allowed them to marry; on the other hand, it has given equal opportunity to homosexuals, while denying them the right to marry. This, indeed, is where Sullivan draws the line. A black or Hispanic child, if heterosexual, has many friends, he writes, but a gay child "generally has no one." And that is why the social stigma attached to homosexuality is different from that attached to race or ethnicity—"because it attacks the very heart of what makes a human being human: the ability to love and be loved." Here is the essence of Sullivan's case. It is a powerful one, even if (as I suspect) his pro-marriage sentiments are not shared by all homosexuals.

Let us assume for the moment that a chance to live openly and legally with another homosexual is desirable. To believe that, we must set aside biblical injunctions, a difficult matter in a profoundly religious nation. But suppose we manage the diversion, perhaps on the grounds that if most Americans skip church, they can as readily avoid other errors of (possibly) equal magnitude. Then we must ask on what terms the union shall be arranged. There are two alternatives—marriage or domestic partnership.

Sullivan acknowledges the choice, but disparages the domestic-partnership laws that have evolved in some foreign countries and in some American localities. His reasons, essentially conservative ones, are that domestic partnerships are too easily formed and too easily broken. Only real marriages matter. But—aside from the fact that marriage is in serious decline, and that only slightly more than half of all marriages performed in the United States this year will be between never-before-married heterosexuals—what is distinctive about marriage is that it is an institution created to sustain child-rearing. Whatever losses it has suffered in *this* respect, its function remains what it has always been.

The role of raising children is entrusted in principle to married heterosexual couples because after much experimentation—several thousand years, more or less—we have found nothing else that works as well. Neither a gay nor a lesbian couple can of its own resources produce a child; another party must be involved. What do we call this third party? A friend? A sperm or egg bank? An anonymous donor? There is no settled language for even describing, much less approving of, such persons.

Suppose we allowed homosexual couples to raise children who were created out of a prior heterosexual union or adopted from someone else's heterosexual contact. What would we think of this? There is very little research on the matter. Charlotte Patterson's famous essay, "Children of Gay and Lesbian Parents" (*Journal of Child Development*, 1992), begins by conceding that the existing studies focus on children born into a heterosexual union that ended in divorce or that was transformed when the mother or father "came out" as a homosexual. Hardly any research has been done on children acquired at the outset by a homosexual couple. We therefore have no way of knowing how they would behave. And even if we had such studies, they might tell us rather little unless they were conducted over a very long period of time.

But it is one thing to be born into an apparently heterosexual family and then many years later to learn that one of your parents is homosexual. It is quite another to be acquired as an infant from an adoption agency or a parent-for-hire and learn from the first years of life that you are, because of your family's position, radically different from almost all other children you will meet. No one can now say how grievous this would be. We know that young children tease one another unmercifully; adding this dimension does not seem to be a step in the right direction.

Of course, homosexual "families," with or without children, might be rather few in number. Just how few, it is hard to say. Perhaps Sullivan himself would marry, but, given the great tendency of homosexual males to be promiscuous, many more like him would not, or if they did, would not marry with as much seriousness. . . .

The courts in Hawaii and in the nation's capital must struggle with all these issues under the added encumbrance of a contemporary outlook that makes law the search for rights, and responsibility the recognition of rights. Indeed, thinking of laws about marriage as documents that confer or withhold rights is itself an error of fundamental importance—one that the highest court in Hawaii has already committed. "Marriage," it wrote, "is a state-conferred legal-partnership status, the existence of which gives rise to a multiplicity of rights and benefits. . . ." A state-conferred legal partnership? To lawyers, perhaps; to mankind, I think not. The Hawaiian court has thus set itself on the same course of action as the misguided Supreme Court in 1973 when it thought that laws about abortion were merely an assertion of the rights of a living mother and an unborn fetus.

I have few favorable things to say about the political systems of other modern nations, but on these fundamental matters—abortion, marriage, military service—they often do better by allowing legislatures to operate than we do by deferring to courts. Our challenge is to find a way of formulating a policy with respect to homosexual unions that is not the result of a reflexive act of judicial rights-conferring, but is instead a considered expression of the moral convictions of a people.

For Better or Worse?

JONATHAN RAUCH

From The New Republic, *May 6, 1996*

Rauch delivers an almost Jesuitical analysis of why same-sex marriage makes sense for conservatives. He is particularly acute in making a social as well as a political argument for the virtues that marriage inculcates—especially in gay men. He is quite comfortable about using the threat of stigma to bring more social order into gay men's lives.

Whether gay marriage makes sense—and whether straight marriage makes sense—depends on what marriage is actually for. Current secular thinking on this question is shockingly sketchy. Gay activists say: marriage is for love, and we love each other, therefore we should be able to marry. Traditionalists say: marriage is for children, and homosexuals do not (or should not) have children, therefore you should not be able to marry. That, unfortunately, pretty well covers the spectrum. I say "unfortunately" because both views are wrong. They misunderstand and impoverish the social meaning of marriage.

So what is marriage for? Modern marriage is, of course, based upon traditions that religion helped to codify and enforce. But religious doctrine has no special standing in the world of secular law and policy (the "Christian nation" crowd notwithstanding). If we want to know what and whom marriage is for in modern America, we need a sensible secular doctrine.

At one point, marriage in secular society was largely a matter of business: cementing family ties, providing social status for men and economic support for women, conferring dowries, and so on. Marriages were typically arranged, and "love" in the modern sense was no prerequisite. In Japan, remnants of this system remain, and it works surprisingly well. Couples stay together because they view their marriage as a partnership: an investment in social stability for themselves and their children. Because Japanese couples don't expect as much emotional fulfillment as we do, they are less inclined to break up. They also take a somewhat more relaxed attitude toward adultery. What's a little extracurricular love provided that each partner is fulfilling his or her many other marital duties?

In the West, of course, love is a defining element. The notion of lifelong love is charming, if ambitious, and certainly love is a desirable element of marriage. In society's eyes, however, it cannot be the defining element. You may or may not love your husband, but the two of you are just as married either way. You may love your mistress, but that certainly doesn't make her your spouse. Love helps make sense of marriage emotionally, but it is not terribly important in making sense of marriage from the point of view of social policy.

If love does not define the purpose of secular marriage, what does? Neither the law nor secular thinking provides a clear answer. Today marriage is almost entirely a voluntary arrangement whose contents are up to the people making the deal. There are few if any behaviors that automatically end a marriage. If a man beats his wife, which is about the worst thing he can do to her, he may be convicted of assault, but his marriage is not automatically dissolved. Couples can be adulterous ("open") yet remain married. They can be celibate, too; consummation is not required. All in all, it is an impressive and also rather astonishing victory for modern individualism that so important an institution should be so bereft of formal social instruction as to what should go on inside of it.

Secular society tells us only a few things about marriage. First, marriage depends on the consent of the parties. Second, the parties are not children. Third, the number of parties is two. Fourth, one is a man and the other a woman. Within those rules a marriage is whatever anyone says it is.

Perhaps it is enough simply to say that marriage is as it is and should not be tampered with. This sounds like a crudely reactionary position. In fact, however, of all the arguments against reforming marriage, it is probably the most powerful.

Call it a Hayekian argument, after the great libertarian economist F. A. Hayek, who developed this line of thinking in his book *The Fatal Conceit*. In a market system, the prices generated by impersonal forces may not make sense from any one person's point of view, but they encode far more information than even the cleverest person could ever gather. In a similar fashion, human societies evolve rich and complicated webs of nonlegal rules in the form of customs, traditions and institutions. Like prices, they may seem irrational or arbitrary. But the very fact that they are the customs that have evolved implies that they embody a practical logic that may not be apparent to even a sophisticated analyst. And the web of custom cannot be torn apart and reordered at will because once its internal logic is violated it falls apart. Intellectuals, such as Marxists or feminists, who seek to deconstruct and rationally rebuild social traditions, will produce not better order but chaos.

So the Hayekian view argues strongly against gay marriage. It says that the current rules may not be best and may even be unfair. But they are all we have, and, once you say that marriage need not be male-female, soon marriage will stop being anything at all. You can't mess with the formula without causing unforeseen consequences, possibly including the implosion of the institution of marriage itself.

However, there are problems with the Hayekian position. It

is untenable in its extreme form and unhelpful in its milder version. In its extreme form, it implies that no social reforms should ever be undertaken. Indeed, no laws should be passed, because they interfere with the natural evolution of social mores. How could Hayekians abolish slavery? They would probably note that slavery violates fundamental moral principles. But in so doing they would establish a moral platform from which to judge social rules, and thus acknowledge that abstracting social debate from moral concerns is not possible.

If the ban on gay marriage were only mildly unfair, and if the costs of changing it were certain to be enormous, then the ban could stand on Hayekian grounds. But, if there is any social policy today that has a fair claim to be scaldingly inhumane, it is the ban on gay marriage. As conservatives tirelessly and rightly point out, marriage is society's most fundamental institution. To bar any class of people from marrying as they choose is an extraordinary deprivation. When not so long ago it was illegal in parts of America for blacks to marry whites, no one could claim that this was a trivial disenfranchisement. Granted, gay marriage raises issues that interracial marriage does not; but no one can argue that the deprivation is a minor one.

To outweigh such a serious claim it is not enough to say that gay marriage might lead to bad things. Bad things happened as a result of legalizing contraception, but that did not make it the wrong thing to do. Besides, it seems doubtful that extending marriage to, say, another 3 or 5 percent of the population would have anything like the effects that no-fault divorce has had, to say nothing of contraception. By now, the "traditional" understanding of marriage has been sullied in all kinds of ways. It is hard to think of a bigger affront to tradition, for instance, than allowing married women to own property independently of their husbands or allowing them to charge their husbands with rape.

Surely it is unfair to say that marriage may be reformed for the sake of anyone and everyone except homosexuals, who must respect the dictates of tradition.

Faced with these problems, the milder version of the Hayekian argument says not that social traditions shouldn't be tampered with at all, but that they shouldn't be tampered with lightly. Fine. In this case, no one is talking about casual messing around; both sides have marshaled their arguments with deadly seriousness. Hayekians surely have to recognize that appeals to blind tradition and to the risks inherent in social change do not, a priori, settle anything in this instance. They merely warn against frivolous change.

So we turn to what has become the standard view of marriage's purpose. Its proponents would probably like to call it a child-centered view, but it is actually an anti-gay view, as will become clear. Whatever you call it, it is the view of marriage that is heard most often, and in the context of the debate over gay marriage it is heard almost exclusively. In its most straightforward form it goes as follows (I quote from James Q. Wilson's fine book *The Moral Sense*):

> A family is not an association of independent people; it is a human commitment designed to make possible the rearing of moral and healthy children. Governments care—or ought to care—about families for this reason, and scarcely for any other.

Wilson speaks about "family" rather than "marriage" as such, but one may, I think, read him as speaking of marriage without doing any injustice to his meaning. The resulting proposition—government ought to care about marriage almost entirely because of children—seems reasonable. But there are problems. The first, obviously, is that gay couples may have children, whether through adoption, prior marriage or (for lesbians) artificial insemination. Leaving aside the thorny issue of gay adoption, the point is that if the mere presence of children is the test, then homosexual relationships can certainly pass it.

You might note, correctly, that heterosexual marriages are more likely to produce children than homosexual ones. When granting marriage licenses to heterosexuals, however, we do not ask how likely the couple is to have children. We assume that they are entitled to get married whether or not they end up with children. Understanding this, conservatives often make an interesting move. In seeking to justify the state's interest in marriage, they shift from the actual presence of children to the anatomical possibility of making them. Hadley Arkes, a political science professor and prominent opponent of homosexual marriage, makes the case this way:

> The traditional understanding of marriage is grounded in the "natural teleology of the body"—in the inescapable fact that only a man and a woman, and only two people, not three, can generate a child. Once marriage is detached from that natural teleology of the body, what ground of principle would thereafter confine marriage to two people rather than some larger grouping? That is, on what ground of principle would the law reject the claim of a gay couple that their love is not confined to a coupling of two, but that they are woven into a larger ensemble with yet another person or two?

What he seems to be saying is that, where the possibility of natural children is nil, the meaning of marriage is nil. If marriage is allowed between members of the same sex, then the concept of marriage has been emptied of content except to ask whether the parties love each other. Then anything goes, including polygamy. This reasoning presumably is what those opposed to gay marriage have in mind when they claim that, once gay marriage is legal, marriage to pets will follow close behind.

But Arkes and his sympathizers make two mistakes. To see them, break down the claim into two components: (1) Two-person marriage derives its special status from the anatomical possibility that the partners can create natural children; and (2) apart from (1), two-person marriage has no purpose sufficiently strong to justify its special status. That is, absent justification (1), anything goes.

The first proposition is wholly at odds with the way society actually views marriage. Leave aside the insistence that natural, as opposed to adopted, children define the importance of marriage. The deeper problem, apparent right away, is the issue of sterile heterosexual couples. Here the "anatomical possibility" crowd has a problem, for a homosexual union is, anatomically speaking, nothing but one variety of sterile union and no different even in principle: a woman without a uterus has no more potential for giving birth than a man without a vagina.

It may sound like carping to stress the case of barren heterosexual marriage: the vast majority of newlywed heterosexual couples, after all, can have children and probably will. But the point here is fundamental. There are far more sterile heterosexual unions in America than homosexual ones. The "anatomical possibility" crowd cannot have it both ways. If the possibility of children is what gives meaning to marriage, then a post-menopausal woman who applies for a marriage license should be turned away at the courthouse door. What's more, she should be hooted at and condemned for stretching the meaning of marriage beyond its natural basis and so reducing the institution to frivolity. People at the Family Research Council or Concerned Women for America should point at her and say, "If she can marry, why not polygamy?"

Obviously, the "anatomical" conservatives do not say this,

because they are sane. They instead flail around, saying that sterile men and women were at least born with the right-shaped parts for making children, and so on. Their position is really a nonposition. It says that the "natural children" rationale defines marriage when homosexuals are involved but not when heterosexuals are involved. When the parties to union are sterile heterosexuals, the justification for marriage must be something else. But what?

Now arises the oddest part of the "anatomical" argument. Look at proposition (2) above. It says that, absent the anatomical justification for marriage, anything goes. In other words, it dismisses the idea that there might be other good reasons for society to sanctify marriage above other kinds of relationships. Why would anybody make this move? I'll hazard a guess: to exclude homosexuals. Any rationale that justifies sterile heterosexual marriages can also apply to homosexual ones. For instance, marriage makes women more financially secure. Very nice, say the conservatives. But that rationale could be applied to lesbians, so it's definitely out.

The end result of this stratagem is perverse to the point of being funny. The attempt to ground marriage in children (or the anatomical possibility thereof) falls flat. But, having lost that reason for marriage, the antigay people can offer no other. In their fixation on excluding homosexuals, they leave themselves no consistent justification for the privileged status of *heterosexual* marriage. They thus tear away any coherent foundation that secular marriage might have, which is precisely the opposite of what they claim they want to do. If they have to undercut marriage to save it from homosexuals, so be it!

For the record, I would be the last to deny that children are one central reason for the privileged status of marriage. When men and women get together, children are a likely outcome; and, as we are learning in ever more unpleasant ways, when children grow up without two parents, trouble ensues. Children are not a trivial reason for marriage; they just cannot be the only reason.

What are the others? It seems to me that the two strongest candidates are these: domesticating men and providing reliable caregivers. Both purposes are critical to the functioning of a humane and stable society, and both are much better served by marriage—that is, by one-to-one lifelong commitment—than by any other institution.

Civilizing young males is one of any society's biggest problems. Whenever unattached males gather in packs, you see no end of trouble; wildings in Central Park, gangs in Los Angeles, soccer hooligans in Britain, skinheads in Germany, fraternity hazings in universities, grope-lines in the military and, in a different but ultimately no less tragic way, the bathhouses and wanton sex of gay San Francisco or New York in the 1970s.

For taming men, marriage is unmatched. "Of all the institutions through which men may pass—schools, factories, the military—marriage has the largest effect," Wilson writes in *The Moral Sense*. (A token of the casualness of current thinking about marriage is that the man who wrote those words could, later in the very same book, say that government should care about fostering families for "scarcely any other" reason than children.) If marriage—that is, the binding of men into couples—did nothing else, its power to settle men, to keep them at home and out of trouble, would be ample justification for its special status.

Of course, women and older men don't generally travel in marauding or orgiastic packs. But in their case the second rationale comes into play. A second enormous problem for society is what to do when someone is beset by some sort of burdensome contingency. It could be cancer, a broken back, unemployment or depression; it could be exhaustion from work or stress under pressure. If marriage has any meaning at all, it is that, when you collapse from a stroke, there will be at least one other person whose "job" is to drop everything and come to your aid; or that when you come home after being fired by the postal service there will be someone to persuade you not to kill the supervisor.

Obviously, both rationales—the need to settle males and the need to have people looked after—apply to sterile people as well as fertile ones, and apply to childless couples as well as to ones with children. The first explains why everybody feels relieved when the town delinquent gets married, and the second explains why everybody feels happy when an aging widow takes a second husband. From a social point of view, it seems to me, both rationales are far more compelling as justifications of marriage's special status than, say, love. And both of them apply to homosexuals as well as to heterosexuals.

Take the matter of settling men. It is probably true that women and children, more than just the fact of marriage, help civilize men. But that hardly means that the settling effect of marriage on homosexual men is negligible. To the contrary, being tied to a committed relationship plainly helps stabilize gay men. Even without marriage, coupled gay men have steady sex partners and relationships that they value and therefore tend to be less wanton. Add marriage, and you bring a further array of stabilizing influences. One of the main benefits of publicly recognized marriage is that it binds couples together not only in their own eyes but also in the eyes of society at large. Around the partners is woven a web of expectations that they will spend nights together, go to parties together, take out mortgages together, buy furniture at Ikea together, and so on—all of which helps tie them together and keep them off the streets and at home. Surely that is a very good thing, especially as compared to the closet-gay culture of furtive sex with innumerable partners in parks and bathhouses.

The other benefit of marriage—caretaking—clearly applies to homosexuals. One of the first things many people worry about when coming to terms with their homosexuality is: Who will take care of me when I'm ailing or old? Society needs to care about this, too, as the AIDS crisis has made horribly clear. If that crisis has shown anything, it is that homosexuals can and will take care of each other, sometimes with breathtaking devotion—and that no institution can begin to match the care of a devoted partner. Legally speaking, marriage creates kin. Surely society's interest in kin-creation is strongest of all for people who are unlikely to be supported by children in old age and who may well be rejected by their own parents in youth.

Gay marriage, then, is far from being a mere exercise in political point-making or rights-mongering. On the contrary, it serves two of the three social purposes that make marriage so indispensable and irreplaceable for heterosexuals. Two out of three may not be the whole ball of wax, but it is more than enough to give society a compelling interest in marrying off homosexuals.

There is no substitute. Marriage is the *only* institution that adequately serves these purposes. The power of marriage is not just legal but social. It seals its promise with the smiles and tears of family, friends and neighbors. It shrewdly exploits ceremony (big, public weddings) and money (expensive gifts, dowries) to deter casual commitment and to make bailing out embarrassing. Stag parties and bridal showers signal that what is beginning is not just a legal arrangement but a whole new stage of life. "Domestic partner" laws do none of these things.

I'll go further: far from being a substitute for the real thing, marriage-lite may undermine it. Marriage is a deal between a couple and society, not just between two people: society recognizes the sanctity and autonomy of the pair-bond, and in exchange each spouse commits to being the other's nurse, social worker and policeman of first resort. Each marriage is its own little society within society. Any step that weakens the deal by granting the legal benefits of marriage without also requiring the public commitment is begging for trouble.

So gay marriage makes sense for several of the same reasons that straight marriage makes sense. That would seem a natural place to stop. But the logic of the argument compels one to go a twist further. If it is good for society to have people attached, then it is not enough just to make marriage available. Marriage should also be *expected*. This, too, is just as true for homosexuals as for heterosexuals. So, if homosexuals are justified in expecting access to marriage, society is equally justified in expecting them to use it. I'm not saying that out-of-wedlock sex should be scandalous or that people should be coerced into marrying. The mechanisms of expectation are more subtle. When grandma cluck-clucks over a still-unmarried young man, or when mom says she wishes her little girl would settle down, she is expressing a strong and well-justified preference: one that is quietly echoed in a thousand ways throughout society and that produces subtle but important pressure to form and sustain unions. This is a good and necessary thing, and it will be as necessary for homosexuals as heterosexuals. If gay marriage is recognized, single gay people over a certain age should not be surprised when they are disapproved of or pitied. That is a vital part of what makes marriage work. It's stigma as social policy.

If marriage is to work it cannot be merely a "lifestyle option." It must be privileged. That is, it must be understood to be better, on average, than other ways of living. Not mandatory, not good where everything else is bad, but better: a general norm, rather than a personal taste. The biggest worry about gay marriage, I think is, is that homosexuals might get it but then mostly not use it. Gay neglect of marriage wouldn't greatly erode the bonding power of heterosexual marriage (remember, homosexuals are only a tiny fraction of the population)—but it would certainly not help. And heterosexual society would rightly feel betrayed if, after legalization, homosexuals treated marriage as a minority taste rather than as a core institution of life. It is not enough, I think, for gay people to say we want the right to marry. If we do not use it, shame on us.

Let Them Wed

THE EDITORS

From the Economist, *January 6, 1996*

The sober, unsentimental, free market conservative British magazine weighs in—for the gay rights movement.

Marriage may be for the ages—but it changes by the year. And never, perhaps, has it changed as quickly as since the 1960s. In western law, wives are now equal rather than subordinate partners; interracial marriage is now widely accepted both in statute and in society; marital failure itself, rather than the fault of one partner, may be grounds for a split. With change, alas, has come strain. In the twenty-five years from 1960, divorce rates soared throughout the West—more than sextupled in Britain, where divorce appears inevitable for the world's most celebrated marriage, that of Charles and Diana Windsor. Struggling to keep law apace with reality, Britain's Tory government is even now advancing another marriage reform, seeking, on the whole sensibly, to make quick or impulsive divorce harder but no-fault divorce easier.

That, however, is not the kind of reform which some decidedly un-Tory people are seeking— and have begun to achieve. Denmark, Norway and Sweden now allow homosexual partners to register with the state and to claim many (though not all) of the prerogatives of marriage. The Dutch are moving in the same direction. In France and Belgium, cities and local governments have begun recognising gay partnerships. And, in the American state of Hawaii, a court case may legalise homosexual marriage itself.

As of today, however, there is no country which gives homosexuals the full right of marriage. And that is what gay activists in more and more places are seeking. Marriage, one might think, is in turbulent enough waters already. Can gay marriage be a good idea—now?

To understand why the answer is yes, first set aside a view whose appealing simplicity is its undoing. "Governments are not elected to arrange nuptial liaisons, much less to untangle them," writes Joe Rogaly in the *Financial Times*. "It is a purely private matter." On this libertarian view, the terms of a marriage contract should be the partners' business, not the state's. With the help of lawyers and sympathetic churchmen, homosexuals can create for themselves what is in all practical respects a marriage; if they lack a government licence, so what?

The government-limiting impulse motivating this view is admirable. But, in truth, the state's involvement in marriage is both inevitable and indispensable. Although many kinds of human pairings are possible, state-sanctioned marriage is, tautologically, the only one which binds couples together in the eyes of the law.

By doing so it confers upon partners unique rights to make life-or-death medical decisions, rights to inheritance, rights to share pensions and medical benefits; just as important, it confers upon each the legal responsibilities of guardianship and care of the other. Far from being frills, these benefits and duties go to the very core of the marriage contract; no church or employer or "commitment ceremony" can bestow them at one blow. If marriage is to do all the things that society demands of it, then the state must set some rules.

Just so, say traditionalists: and those rules should exclude homosexuals. Gay marriage, goes the argument, is both frivolous and dangerous: frivolous because it blesses unions in which society has no particular interest; dangerous because anything which trivialises marriage undermines this most basic of institutions. Traditionalists are right about the importance of marriage. But they are wrong to see gay marriage as trivial or frivolous.

It is true that the single most important reason society cares about marriage is for the sake of children. But society's stake in stable, long-term partnerships hardly ends there. Marriage remains an economic bulwark. Single people (especially women) are economically vulnerable, and much more likely to fall into the arms of the welfare state. Furthermore, they call sooner upon public support when they need care—and, indeed, are likelier to fall ill (married people, the numbers show, are not only happier but considerably healthier). Not least important, marriage is a great social stabiliser of men.

Homosexuals need emotional and economic stability no less than heterosexuals—and society surely benefits when they have it. "Then let them 'unchoose' homosexuality and marry someone of the opposite sex," was the old answer. Today that reply is untenable. Homosexuals do not choose their condition; indeed, they often try desperately hard, sometimes to the point of suicide, to avoid it. However, they are less and less willing either to hide or to lead lives of celibacy. For society, the real choice is between homosexual marriage and homosexual alienation. No social interest is served by choosing the latter.

To this principle of social policy, add a principle of government. Barring a compelling reason, governments should not discriminate between classes of citizens. As recently as 1967, blacks and whites in some American states could not wed. No one but a crude racist would defend such a rule now. Even granting that the case of homosexuals is more complex than the case of miscegenation, the state should presume against discriminating—especially when handing out something as important as a marriage licence. Thus the question becomes: is there a compelling reason to bar homosexuals from marriage?

One objection is simply that both would-be spouses are of the same sex. That is no answer; it merely repeats the question. Perhaps, then, once homosexuals can marry, marital anarchy will follow? That might be true if homosexual unions were arbitrary configurations, mere parodies of "real" marriage. But the truth is that countless homosexual couples, especially lesbian ones, have shown that they are as capable of fidelity, responsibility and devotion as are heterosexual couples—and this despite having to keep their unions secret, at least until recently. Would gay marriage weaken the standard variety? There is little reason to think so. Indeed, the opposite seems at least as likely: permitting gay marriage could reaffirm society's hope that people of all kinds settle down into stable unions.

The question of children in homosexual households—adoption, especially—is thorny. That question, however, is mainly separate from the matter of marriage as such. In settling a child with guardians who are not the natural parents, the courts and adoption agencies will consider a variety of factors, just as they do now; a couple's homosexuality may be one such factor (though it need not, by itself, be decisive).

In the end, leaving aside (as secular governments should) objections that may be held by particular religions, the case against homosexual marriage is this: people are unaccustomed to it. It is strange and radical. That is a sound argument for not pushing change along precipitously. Certainly it is an argument for legalising homosexual marriage through consensual politics (as in Denmark), rather than by court order (as may happen in America). But the direction of change is clear. If marriage is to fulfill its aspirations, it must be defined by the commitment of one to another for richer for poorer, in sickness and in health—not by the people it excludes.

Homosexuality: The Policy Questions
RICHARD A. POSNER

From Sex and Reason, *by Richard A. Posner, 1992*

Posner, a legal theorist best known for his pioneering work in law and economics, makes a case for limited tolerance—abolishing sodomy laws but retaining marriage rights as exclusively heterosexual. Even so, Posner is tentative in opposing marriage rights, and he puts great store by the settled instincts of a conservative populace.

There are three differences between punishing sodomy and confining the right to marry to heterosexuals. The first is that permitting homosexual marriage would be widely interpreted as placing a stamp of approval on homosexuality, while decriminalizing sodomy would not, at least not to anywhere near the same extent. To say that an act is not a crime is not to commend it; a great deal of behavior that is disgusting or immoral or both is nevertheless not criminal. But marriage, even though considered sacramental only by Catholics, is believed by most people in our society to be not merely a license to reproduce but also a desirable, even a noble, condition in which to live. To permit persons of the same sex to marry is to declare, or more precisely to be understood by many people to be declaring, that homosexual marriage is a desirable, even a noble, condition in which to live. This is not what most people in this society believe; and for reasons stated earlier it would be misleading to suggest that homosexual marriages are likely to be as stable or rewarding as heterosexual marriages, even granting as one must that a sizable fraction of heterosexual marriages in our society are not stable and are not rewarding. I do not suggest that government's pronouncing homosexual marriage a beatific state would cause heterosexuals to rethink their sexual preference. My concern lies elsewhere. It is that permitting homosexual marriage would place government in the dishonest position of propagating a false picture of the reality of homosexuals' lives.

Against this it can be argued that as heterosexual marriage becomes ever more unstable, temporary, and childless, the suggestion that it differs fundamentally from what homosexual marriages could be expected to be like becomes ever more implausible. And this is true. But it is a point in favor not of homosexual marriage but of chucking the whole institution of marriage in favor of an explicitly contractual approach that would make the current realities of marriage transparent.

The second difference between the sodomy and marriage issues will strike many readers as a trivial addendum to the first.

It is that the more broadly *marriage* is defined, the less information it and related terms convey. When we read that Mr. X is married or that Ms. Y is married, we know immediately that X's spouse is a woman and Y's a man. If we invite people to a party and ask them to bring their spouses, we know that each man will either come alone or bring a woman and that each woman will either come alone or bring a man. So a homosexual man will come alone and likewise a homosexual woman. If we do not care to limit the additional guests to spouses, we ask the invitees to bring not their spouses but their "guests." If our son or daughter tells us that he or she is getting married, we know the sex of the prospective spouse. All these understandings would be upset by permitting homosexual marriage. This of course is one reason homosexual rights advocates want homosexual marriage to be permitted. All I wish to emphasize is that there is an information cost to the proposal.

But there is also an information benefit. The denial of marriage to homosexuals prevents a homosexual couple from signaling the extent of their commitment. If marriage were abolished, heterosexual cohabitation would denote indifferently the briefest and the most permanent of relationships. If the "freedom to marry" of which the Supreme Court spoke in *Loving v. Virginia* were taken seriously, the deprivation to the homosexual couple denied the right to marry would carry a heavy weight; but of course the Court was thinking of heterosexual marriage.

The third difference between the sodomy and marriage issues is the most important. Abolishing the sodomy laws would have few collateral effects, though I have suggested that it would have one: it would make it easier for homosexuals to obtain jobs in fields at present closed to them. Authorizing homosexual marriage would have many collateral effects, simply because marriage is a status rich in entitlements. It would have effects on inheritance, social security, income tax, welfare payments, adoption, the division of property upon termination of the relationship, medical benefits, life insurance, immigration, and even testimonial privilege. (The *Commercial-News* of Danville, Ohio, carried an article under the intriguing banner "Homosexual Loses Court Battle over Use of Mate's Testimony." The mate in question was another man.) These incidents of marriage were designed with heterosexual marriage in mind, more specifically heterosexual marriages resulting in children. They may or may not fit the case of homosexual marriage; they are unlikely to fit it perfectly. Do we want homosexual couples to have the same rights of adoption and custody as heterosexual couples? Should we worry that a homosexual might marry a succession of dying AIDS patients in order to entitle them to spouse's medical benefits? These questions ought to be faced one by one rather than elided by conferring all the rights of marriage in a lump on homosexuals willing to undergo a wedding ceremony.

None of these points is decisive against permitting homosexual marriage. All together may not be. The benefits of such marriage may outweigh the costs. Nonetheless, since the public hostility to homosexuals in this country is too widespread to make homosexual marriage a feasible proposal even if it is on balance cost-justified, maybe the focus should be shifted to an intermediate solution that would give homosexuals most of what they want but at the same time meet the three objections I have advanced.

Denmark and Sweden, not surprisingly, provide the model. What in Denmark is called registered partnership and in Sweden homosexual cohabitation is in effect a form contract that homosexuals can use to create a simulacrum of marriage. The Danish law goes further than the Swedish: it places the registered partners under all the provisions of the marriage code except those relating to children, although a question has arisen whether the registered partner has the same beneficial rights in his (or her) partner's private pension that a spouse would have. Sweden, which already has defined a quasi-marital status for cohabitating heterosexuals, allows cohabiting homosexuals to elect that status, the main feature of which is an even division, upon the dissolution of the relationship, of what in this country would be called community property. The Danish approach is mechanical in assuming that the presence of children is the only thing that distinguishes heterosexual from homosexual marriage. The Swedish approach assumes, realistically I think, that a homosexual relationship, even when meant to last, is more like heterosexual cohabitation than like heterosexual marriage, so the forms that the Swedes have worked out to regularize what is after all an extremely common relationship in their country provide the appropriate model for homosexuals who want to live together in ours. It may indeed offer an increasingly attractive model for heterosexuals as well. . . .

Same-Sex Marriage Nears

WILLIAM SAFIRE

From The New York Times, *April 29, 1996*

*Conservative columnist William Safire comes out in favor of
domestic partnerships—but draws the line at marriage. But
notice his dismissal of some conservative arguments that the
changes in Hawaii are a result of "hyperactivist judges."*

As the legislative session headed toward a midnight close Friday night, opponents of homosexual marriage insisted on a recorded vote. Supporters of gay rights won. Hawaii's state senators voted 15 to 10 against the more conservative House's bill to ban the licensing of marital unions of persons of the same sex.

As a result, the state's lawyers will find it harder to assert a "compelling state interest" in limiting marriage to one man and one woman. *Baehr v. Miike* comes before Judge Kevin Chang in August; the likelihood increases that he will rule that the state Constitution's provision against sex discrimination precludes the state from refusing to issue marriage licenses to gay couples.

No longer can defenders of one-man, one-woman marriage claim that the institution is being threatened by hyperactivist judges. One state's duly elected representatives have just paved the way, and under the U.S. Constitution's "full faith and credit" clause, a judicial proceeding held in one state is to be honored in all states.

Nor is the movement limited to the United States. In The Hague last week, a majority of the Dutch Parliament called on the government to submit legislation permitting homosexual marriage. That would affect all members of the European Union; British gays could marry in Amsterdam and claim spousal status in London.

The Hawaii solons, in a tense conference just before the deadline, considered a compromise. Homosexuals in contracted "domestic partnerships" were not to be denied pension or insurance benefits or inheritance or other state tax deductions available to spouses, thereby assuring fairness as taxpayers and equal treatment as employees—but not including a state of matrimony. The compromise, which might have affected the outcome of the court case, failed. That was unfortunate because that is the way this issue should be resolved.

Libertarians like me have a tough time with same-sex marriage because we despise discrimination, cherish privacy and reject homophobia. When we express reluctance to rush to make a fundamental change in the legal and religious definition of a family, editorialists assail "entrenched anti-gay bigotry" and shrilly accuse all who fail to embrace S.S.M. of being "driven by social intolerance." Such straight-bashing neither contributes to civil discourse nor persuades us we are morally obtuse.

To the heart of the matter: Why break the age-old pattern of defining marriage as the union of one man, one woman? Or, to slant the question the other way: Why should heterosexuals have a lock on wedlock?

Serious arguments presented by supporters of same-sex marriage have force: In times of casual cohabitation, marriage would encourage homosexual couples to stay together and build stable, mutually supportive lives. Moreover, when so many children need loving parents, society's sanction of marriage would make adoption much easier, though not everyone agrees that gay adoptive parents would not influence the sexual orientation of a child.

Religion aside, the state's interest in marriage is to create a unit for mutual care and the bearing and rearing of children. Tax and inheritance incentives have long been offered to bolster these "family values," which are under great strain, and nothing should be done now to further weaken the traditional family.

Underlying this disagreement, and giving the debate its bitterness, is the belief that what is at stake is not just tax and pension fairness (in the works for domestic partners who take contractual vows) but the reach for unequivocal social and theological approbation. Gays understandably want not just equal economic treatment but equal moral status; most Americans are not ready to go beyond toleration to active approval. That division is not in dispute.

Will S.S.M. be a political issue? Hawaii, dominated by Democrats, has shown it already is. In the national campaign, Republicans will oppose gay marriage, perhaps in a platform plank; if Bill Clinton ever holds a press conference and is asked about this, he can be expected to straddle, saying he "personally" opposes same-gender legal liaison, but it is a state issue and he's for states' rights.

The nation and its gay minority would be best served by the compromise Hawaii just scorned.

Gay Marriages and the Affirmation of an Ideal

AMY E. SCHWARTZ

From the Washington Post, *June 3, 1996*

A straight woman argues that gay marriage would be far more likely to make homosexuals like heterosexuals than the other way around.

When the Joe Camel character first started appearing on cigarette packs, along with mischievous rumors as to what the picture really showed, I yielded to prurient curiosity and bought a pack. Holding it in my hand, I discovered something peculiar: Though I had never in my life smoked a cigarette, let alone bought any, the sight of my own fingers clasped around a pack of Camels touched off an incredible wash of cultural familiarity, of rightness, that was utterly at odds with anything I'd heard about smoking in at least a decade.

Talk about a lesson in the workings of cultural pressure. Without knowing it, I had soaked up over the years—from ads, movies, who knows?—a terrific subconscious sense that the society around me supported this purchase, that I was doing what people do. It was ridiculous, of course; the feeling went away when I put the cigarettes out of sight in a drawer. But it left me with a healthy respect for the anti-tobacco people's arguments about the cumulative beneath-the-surface power of advertising (who knew that this, of all things, was still sloshing around in the zeitgeist?) and in general for the proposition that you can be unaware of a powerful, mostly invisible undertow of social reinforcement until you happen to stumble into it by mistake.

I wish something of the sort would happen to the people who have spent this political season wailing and gnashing their teeth over the lack of societal support for and the need to "defend" and "strengthen" the institution of marriage. Some of these worries appear heartfelt; others, like the "defense of marriage" tag stuck on the congressional bill to block legalization of gay marriages, seem transparent efforts to harness the societal interest in marriage to assertions of a "harm" both implausible and theoretical. To get engaged to be married in the midst of this debate, as I recently did, is a little like picking up that Camel pack. First, you immediately become aware of a fierce river of support that is totally at odds with the public plaints. Second, you get a glimpse, from feeling it, of how the support mechanism actually works, a close-up of the culture cranking itself efficiently from generation to generation.

And that glimpsed close-up in turn makes killingly clear—in case I had had any doubts to begin with—that the assertions about gay marriage hurting that mechanism, undermining that support, assume a process that has the mechanism exactly backward.

Conservative critics on every side wail that marriage and the family are under attack or in disrepute, succumbing to the onslaught of divorce, self-indulgence and the collapse of traditional sexual norms, not to mention the perfidious influence of gay rights. Are they kidding? The society is marriage-mad. Being single and considering whether to marry some particular person is like standing in a gale; say yes, and the gale picks you up and flings you through the air like one of those cows in *Twister*. The announcement of one's intention to marry brings floods of warmth and pleasure not just from friends and loved ones but from casual acquaintances and even strangers, as if (and on some level it's obviously true) you're doing something not just for yourselves but for everybody.

Signature purchases like rings touch off an internal buzz of recognition 100 times as deafening as that of the Camel pack. As you plunge into the fervid territory controlled by the bridal industry you notice that much of what it does is ideally suited to ease you up and over large personal transitions, siphoning off your anxieties into details about reception halls, propelling you forward to the goal like those cheering spectators who line the last mile of marathons.

And it works. Some serious-minded critics worried about divorce statistics actually think the mechanism propelling couples forward from engagement to ceremony is a bit too strong. One rabbi of my acquaintance will occasionally refuse to perform a wedding ceremony for a couple she doesn't think is ready; she tells them they are welcome to seek another officiant, she says, but several such couples, on hearing so unexpected a challenge from their rabbi, have taken the escape hatch thus offered and have split up.

Though perhaps less inclined to such direct action, many of the people whose worries about the state of marriage are heartfelt—as distinct from those using those worries as a club to beat gay visibility—would agree that all this support for forming new marriages isn't their point; rather, what is needed is more help in sustaining the marriages once they're formed. What you need, in other words, isn't a lot of cheering at the marathon starting point but more of it on the uphill stretches and from other, more experienced runners.

Which is why the "defense of marriage" argument against gay marriage strikes me as so perverse, because, if the adult world's response to an engagement amounts to a burst of sustained cheering for the serious task ahead—Go for it, you can do it, we did it, everyone should do it, go for it!—then it is hard to see anything but destructiveness in substituting the message: Some people must never be allowed to do this.

Better, surely, to cheer the common denominator, to think what helped this rushing river of support might give gay couples in the struggle for serious goals like monogamy and fidelity—and also what their achievement of those goals might give back to the rest of us. The evidence of a gay couple's desire to leap into lifelong commitment seems to me yet another bridge to that couple's humanity, an affirmation for the ideal of marriage that underlines a previously unnoticed kinship. Doesn't every successfully, publicly monogamous couple committed for life bolster the resolve of every other couple that aspires to that achievement?

Don't Say I Didn't Warn You
KATHA POLLITT

From the Nation, *April 29, 1996*

Why the stigmatization of the unmarried in conservative ideology could hurt gays—as well as straights.

When gay friends argue in favor of same-sex marriage, I always agree and offer them the one my husband and I are leaving. Why should straights be the "only" ones to have their unenforceable promise to love, honor and cherish trap them like houseflies in the web of law? Marriage will not only open up to gay men and lesbians whole new vistas of guilt, frustration, claustrophobia, bewilderment, declining self-esteem, unfairness and sorrow, it will offer them the opportunity to prolong this misery by tormenting each other in court. I know one pair of exes who spent in legal fees the entire value of the property in dispute, and another who took five years and six lawyers to untie the knot. Had these couples merely lived together they would have thrown each other's record collections out the window and called it a day. Clearly something about marriage drives a lot of people round the bend. Why shouldn't some of those people be gay?

Legalizing gay marriage would be a good idea even if all it did was to chasten conservative enthusiasts like Andrew Sullivan and Bruce Bawer, who imagine that wedlock would do for gays what it is less and less able to do for straights—encourage monogamy, sobriety and settled habits. Gay conservatives are quick to criticize hetero offenders against the socio-marital order, like divorced and single parents and poor women who nonetheless have children. Legalizing gay marriage will do a lot to open these men's eyes: Soon they'll be divorcing, single parenting and bankrupting each other like the rest of us. Maybe we'll hear less about restoring the stigma of "illegitimacy" and divorce over at *The New Republic* when gay men find themselves raising kids with no help from a deadbeat co-dad.

I'm for same-sex marriage because I'd be a hypocrite not to be: I married, after all, for reasons that apply to gay couples—a mix of love, convention and a practical concern for safeguarding children, property, my husband and myself from unforeseen circumstances and strange legal quirks. I don't see why gays shouldn't be able to make the same choice, and I've yet to see an argument on the other side that doesn't dissolve into bias and prejudice and thinly disguised religious folderol. In a recent *New York Times* Op-Ed, former Quayle speechwriter Lisa

Schiffren attacked the idea of gay marriage by defining marriage as about procreation, with the many non-procreating couples—infertile, voluntarily childless, middle-aged and elderly—included out of politeness. (It was a banner weekend for Schiffren at the *Times*—the very next day the *Magazine* published her essay claiming that the legalization of abortion explains why no one offered her a subway seat when she was pregnant.) In a particularly overwrought 1991 *Commonweal* essay, Jean Bethke Elshtain depicted gay marriage as "antinatal—hostile to the regenerative female body." Haven't these writers ever heard of Heather's two mommies and Daddy's roommate? *Lots* of gay and lesbian couples are raising children together these days. Interestingly, neither of these defenders of the hearth mentions love—maybe gays are the last romantics, after all.

For social conservatives like Elshtain and Schiffren, opposition to gay marriage is more than homophobia. It's a move in a larger, high-stakes policy struggle over the family. The kernel of truth grasped by anti-gay-marriage conservatives is that same-sex wedlock is part of the modern transformation of marriage from a hierarchical, gender-polarized relationship whose permanence was enforced by God, law, family and community into a more equal, fluid and optional relationship whose permanence depends on the mutual wishes of the partners. Whatever its conservative champions think, gay marriage could never have become a realistic political issue, with considerable popular support from straights, without the breakdown of traditional family values—widespread divorce, nonmarital births, cohabitation, blended families, double-income couples, interracial and interfaith and no-faith unions, abortion, feminism. When it becomes legal, as I believe it will, same-sex marriage will be the result, not the cause, of a change in the meaning of marriage. The reason arguments against it sound so prudish and dated and irrational is that they are. . . .

The truth is, we are moving toward a society in which the old forms of human relationships are being disrupted and re-shaped, and sooner or later the law must accommodate that reality. Legalizing gay marriage is part of the process, but so is diminishing the increasingly outmoded privileged status of marriage and sharing out its benefits along different, more egalitarian lines. Andrew Sullivan and Bruce Bawer may have more in common with single mothers than they would like to think.

CHAPTER SIX

Can Hawaii Be Stopped?

THE DEFENSE OF MARRIAGE ACT: THE NATIONAL DEBATE BEGINS

In some sense all the debate on same-sex marriage that went on before the advent of the Defense of Marriage Act was a warm-up. This legislation was introduced in May 1996 in the U.S. House of Representatives to ensure that legal same-sex marriages in Hawaii could not be upheld in other states under the Full Faith and Credit clause of the U.S. Constitution. As a matter of law, it seems highly implausible that states would have been compelled to uphold same-sex marriages by such means, as the arguments of Chapter 10 make clear. But the mere threat was enough to provoke uproar in Washington and around the country. Was such a law necessary—or even constitutional? And was the country ready for same-sex marriage anywhere?

This chapter begins with the arguments for (Jay Alan Sekulow) and against (Cass Sunstein) the constitutionality of the Defense of

Marriage Act—or DOMA, as it became known. Transcripts from the House hearings are excerpted: Congressman Barney Frank's passionate attack on the political animus behind the bill; Congressman Henry Hyde's defense of informal living arrangements between gay people; Congressman Bob Inglis's explosion about the miscegenation analogy. But perhaps the most telling exchange of the entire debate is between Congressmen Sonny Bono and Barney Frank as Bono wrestles with his own conflicts between his gut and his conscience. Finally, Senators Byrd, Lewis, Robb, and Gramm vie with one another in a debate of remarkable eloquence and emotion about the meaning of marriage and discrimination in America.

The Defense of Marriage Act was passed by overwhelming margins in both the House and the Senate and was signed into law by President Clinton in September 1996 in the middle of the night.

H.R. 3396: To Define and Protect the Institution of Marriage
May 7, 1996

The text of the Defense of Marriage Act. There are two sections: the first outlines states' rights not to recognize the same-sex marriages of other states; the second defines marriage, for federal purposes, as an arrangement made between a man and a woman. This bill was the first in the nation's history to define marriage at a federal level. The issue had previously always been left to the states to decide.

H.R. 3396

To define and protect the institution of marriage.

IN THE HOUSE OF REPRESENTATIVES

MAY 7, 1996

Mr. BARR of Georgia (for himself, Mr. LARGENT, Mr. SENSENBRENNER, Mrs. MYRICK, Mr. VOLKMER, Mr. SKELTON, Mr. BRYANT of Tennessee, and Mr. EMERSON) introduced the following bill; which was referred to the Committee on the Judiciary

---

A BILL

To define and protect the institution of marriage.

Be it enacted by the Senate and House of Representatives of the United States of America in Congress assembled,

SECTION 1. SHORT TITLE.

This Act may be cited as the "Defense of Marriage Act."

SEC. 2. POWERS RESERVED TO THE STATES.

(a) IN GENERAL.—Chapter 115 of title 28, United States Code, is amended by adding after section 1738B the following:

"§ 1738C. CERTAIN ACTS, RECORDS, AND PROCEEDINGS AND THE EFFECT THEREOF

"No State, territory, or possession of the United States, or Indian tribe, shall be required to give effect to any public act, record, or judicial proceeding of any other State, territory, possession, or tribe respecting a relationship between persons of the same sex that is treated as a marriage under the laws of such other State, territory, possession, or tribe, or a right or claim arising from such relationship."

(b) CLERICAL AMENDMENT.—The table of sections at the beginning of chapter 115 of title 28, United States Code, is amended by inserting after the item relating to section 1738B the following new item:

"1738C. Certain acts, records, and proceedings and the effect thereof."

SEC. 3. DEFINITION OF MARRIAGE.

(a) IN GENERAL.—Chapter 1 of title 1, United States Code, is amended by adding at the end the following:

"§ 7. DEFINITION OF 'MARRIAGE' AND 'SPOUSE'

"In determining the meaning of any Act of Congress, or of any ruling, regulation, or interpretation of the various administrative bureaus and agencies of the United States, the word 'marriage' means only a legal union between one man and one woman as husband and wife, and the word 'spouse' refers only to a person of the opposite sex who is a husband or a wife."

(b) CLERICAL AMENDMENT.—The table of sections at the beginning of chapter 1 of title 1, United States Code, is amended by inserting after the item relating to section 6 the following new item:

"7. Definition of 'marriage' and 'spouse'."

Defending Marriage

JAY ALAN SEKULOW

From the written testimony provided to the House Judiciary Committee from the American Center for Law and Justice, May 15, 1996

Here the chief lawyer for the Religious Right defends the Defense of Marriage Act (DOMA). Deflecting the accusation that DOMA was a purely political ploy, Sekulow claims that without it the Constitution would soon have wreaked havoc on the marriage laws of the nation.

A decision for the same-sex couples who are plaintiffs in *Baehr* will, very likely, have nationwide ramifications. Those ramifications are due to one provision of the United States Constitution, and its role in a directed nationwide effort to change the laws of fifty states regarding the nature of a legal relationship, marriage. The constitutional provision states:

> Full faith and credit shall be given in each state to the public acts, records, and judicial proceedings of every other state. And the Congress may by general laws prescribe the manner in which such Acts, Records, and proceedings shall be proved, and the effect thereof.

It is possible, because nationally organized efforts are intent on pushing the issue to the limits, that under the Full Faith and Credit Clause, other states will have to recognize as valid Hawaiian "marriages" between same-sex couples, and thus accord those couples all the benefits and protections accorded any other married couples. Several writers already have advanced, or at least discussed, this argument in law review articles. . . .

The threat that same-sex couples married in Hawaii will seek to have their marriages recognized in other states is real. Indeed, given the intensity with which the homosexual community has been focusing on the developments in *Baehr*, it is no exaggeration to suggest that *Baehr* simply is part of an orchestrated attempt to gain nationwide recognition (ultimately, acceptance) of same-sex marriages.

This strategy is not a figment of an overwrought imagination, whether mine or another's. The evidence of such a strategy is plain, for its proponents disdain to hide their purposes. The Marriage Project of the Lambda Legal Defense and Education Fund puts its goal in its name.

That organization, LLDEF, and its Marriage Project have been closely involved in the *Baehr* litigation. If successful, according to Lambda, "[c]ommon sense, constitutional doctrines, and legal precedent suggest that when [same-sex] marriages are lawfully performed in Hawaii, they will have to be recognized by other states. . . ."

Other statements show that homosexuals are eagerly awaiting the decision in *Baehr* to take advantage of the opportunity for "marriage" that a decision in *Baehr* may offer. For example, lesbian columnist Deb Price, referring to the plans she has with her lesbian partner, wrote, "We'll be on the first plane out! So many of us are just waiting for the day that our relationships are legally recognized."...

Moreover,

Gays and lesbians . . . eagerly wait word from Hawaii and many plan to head for the islands once and if licenses become available. "We'd go right away," John Holden and Michael

Galluccio said. "We've even asked my mother to be prepared to watch the baby at a moment's notice. And if it doesn't become legal until next year, we'll take Adam along, because by then he'll be old enough for the trip.". . .

Some have predicted not a trickle of such Hawaii same-sex marriage junkets, but a flood. And one magazine targeted to the gay and lesbian community reported in 1990 that eighty-three percent of the reader-respondents to a survey stated that if same-sex marriage was legalized they would marry. . . .

For Mr. Wolfson, who heads up Lambda's Marriage Project, the question of winning the right of same-sex couples to marry is apparently rather more than just being allowed to marry. In a recent article, Mr. Wolfson set the tone for his piece by quoting the lyrics of a song. Those lyrics allow us to peek behind the facade of the Marriage Project's stated goal of obtaining equal marriage rights for homosexuals to the deeper and more disturbing motivations behind Mr. Wolfson's press for legalization: "How can the world change, It can change like that, Due to one little word: 'Married.'"

Like the vapors Pandora had wished not to have let loose, Mr. Wolfson is clear about one thing: his goal of revolutionizing society, served in part by revolutionizing marriage, is a no-holds-barred, take-no-prisoners struggle: "[A]s [Martin Luther King, Jr.] put it, 'In this Revolution, no plans have been written for retreat,' we must ready ourselves to defend our victory and advance toward other goals.". . .

The point of this strategy, for homosexuals, was stated by Michelangelo Signorile in *Out* magazine:

> [Homosexuals must] fight for same-sex marriage and its benefits and then, once granted, redefine the institution of mar-

riage completely . . . to debunk a myth and radically alter an archaic institution. . . . The most subversive action lesbians and gays can undertake—and one that would perhaps benefit all of society—is to transform the notion of "family."

Thus, the strategy to recognize same-sex marriage is nothing less than a strategy to discard the traditional idea of "family" that has served to hold this society together. . . .

Will this strategy succeed? Can it be that over two hundred years of national unity and previous centuries of common law regarding the nature of marriage and the matrimonial relationship would fall victim to the latest round of judicial retrofitting of a *state* constitutional requirement of equality under the law? Right now, that is an open question. Clearly there are those who argue that, under the Full Faith and Credit Clause, states would be required to recognize same-sex marriages performed in Hawaii. To those arguments it is a fair response that there is a "public policy" exception to the Full Faith and Credit requirement. According to the *Restatement (Second) of Conflict of Laws* § 283 (1971), a state that had a "significant relationship to the spouses and the marriage at the time of the marriage" need not recognize a marriage if the marriage contravenes "the strong public policy" of that state.

It is not possible to predict with certainty, however, how courts will apply this exception to same-sex marriages. Section 2 of the Defense of Marriage Act removes this uncertainty by providing in essence that states are not bound, as a matter of federal law, to recognize same-sex marriages performed in another state. But that certainty does not come at the expense of state prerogatives. DOMA does not prevent states from choosing to recognize same-sex marriages. A state still would be free, as a matter of state law, to accord those marriages whatever status the state wishes. By removing the confusion surrounding the application of the Full Faith and Credit clause, the states will be free and empowered to develop their own policy on same-sex marriages. In this respect, Congress eschews any role in compelling states to adopt Hawaii's policy as their own, and insures that neither Hawaii nor any other state can cause this intended revolution through "ordinary litigation between parties. . . ."

Beyond the direct and odious consequences of a certain Supreme Court decision with which he disagreed, Abraham Lincoln had rather more to say about a role for the judiciary that he feared the citizenry might pass to it by default. In his first inaugural address, he explained:

> At the same time the candid citizen must confess that if the policy of the government, upon vital questions, affecting the whole people, is to be irrevocably fixed, by decisions of the Supreme Court, the instant they are made, in ordinary litigation between parties, in personal action, the people will have ceased, to be their own rulers, having, to that extent, practically resigned their government, into the hands of that eminent tribunal. Nor is there, in this view, any assault upon the court, or the judges. It is a duty, from which they may not shrink, to decide cases properly brought before them; and it is no fault of theirs, if others seek to turn their decisions to political purposes.

The only real question here is whether Congress has the power, under the Full Faith and Credit Clause, to define what effect a same-sex marriage validly created in one jurisdiction will have in another. For these purposes, the key language of the clause states, "Congress may by general laws prescribe the manner in which such acts, records, and proceedings [of every state]

shall be proved [in every other state], and the effect thereof."
While this language enables Congress to regulate the effect of
proofs of foreign, that is, sister-state judgments under the Full
Faith and Credit Clause, Congress has only exercised this authority three times. The first usage was in 1790 when Congress
codified the functions of the Full Faith and Credit clause...,
again in 1980 with the Parental Kidnapping Prevention Act...,
and finally, with the Full Faith and Credit Child Support Orders
Act of 1994.... This bill would create ... and allow for a further exercise of Congress' authority to "prescribe the manner
in which ... acts, records, and proceedings" of one state are
proved in another state.

The fact that the authority is rarely used does not mean that
the authority does not exist. The enabling language is clear; it
has been noted, however, that "there are few clauses of the Constitution, the literal possibilities of which have been so little developed as the Full Faith and Credit clause."...

Don't Panic
CASS SUNSTEIN

*From oral testimony given by the professor of
jurisprudence at the University of Chicago Law
School at the hearings held by the Senate Judiciary
Committee, July 11, 1996*

*Here Sunstein argues that DOMA is unnecessary, and its
claim of authority to regulate marriage federally under the
Full Faith and Credit clause is probably unconstitutional.*

I'm going to be talking . . . about the constitutional issues, the question of congressional power. I won't say a word about the policy questions or the underlying issues about the nature or definition of marriage. The first point to note about this legislation is that it's remarkably unprecedented. In the nation's entire history, now well over two hundred years, Congress has never passed legislation whose purpose in effect was to negate the application of one state's judgment in other states. Congress has legislated under the full faith and credit clause. This negating or nullifying power has never been exercised once.

This legislation risks two dangers. One is it may well be pointless, and if it's not pointless, it raises very serious constitutional problems.

If it's pointless, it's because states have grappled with this problem for a long time. This is an old problem, not a new one; it's familiar. And states that have significant geographical connections with people don't have to recognize marriages among people when those marriages violate the public policy of the state. In cases involving incest, polygamy, adultery, and more, states have grappled successfully with this problem without national intervention. This particular issue, the issue of same-sex marriages, falls into a class of cases with which the federal system has dealt successfully without national legislation.

If the statute isn't pointless, it's very problematic from the constitutional point of view. There's a good reason to think that the full faith and credit clause gives Congress broad power to extend the application of judgments in one state. There's good reason to think that Congress has not been given the power to negate judgments by one state insofar as they're applied in other states. If Congress does have the power to do this under the full faith and credit clause, there's a big problem under the equal protection of the components of the due process clause, as construed just a few weeks ago by the Supreme Court in *Romer v.*

Evans. If Congress does this, it seems like a limited measure just involving same-sex marriage, there could be very large future consequences in areas involving product liability, punitive damages, marriage and divorce, where there are interest groups all over the nation who would be extremely thrilled to see the possibility that Congress can nullify the extraterritorial application of one state's judgments.

Let me just say a few words now by way of elaboration. On pointlessness, as I say, this is not a new problem, it's an old one. In areas involving minors, incestuous or bigamous marriages, states have dealt with this very successfully and very frequently. There are volumes and volumes of cases. They don't involve congressional legislation. When a marriage violates a state's policy and when the state has a geographical connection with the parties, the state is not obliged to recognize the marriage. That is the tradition. It's extremely well settled law. It's in (both restatements ?) of the conflicts of law. It suggests the very serious possibility that this legislation has no purpose. If it does have a purpose, it is problematic from the constitutional point of view. There has been no serious suggestion that this is okay under the commerce clause. It would be an exotic understanding of the commerce clause to say that marriage falls within that domain.

The full faith and credit clause does, as you say, Senator Hatch, have the word "effects" in it, and Congress does have power to prescribe the effect of a judgment, and that might seem textually to give Congress power here, but I think there are some reasons to think that that is more word play or a verbal trick than an accurate understanding of the Constitution.

The full faith and credit clause, above all, has a unifying purpose, not a disunifying purpose. It's part of the move from the Articles of Confederation to the Constitution. If you look at the purpose of the clause, it's not to allow nullification, it's to allow extension of judgments, not to negate them. If you look at the history of the clause back when the framers were writing, Madison and the others, they spoke about congressional extension and enforcement of judgments. They spoke not at all about congressional nullification of judgments. There's a big dog that didn't bark in the framer's night, and that's the bark of nullification.

If history and purpose aren't conclusive, let's look just at Congress's practice for now well over two hundred years. Congress has never once nullified the extraterritorial application of a state judgment. Congress has acted under the full faith and credit clause a fair bit. It's always been in the interest of extension. The consequences of nullifying rather than extension could be very extreme. Californian divorces, Idaho punitive damage judgments, Illinois product liability judgments, all of them would henceforth be up for grabs.

That's why from the standpoint of federalism this is a very large as well as a very new bit of legislation. If for the first time in the country Congress is going to act to nullify a judgment in its extraterritorial applications, there is a problem under the equal protection clause. The Court said just a few weeks ago that Congress may not enact measures that have the peculiar property of imposing a broad disability on a single group. This is an invalid form of legislation. If Congress hasn't legislated for polygamous, incestuous marriages or marriages among minors, then it has raised the question of discrimination. In conclusion, this legislation has never been—nothing like it has ever been done. It's unprecedented. It may well be pointless. This problem has been handled by the states for well over two hundred years. If it has a point, it risks unconstitutionality. From the standpoint of federalism and constitutional law, it is ill advised.

The Hearings of the House Judiciary Committee on the Defense of Marriage Act

May 15, 1996

The Hearings of the House Judiciary Committee proved to be memorable. The raw emotions of gay men and lesbians and of House members and others on both sides of the issue electrified Capitol Hill for a day. It was the first time in history that the real lives of homosexuals were addressed so forthrightly in the halls of Congress. What follows is an edited transcript of the highlights. The featured speakers are Congressman Barney Frank of Massachusetts, one of two openly gay members of Congress; Hadley Arkes, an Amherst College professor; Congressman Henry Hyde, a Republican of fervent Roman Catholic faith; the highly conservative Republican Congressman from South Carolina, Bob Inglis; and the executive director of the Human Rights Campaign, the nation's largest gay rights lobby, Elizabeth Birch.

Rep. Barney Frank: We are dealing with a couple of related events today. This legislation and Senator Dole's apparent resignation from the Senate. They are both indications that the Republican national campaign is not doing very well, and there is a significant effort to change the subject. There are issues that ought to be discussed around the question of marriage, same-sex marriage. They ought to be discussed in a reasonable and unhurried way. First, let's be clear that the crisis that is being invoked to justify this drafting of this committee into the Republican campaign effort is greatly exaggerated. Same-sex marriage is nowhere legal in America today, and is not likely to become legal within the next couple of months in a final and binding way.

Why the hurry then? Particularly why the hurry in a Congress which has not been known for its capacity rapidly to dispose of important issues? Because we have a campaign that is hurting, and this is part of that effort. That's reflected, in part, in the very nature of the bill. There is a desperate effort here to find an issue. So we are apparently going to be asked to give the states a power which everybody who is for the bill thinks the states already have. We are told we must empower the states to reject, under their exception to the full faith and credit clause, marriages in Hawaii. But everybody who is talking about giving the states that power, in fact, thinks the states already have it.

What my friends have here is an elephant stick. Now, an elephant stick is the big stick someone is carrying walking around the White House. And when asked what it's for, he says, "Well, it keeps all the elephants off Pennsylvania Avenue." And when the answer is "There are no elephants," they say, "See, my stick worked."

Well, that's what they've got. They seek to empower to do what they believe the states can already do. In fact, if you took this seriously, it would be undermining the states' power. Because if, in fact, you accept as a reality that the states have the power to do this, . . . what we are now saying to the states is, "Oh, no, you must get permission from us."

Authors of this bill have written and said, "This is a bill to allow the states to do this." Well, passing a bill that allows the states to do something logically assumes that the states cannot do it in the absence of that permission. If we need to pass a bill to allow the states, then the states apparently can't do it without us.

Now, no one thinks that. So, why are we passing a bill to do what the people who want the bill passed think the states can already do? Because what they are worried about is not what the states decide to do with regard to marriage. They are worried about how the state decides to allocate its electoral votes. And this is an effort to influence not marriage in the states, but whether the Democratic or Republican tickets win. We'll deal with that more. But I also want to talk about the substance.

This is entitled, "Protect the institution of marriage," to "define and protect." "Define," I would have no semantic objection. We could debate this. But the notion that same-sex marriage somehow constitutes an assault on marriage between a man and a woman is very bizarre.

Apparently, the only logic I could think of is that people are afraid that men and women who are now married or contemplating marriage will, if they learn that they could get a tax advantage from marrying someone of the same sex, change their minds about marrying someone of the opposite sex and go off and marry someone of the same sex.

Because how can it be? Against what are you protecting marriage? I mean, those who believe in the importance of a man and a woman in love coming together in a union that is emotional and reinforced legally, how in the world is it a threat? And I will say, in terms of the priorities here—and I understand why they want to change the subject, things aren't going well with regard to Medicare or the environment or education and a lot of other issues. I talk, obviously as others do, to people in my district, and I have people tell me:

> "I am worried about losing my Medicare."
> "I am worried about losing my job."
> "I am worried about the lack of safety on the streets."

"I am worried that there is not enough money
now to continue with toxic waste cleanup."

Never yet has someone come to me and said, "Congressman, I am terribly threatened. There are two women who are deeply in love a couple of miles away from me. And if you do not prevent them from formalizing their union, this will be terrible for me, and, in fact, will threaten my marriage." I know of no heterosexual marriage, the form of marriage that we have that has sustained us, that is threatened by this.

Herb and I entertained on Sunday 21 members of my family. A large majority of them were, in fact, heterosexual couples and the children of those heterosexual couples. I must tell you that having spent several hours in Herb's and my company none of them left with their marriages in jeopardy. In no case were the marital bonds any weaker than before. In no case did these people, who range in age from a couple of toddlers who might be too young, but from a four-year-old to a twenty-year-old on to Herb's parents, in no case was this disruptive. So that's why I reiterate that this is largely political in motivation. There is no need to empower the states to do what the states want. I do believe there is a constitutional issue here. But the constitutional issue is not one for the role of the Congress. There are people who believe that under the full faith and credit clause the states must accept same-sex marriage if any state does it. There are other people who believe that under the public policy exceptions that states have been allowed to have that would not be binding.

That is something that will be litigated directly between the states and the Supreme Court. There is no constitutional role for the Congress in this, whether or not—I mean, apparently what this is, is an amicus brief. I've never heard of Congress passing an amicus brief and calling it a law. Because that's all it could mean.

So this part about the states is either a nullity, if you believe that the states have no such power, or if you believe that the Supreme Court would uphold the states' rights here, as it has in other cases, then it's totally unnecessary.

So we have a totally unnecessary bill to ward off something, which is now, in effect, being rushed through a Congress which is unable to even get the gas tax repealed because they are unable to function, and therefore they are looking desperately for an alternative political issue. And that's it. And it is, I think, an issue which in addition is exaggerated in its defense. Because the notion that two men who have an emotional bond live together, or two women, threatens marriage is of a piece with the illogic of the rest of this bill . . .

Mr. Hadley Arkes: There was a family, a situation in Virginia not long ago, of a forty-year-old mother married to her nineteen-year-old son. They were forced to separate. I suppose people could argue that their presence wasn't going to disintegrate the institution of marriage.

To make our point, again, we are not predicting that there is going to be an erosion of marriage, but I think the melancholy point is this, that the notion of marriage may not be extended to take in, to accommodate the concern for gay marriage without setting off many other kinds of changes, and as a result of those changes, I think we would find that marriage would not have that special kind of significance that makes it an object right now of such craving. As Dennis [Prager] suggested, it is not that you are going to sort of undercut families that exist, but as the society keeps offering many alternatives and notions of sexuality outside of the framework of marriage, we move away from the sense that there is something portentous about the generation of new life, something that commands that this be pursued within a framework of commitment where the child understands that her parents are committed to her nurturance for the same reason that they are committed to one another. That they have quit their freedom to be rid of that relationship when it no longer suits their convenience. Now, if you think that all of this might undercut in time, or erode our conviction about the importance of that framework, about the generation of children as opposed to the notion that our children are simply spawned with no particular responsibility, remind ourselves that even in those melancholy situations when marriages dissolve, the framework of lawfulness at least has this advantage, that it fixes the question of who bears responsibility for the children.

Another point, I just might say that in response to Andrew [Sullivan] and, again, Andrew is a man of just impeccable arguments and I respect his judgments on many things, but I thought the concern here is about the debate being stifled by being drawn into the cloister of the courts, where it is handled, according to the formulas that are familiar to lawyer and judges, and that I thought it would be quite consistent with the spirit of liberalism, as Justice Brennan used to say, that robust arena of public discussion that we bring things out of the cloister of the courts, and bring them back into the public arena of discussion where it is matter of discussion not merely for lawyers.

Rep. Henry Hyde: Professor, I have known people in my life who have been deeply in love, not married, men and women, an enduring love, a powerful love, into their old age. What is stopping people, two men who love each other, or two women, from having that commitment of the soul as well as of the body, what do they need marriage for to solemnize it? Why can't they have this relationship which can be as fulfilling as if they have gotten a marriage license and taken an oath, and that is all marriage is, you are swearing to each other before an official witness, that they will love, honor and obey, or cherish, or whatever the word is. You can see how long ago it was that I got married. But what is the big deal?

Mr. Hadley Arkes: I think you are inviting me to, I don't want to go [over] ground I have already traversed, but to point out that, as I said, we understand that there are many relations of deep love between men and men, between women and women, grandparents and grandchildren, and, as I said, in the nature of things, not merely a matter of opinion, in the nature of things, those loves cannot be diminished as loves because they are not manifested properly in marriage. So I think I would agree with that wholly. . . .

Rep. Inglis: I must tell you that it offends me tremendously to have homosexuals compare themselves to the historic struggle for civil rights among black people.

Ms. Birch: Why?

Rep. Inglis: Because black people were economically disenfranchised and cut out of this society, whereas homosexuals, by most studies that I am aware of, have a higher standard of living than heterosexuals. So the comparison offends me tremendously—

Ms. Birch: Yeah, well, your information, sir, is inaccurate.

Rep. Inglis: —that you can persist in this comparison to this historic struggle of blacks to achieve equality in this country. The fact is, that [it] is not a choice to be black, but it is a choice—I know you don't like this, but it is obviously a choice to be homosexual.

Ms. Birch: Wrong.

Rep. Inglis: And that is simply, you are wrong to assert that it is not a choice.

Ms. Birch: Representative, I don't think you know anything about it.

Rep. Inglis: You are absolutely wrong to assert that. So therefore—

Ms. Birch: And if you would like to talk about the law, I would like to respond to that. I don't think you know anything about the struggle of African-Americans in this country *vis-à-vis* gay Americans.

Rep. Inglis: I know, because you are the head victim, I know, you are in charge of victims, so you will decide who can speak for that, not anybody else.

Ms. Birch: I would expect a little dignity and respect.

Rep. Inglis: But I think that the point that should be made here, and really what this all boils down to is, is it a choice or is it a condition? And if you would please make the honest argument—you would say, listen, it is a wonderful condition, let's all be gay, but you are not making that argument. You are making the argument, we are poor and pitiful and you must accept us the way we are, so you are admitting that it is not a desirable lifestyle, and there is something wrong with it, by arguing that it is not a choice. So I think if you analyze that honestly, it is essential to me because I hope that many can be rescued from that lifestyle and returned to where they can have a happy lifestyle because I think it is inherently destructive.

Ms. Birch: Mr. Chairman, may I respond?

Rep. Canady: I am sorry, the thirty minutes has gone—I am sorry the thirty seconds has gone.

Transcript of the Mark-Up Record of the Defense of Marriage Act
House Judiciary Committee, June 12, 1996

Every so often in a public debate, an interchange occurs that seems to encapsulate all the tensions surrounding the issue. This dialogue between Congressmen Sonny Bono and Barney Frank is one of those moments. Bono seems to concede Frank's arguments in defense of same-sex marriage, but emotionally holds something back. Since Bono is the father of a lesbian, his conflicts are even deeper than most—and his honesty is truly remarkable.

Mr. Bono: I . . . this has been an amazing experience for me because I'm immersed in legal rhetoric that is interpreting the Constitution, and it's staggering how brilliant everyone is and how well they know their craft, and I wouldn't dare venture into their craft.

And it's clear to me, Mr. Chairman, that your job here, or my job here, is to try to interpret the Constitution and then act on that interpretation, representing the people. But it seems like the rhetoric has gone on to a point—sometimes things go way beyond where they should go, and an impasse is an impasse. And if there was ever an obvious impasse, this is it.

And what seems to have occurred here is that this subject is a rough subject because, if you're not a homosexual, you have strong feelings one way; if you are a homosexual, you have strong feelings the other way. But I would just like to go on the record and say this: that when things like this come out, it certainly makes a minority feel like everyone thinks they're less. And I think for someone to defend that is absolutely natural.

And Barney's a good friend of mine—or I consider him a good friend of mine. And I see his point of view, and I appreciate his fight. He's fighting as hard as he can because he's a human being; he has these feelings; he's gay; my daughter's gay. He has to live this way. So society hasn't quite accepted all of this.

So I think we go beyond the Constitution here. I think we go beyond all these brilliant interpretations here, and I think we have hit feelings, and we've hit what people can handle and what they can't handle, and it's that simple. And no matter how you justify what you say legally or whether it represents the Constitution, I think it breaks down to whether you're able to handle something or whether you're not able to handle something. I don't love my daughter any less because she's gay, and I don't dislike Barney any more because he's gay. I have, again, a tremendous respect.

And I want to reiterate that, no matter how strong of a person you are, these kind of bills and this kind of legislation is going to make someone defensive and going to make them feel like other people are trying to make them less, and Barney's not less.

And so I think that sometimes we have to now go beyond the law and get into a sensitivity and just say it like it is, tell the truth, and go on with it. I mean, what is obvious here is the votes are going to be the way they're going to be. And we can talk for hours and hours and hours, and you'll hear both sides brilliantly discussed—

Mr. Gekas: Will the gentleman yield for a moment?

Mr. Bono: Let me just finish, and I'll be happy to yield.

I just want to say this; I owe this to Barney, and I want to go on record that I'm not homophobic; I'm not a bigot, and I'm not pandering to hatred, and I like—I like Barney, and I love my daughter. I simply can't handle it yet, Barney. It's nothing—nothing else, but at least I want to honestly say that to you, and throw aside all the legal rhetoric. I wish I was ready, but I can't tell my son it's okay, or I don't think I can yet. So if I could—

Mr. Frank: Would you yield to me?

Mr. Bono: Yes.

Mr. Frank: I would ask that the gentleman have an additional minute, and I thank the gentleman and I appreciate candor and the decency that motivates it.

I would say two things. It's not that I feel less. This bill says I and many others are less. It says that—and no one is asking for a stamp of approval. What we're saying is, if we pay taxes, if we work, we simply want to be able to get the same financial benefits and the same responses other people do.

And, secondly, in terms of handling it—and I understand that, but no one is asking you or any of the others to do any more than leave us alone and let us have the same rights as anyone else. Let us have the rights in any State that decides, because that's all this amendment says. If the State—if we can persuade a State legislature to do it, if we can win a referendum, if we can have a court decision not be overturned, let us be like anyone else. So no one is asking you to do anything else, and if it bothers people, turn your head, but don't inflict legal disabilities that carry out that feeling.

Mr. Bono: I ask for an additional thirty seconds.

Chairman Hyde: Without objection.

Mr. Bono: I hear you. I really do hear you. And my response back to you is, you're absolutely right, but the other side of it is this has taken people to as far as they can go, and then no justifiers— I don't want to justify it because I can't. You just go as far as you can go, and then that's why I want to say to you again, honestly, I can't go this far as you deserve even, but—and I'm sorry, but I think that's the whole situation here, and I think we could argue it legally for hours and days, but that's what it's going to get down to.

House Debate on the Defense of Marriage Act
May 30, 1996

Congressman Frank accuses his opponents of political cynicism. Congressman Hyde explodes with indignation.

Mr. Frank: We are talking here about a desperate search for a political issue.

Mr. Hyde: Political! I wish I had never heard of this issue. This is a miserable, uncomfortable, queasy issue. There is no political gain. But there is a moral issue. . . . Nobody wants to talk about it. We are forced to talk about it by the courts. . . .

Don't assume that people are doing this for political profit. People don't think that the traditional marriage ought to be demeaned or trivialized by same-sex unions. If two men want to love each other, go right ahead. If you want to solemnize your love affair by some ceremony, create one. But don't take marriage, which for centuries has been a union between man and woman, and certainly is in this country, and try to say that what you're doing is American.

Mr. Frank: I guess my problem is this. There are plenty of people here who have had marriages that have meant a great deal to them. I salute that. I don't for a minute understand how it demeans, and I would ask the gentleman to explain that to me. The gentleman's marriage, the marriages of other members here are based on a deep love, a bond between two people. I don't think

I demean it. I don't know how I could demean it. How does anything I do in which I express my feelings toward another demean the powerful bond of love and emotion and respect of two other people?

To accuse someone of demeaning something so powerful as the marriage of two people, that is a fairly tough accusation. And I must tell [you], my friend, I don't think it is deserved.

Mr. Hyde: A loving relationship between people of the same sex ought to be their relationship. It ought to be private, and keep it private.

Mr. Frank: You use the word "demean." How does it demean you?

Mr. Hyde: Because many of us feel that there is an immoral—

Mr. Frank: How does it demean your marriage? If other people are immoral, how does it demean your marriage? That's what you are saying.

Mr. Hyde: It demeans the institution. It doesn't demean my marriage. My marriage was never demeaned. The institution of marriage is trivialized by same-sex marriage.

House Debate on the Defense
of Marriage Act
July 11, 1996

*In arguing against the oppression of homosexuals through
what he refers to as a "mean-spirited bigots act," African-
American congressman John Lewis cites the Declaration of
Independence to invoke the rights of homosexuals to "life, liberty and the pursuit of happiness" and quotes Martin Luther
King, Jr.'s sentiments on the subject of interracial marriage,
too.*

Congressman John Lewis of Georgia

Let me say that when I was growing up in the south during the
1940s and the 1950s, the great majority of the people in that
region believed that black people should not be able to enter
places of public accommodation, and they felt that black people
should not be able to register to vote, and many people felt that
was right but that was wrong. I think as politicians, as elected
officials, we should not only follow but we must lead, lead our
districts, not put our fingers into the wind to see which way the
air is blowing but be leaders.

Mr. Chairman, this is a mean bill. It is cruel. This bill seeks
to divide our nation, turn Americans against Americans, sow the
seeds of fear, hatred and intolerance. Let us remember the Pre-
amble of the Declaration of Independence: We hold these
truths self-evident that all people are endowed by their creator
with certain inalienable rights. Among these are life, liberty and
the pursuit of happiness.

This bill is a slap in the face of the Declaration of

Independence. It denies gay men and women the right to liberty and the pursuit of happiness. Marriage is a basic human right. You cannot tell people they cannot fall in love. Dr. Martin Luther King, Jr., used to say when people talked about interracial marriage and I quote, "Races do not fall in love and get married. Individuals fall in love and get married."

Why do you not want your fellow men and women, your fellow Americans to be happy? Why do you attack them? Why do you want to destroy the love they hold in their hearts? Why do you want to crush their hopes, their dreams, their longings, their aspirations?

We are talking about human beings, people like you, people who want to get married, buy a house, and spend their lives with the one they love. They have done no wrong.

I will not turn my back on another American. I will not oppress my fellow human being. I have fought too hard and too long against discrimination based on race and color not to stand up against discrimination based on sexual orientation.

Mr. Chairman, I have known racism. I have known bigotry. This bill stinks of the same fear, hatred and intolerance. It should not be called the Defense of Marriage Act. It should be called the defense of mean-spirited bigots act.

I urge my colleagues to oppose this bill, to have the courage to do what is right. This bill appeals to our worst fears and emotions. It encourages hatred of our fellow Americans for political advantage. Every word, every purpose, every message is wrong. It is not the right thing to do, to divide Americans.

We are moving toward the twenty-first century. Let us come together and create one nation, one people, one family, one house, the American house, the American family, the American nation.

Senate Debate on the Defense of Marriage Act
October 9, 1996

These three Senate speeches express the full range of views on same-sex marriage: Senator Gramm's cool hostility, Senator Byrd's spluttering incomprehension, and Senator Robb's dissent from the majority view. Robb claims to be speaking with an eye on history.

Mr. Gramm

. . . We are here today because the traditional family is important to America. Further, it has always been important to civilization. Our Founders recognize that, and they set out a procedure in the Constitution which is as clear as any procedure could be as to what is Congress' role in this matter.

Let me begin by referring you to article IV, section 1, of the Constitution. Article IV, section 1 says: "Full faith and credit shall be given in each State to the public Acts, Records, and judicial Proceedings of every other State. And the Congress may by general Laws prescribe the Manner in which such Acts, Records, and Proceedings shall be proved, and the Effect thereof."

In other words, article IV, section 1 of the Constitution requires States to recognize the contracts, the judicial proceedings, and the public records of every other State. Obviously, at the top of this list would be marriages. But it specifically gives Congress the power to prescribe under what circumstances such recognition will occur.

My first point is, those who say Congress has no role in this issue need only read the second sentence of article IV, section 1 of the Constitution to see that Congress has the only role in prescribing the circumstance under which one State must recognize a marriage that occurs in another State. We are here today doing exactly what the Founding Fathers prescribed in the Constitution that we should do.

Now, where did this issue come from? Well, its roots come from the fact that the Hawaiian constitution outlaws discrimination based on sex—basically, they have an equal rights amendment. In 1991, three different groups of people argued that they, in trying to engage in a same-sex marriage, were being discriminated against on the basis of sex, and that this violated the equal rights amendment written into the constitution of Hawaii. Essentially, their argument was that when two women or two men are denied a marriage license, one of them is being discriminated against based on the fact that they are of the same sex as the other person applying for the license. This is the foundation of the current judicial proceedings in Hawaii. . . .

The point is if the Hawaii court rules under the equal rights amendment of the Hawaii constitution—a provision that is not in the U.S. Constitution, though it was long debated as a potential addition—if the court rules in favor of single-sex marriages on the basis of sex discrimination, a failure to pass the Defense of Marriage Act here today will require the State of Texas, the State of Kansas, and every other State in the Union to recognize and give full faith and credit to single-sex marriages which occur in Hawaii.

There are those who say this is not a congressional matter, that it should be left up to the courts, but if this is left up to the courts, under article IV, section 1 of the U.S. Constitution, they will have no choice except to impose same-sex marriages on Texas, so long as they are sanctioned by Hawaii.

The Constitution allows Congress—in fact, gives us the responsibility—to prescribe the manner in which such acts, records, and proceedings shall be proved and the effect thereof. What we are doing today in this bill is saying three things: No. 1, we are saying that there can be no question, as far as Federal law is concerned, that States have the right to ban same-sex marriages.

No. 2, we are saying that marriage is defined as a union between a man and a woman, and, therefore, with regard to the requirements of the full faith and credit clause, no matter what happens in Hawaii or any other State, no other State will be required to recognize a same-sex marriage as a traditional marriage.

Finally, we are saying that the Federal Government, itself, will recognize only marriages that occur between a man and a woman . . .

So here are the issues in very simple fashion: No. 1, is there anything unique about the traditional family? For every moment of recorded history, we have said yes. In every major religion in history, from the early Greek myths of the "Iliad" and the "Odyssey" to the oldest writings of the Bible to the oldest teachings of civilization, governments have recognized the traditional family as the foundation of prosperity and happiness, and in democratic societies, as the foundation of freedom. Human beings have always given traditional marriage a special sanction. Not that there cannot be contracts among individuals, but there is something unique about the traditional family in terms of what it does for our society and the foundation it provides—this is something that every civilized society in five thousand years of recorded history has recognized. Are we so wise today that we are ready to reject five thousand years of recorded history? I do not think so. I think that even the greatest society in the history of the world—which we have here today in the United States of

America—that even a society as great as our own trifles with the traditional family at great peril to itself. . . .

Mr. Byrd

. . . Obviously, human beings enter into a variety of relationships. Business partnerships, friendships, alliances for mutual benefits, and team memberships all depend upon emotional unions of one degree or another. For that reason, a number of these relationships have found standing under the laws of innumerable nations.

However, in no case has anyone suggested that these relationships deserve the special recognition or the designation commonly understood as "marriage." The suggestion that relationships between members of the same gender should ever be accorded the status or the designation of marriage flies in the face of the thousands of years of experience about the societal stability that traditional marriage has afforded human civilization. To insist that male-male or female-female relationships must have the same status as the marriage relationship is more than unwise, it is patently absurd.

Out of such relationships children do not result. Of course, children do not always result from marriages as we have traditionally known them. But out of same-sex relationships no children can result. Out of such relationships emotional bonding oftentimes does not take place, and many such relationships do not result in the establishment of "families" as society universally interprets that term. Indeed, as history teaches us too often in the past, when cultures waxed casual about the uniqueness and sanctity of the marriage commitment between men and women, those cultures have been shown to be in decline. This was particularly true in the ancient world in Greece and, more particularly, in Rome. In both Greece and Rome, same-sex relationships were not uncommon, particularly among the upper classes. Plato and Aristotle referred to the existence of such relationships in their writings, as did Plutarch, the Greek biographer.

Homer, the Greek epic poet, in the "Iliad," wrote of the love relationship that existed between Achilles and Patroclus. Homer relates that after Patroclus was slain by Hector, Patroclus appeared to Achilles in a dream saying, "Do not lay my bones apart from yours, Achilles. Let one urn cover my bones with yours, that golden, two-handled urn that your mother so graciously gave you."

As to the Romans, Cicero mentioned casually that a former consul, who was Catiline's lover, approached him on Catiline's behalf. This was undoubtedly during the time of the "Catiline Conspiracy," which took place in the years 63 and 62 A.D.

Suetonius, the Roman biographer, relates that Julius Caesar prostituted his body to be abused by King Nicomedes of Bithynia, and that Curio the Elder, in an oration, called Caesar "a woman for all men and a man for all women."

While same-sex relations were not unknown, therefore, to the ancients, same-sex marriages were a different matter. But they did sometimes involve utilization of the forms and the customs of heterosexual marriage. For example, the Emperor Nero, who reigned between 54 and 68 A.D., took the marriage vows with a young man named Sporus, in a very public ceremony, with a gown and a veil and with all of the solemnities of matrimony, after which Nero took this Sporus with him, carried on a litter, all decked out with ornaments and jewels and the finery normally worn by empresses, and traveled to the resort towns in Greece and Italy, Nero, "many a time, sweetly kissing him."

Juvenal, the Roman satirical poet, wrote concerning a same-sex wedding, by way of a dialog:

"I have a ceremony to attend tomorrow morning."

"What sort of ceremony?"

"Nothing special, just a gentleman friend of mine who is marrying another man and a small group has been invited."

Subsequently in the dialog, "Gracchus has given a dowry of 400 sesterces, signed the marriage tablets, said the blessing, held a great banquet, and the new bride now reclines on his husband's lap."

Juvenal looked upon such marriages disapprovingly, and as an example that should not be followed.

Mr. President, the marriage bond as recognized in the Judeo-Christian tradition, as well as in the legal codes of the world's most advanced societies, is the cornerstone on which the society itself depends for its moral and spiritual regeneration as that culture is handed down, father to son and mother to daughter.

Indeed, thousands of years of Judeo-Christian teachings leave absolutely no doubt as to the sanctity, purpose, and reason for the union of man and woman. One has only to turn to the Old Testament and read the word of God to understand how eternal is the true definition of marriage.

Mr. President, I am rapidly approaching my 79th birthday, and I hold in my hands a Bible, the Bible that was in my home when I was a child. This is the Bible that was read to me by my foster father. It is a Bible, the cover of which having been torn and worn, has been replaced. But this is the Bible, the King James Bible. And here is what it says in the first chapter of Genesis, 27th and 28th verses:

> So God created man in his own image, in the image of God created he him; male and female created he them.
>
> And God blessed them, and God said unto them, Be fruitful, and multiply, and replenish the earth. . . .

And when God used the word "multiply," he wasn't talking about multiplying your stocks, bonds, your bank accounts or your cattle on a thousand hills or your race horses or your acreages of land. He was talking about procreation, multiplying, populating the Earth.

And after the flood, when the only humans who were left on the globe were Noah and his wife and his sons and their wives, the Bible says in chapter 9 of Genesis:

> And God blessed Noah and his sons, and said unto them,
> Be fruitful, and multiply, and replenish the earth.

Christians also look at the Gospel of Saint Mark, chapter 10, which states:

> But from the beginning of the creation God made them male and female.
> For this cause shall a man leave his father and mother, and cleave to his wife:
> And they twain shall be one flesh: so then they are no more twain, but one flesh.
> What therefore God hath joined together, let not man put asunder.

Woe betide that society, Mr. President, that fails to honor that heritage and begins to blur that tradition which was laid down by the Creator in the beginning. . . .

This reflects a demand for political correctness that has gone berserk. We live in an era in which tolerance has progressed beyond a mere call for acceptance and crossed over to become a demand for the rest of us to give up beliefs that we revere and hold most dear in order to prove our collective purity.

At some point, a line must be drawn by rational men and women who are willing to say, "Enough!"

Mr. Robb

. . . Mr. President, scientists have not yet discovered what causes homosexuals to be attracted to members of their own sex. For the vast majority of us who don't hear that particular drummer it's difficult to fully comprehend such an attraction.

But homosexuality has existed throughout human history. And even though medical research hasn't succeeded in telling us why a small but significant number of our fellow human beings have a different sexual orientation, the clear weight of serious scholarship has concluded that people do not choose to be homosexual, any more than they choose their gender or their race. Or any more than we choose to be heterosexual. And given the prejudice too often directed toward gay people and the pressure they feel to hide the truth—their very identities—from family, friends and employers, it's hard to imagine why anyone would actually choose to bear such a heavy burden unnecessarily.

The fact of the matter is that we can't change who we are, or how God made us and that realization is increasingly accepted by succeeding generations. It has been my experience that more and more high school and college students today accept individual classmates as straight or gay without emotion or stigma. They accept what they cannot change as a fact of life. Which brings to mind one of my favorite prayers:

God, grant me the serenity to accept the things I cannot change
The courage to change the things I can,
And the wisdom to know the difference.

I suspect that for older generations fear has often kept this issue from being discussed openly before now—fear that anyone who expressed an understanding view of the plight of homosexuals was likely to be labeled one. Because of this fear, the battle against discrimination has largely been left to those who were directly affected by it. Mr. President, I believe it is time for those of us who are not homosexual to join the fight. A basic respect for human dignity—which gives us the strength to reject racial, gender and religious intolerance—dictates that in America we also eliminate discrimination against homosexuals. I believe that ending this discrimination is the last frontier in the ultimate fight for civil and human rights. . . .

Ultimately, Mr. President, immorality flows from immoral choices. But if homosexuality is an inalienable characteristic, which cannot be altered by counseling or willpower, then moral objections to gay marriages do not appear to differ significantly from moral objections to interracial marriages. . . .

Unfortunately, Mr. President, discrimination is not new in this country. Countless courageous Americans have risked their careers and even their lives to defy discrimination. We forget today how difficult these acts were in their own time. We forget how different our world would be if these pioneers had taken the easy path. One thing we do know, Mr. President, is that time has been the enemy of discrimination in America. It has allowed our views on race and gender and religion to evolve dramatically, inevitably, in the American tradition of progress and inclusion.

We're not there yet, Mr. President. In matters of race, gender, and religion, we've passed the laws, implemented the court decisions, signed the executive orders. And every day we work to battle the underlying prejudice that no law or judicial remedy or executive act can completely erase. But we've made the greatest strides forward when individuals, faced with their moment in history, were not afraid to act. And time has allowed us to see more clearly the humanity that binds us, rather than the religious, gender, racial, and other differences that distinguish us. But I fear, Mr. President, that if we don't stand here against this bill, we will stand on the wrong side of history, not unlike the majority of the Supreme Court who upheld the "separate but equal," doctrine in *Plessy v. Ferguson*. And with the benefit of time, the verdict of history is not likely to be as forgiving as we might believe it to be today. . . .

CHAPTER SEVEN

Not in Front of the Children?
SAME-SEX MARRIAGE AND PARENTHOOD

In the trial court hearings in Hawaii in September 1996, a large part of the state of Hawaii's argument against legal same-sex marriage centered on the expected effect on children. And, indeed, when the issue of homosexuality is raised, the problem of parenting is rarely far behind. Legalizing same-sex marriage would logically mean granting homosexuals adoption and parenting rights, and the implications of such a move have yet to be fleshed out. Unfortunately, most of the existing studies of children born of lesbian or gay parents have consisted of small samples of dubious extraction. Nevertheless, the unanimity of such studies is striking: there seems to be no appreciable difference between children brought up in stable homosexual homes and those brought up in stable heterosexual ones.

Many of these studies are laborious to read, laden with social science jargon and statistics. The best summary, however, is Professor Charlotte Patterson's account for the American Psychological Association; it begins this section. Also included is by far the best recent study comparing children in stable two-parent heterosexual homes with those in stable two-parent lesbian homes. Following these pieces is a telling critique by a group of scholars, from the Journal of Divorce and Remarriage, *arguing that almost all the studies Patterson cites do not meet basic guidelines for statistical validity, and the few that do support conclusions somewhat different than Patterson's. The chapter finishes with real-life accounts of the extreme tensions, difficulties, and triumphs of gay and lesbian family units— and an extract from one of the rulings in the now famous Sharon Bottoms case.*

Children of Lesbian and Gay Parents: Summary of Research Findings
CHARLOTTE PATTERSON

From Lesbian and Gay Parenting: A Resource for Psychologists, *American Psychological Association,* 1995

Patterson provides the most comprehensive survey of most of the existing social science studies on the adjustment of children brought up in lesbian or gay families.

One belief that often underlies both judicial decision-making in custody litigation and public policies governing foster care and adoption has been the belief that lesbians and gay men are not fit to be parents. In particular, courts have sometimes assumed that gay men and lesbians are mentally ill, that lesbians are less maternal than heterosexual women, and that lesbians' and gay men's relationships with sexual partners leave little time for ongoing parent-child interactions. Results of research to date have failed to confirm any of these beliefs. . . .

The first general concern is that development of sexual identity will be impaired among children of lesbian or gay parents—for instance, that children brought up by gay fathers or lesbian mothers will show disturbances in gender identity and/or in gender role behavior. It has also been suggested that children brought up by lesbian mothers or gay fathers will themselves become gay or lesbian.

A second category of concerns involves aspects of children's personal development other than sexual identity (Falk, 1989; Editors of the *Harvard Law Review,* 1990; Kleber et al., 1986). For example, courts have expressed fears that children in the custody of gay or lesbian parents will be more vulnerable to mental breakdown, will exhibit more adjustment difficulties and behavior problems, and will be less psychologically healthy than children growing up in homes with heterosexual parents.

A third category of specific fears expressed by the courts is that children of lesbian and gay parents may experience difficulties in social relationships. For example, judges have repeatedly expressed concern that children living with lesbian mothers may be stigmatized, teased, or otherwise traumatized by peers. Another common fear is that children living with gay or lesbian parents may be more likely to be sexually abused by the parent or by the parent's friends or acquaintances.

Three aspects of sexual identity are considered in the research: gender identity concerns a person's self-identification as male or female; gender-role behavior concerns the extent to which a person's activities, occupations, and the like are regarded by the culture as masculine, feminine, or both; sexual orientation refers to a person's choice of sexual partners—i.e., heterosexual, homosexual, or bisexual (Money & Earhardt, 1972; Stein, 1993). To examine the possibility that children in the custody of lesbian mothers or gay fathers experience disruptions of sexual identity, research relevant to each of these three major areas of concern is summarized below.

Gender Identity. In studies of children ranging in age from five to fourteen, results of projective testing and related interview procedures have revealed normal development of gender identity among children of lesbian mothers (Green, 1978; Green, Mandel, Hotvedt, Gray, & Smith, 1986; Kirkpatrick, Smith, & Roy, 1981). More direct assessment techniques to assess gender identity have been used by Golombok, Spencer, and Rutter (1983) with the same result: all children in this study reported that they were happy with their gender, and that they had no wish to be a member of the opposite sex. There was no evidence in any of the studies of gender identity difficulties among children of lesbian mothers. No data have been reported in this area for children of gay fathers.

Gender-Role Behavior. A number of studies have examined gender-role behavior among the offspring of lesbian mothers (Golombok et al., 1983; Gottman, 1990; Green, 1978; Hoeffer, 1981; Kirkpatrick et al., 1981; Patterson, 1994a). These studies reported that such behavior among children of lesbian mothers fell within typical limits for conventional sex roles. For instance, Kirkpatrick and her colleagues (1981) found no differences between children of lesbian versus heterosexual mothers in toy preferences, activities, interests, or occupational choices.

Rees (1979) administered the Bem Sex Role Inventory (BSRI) to 24 adolescents, half of whom had divorced lesbian and half of whom had divorced heterosexual mothers. The BSRI yields scores on masculinity and femininity as independent factors and an androgyny score from the ratio of masculinity to femininity. Children of lesbian and heterosexual mothers did not differ on masculinity or on androgyny, but children of lesbian mothers reported greater psychological femininity than did those of heterosexual mothers. This result would seem to run counter to expectations based on stereotypes of lesbians as lacking in femininity, both in their own demeanor and in their likely influences on children.

Sex role behavior of children was also assessed by Green and his colleagues (1986). In interviews with the children, no differences between 56 children of lesbian and 48 children of heterosexual mothers were found with respect to favorite television programs, favorite television characters, or favorite games or toys. There was some indication in interviews with children themselves that the offspring of lesbian mothers had less sex-typed preferences for activities at school and in their neighborhoods than did children of heterosexual mothers. Consistent with this result, lesbian mothers were also more likely than heterosexual mothers to report that their daughters often participated in rough-and-tumble play or occasionally played with "masculine" toys such as trucks or guns; however, they reported no differences in these areas for sons. Lesbian mothers were no more or less likely than heterosexual mothers to report that their children often played with "feminine" toys such as dolls. In both family types, however, children's sex-role behavior was seen as falling within normal limits.

In summary, the research suggests that children of lesbian mothers develop patterns of gender-role behavior that are much like those of other children. No data are available as yet in this area for children of gay fathers.

Sexual Orientation. A number of investigators have also studied a third component of sexual identity: sexual orientation (Bailey,

Bobrow, Wolfe, & Mikach, 1995; Bozett, 1980, 1982, 1987, 1989; Gottman, 1990; Golombok et al., 1983; Green, 1978; Huggins, 1989; Miller, 1979; Paul, 1986; Rees, 1979). In all studies, the great majority of offspring of both gay fathers and lesbian mothers described themselves as heterosexual. Taken together, the data do not suggest elevated rates of homosexuality among the offspring of lesbian or gay parents. For instance, Huggins (1989) interviewed 36 teenagers, half of whom were offspring of lesbian mothers and half of heterosexual mothers. No children of lesbian mothers identified themselves as lesbian or gay, but one child of a heterosexual mother did; this difference was not statistically significant. In a recent study, Bailey and his colleagues (1995) studied adult sons of gay fathers and found more than 90 percent of the sons to be heterosexual. Because the heterosexual and nonheterosexual sons did not differ in the length of time they had resided with their fathers, the effects of the exposure to the fathers' sexual orientation on the sons' sexual orientation must have been either very small or nonexistent. . . .

Studies assessing potential differences between children of gay and lesbian versus heterosexual parents have sometimes included assessments of children's social relationships. The most common focus of attention has been on peer relations, but some information on children's relationships with adults has also been collected. Research findings that address the likelihood of sexual abuse are also summarized in this section.

Research on peer relations among children of lesbian mothers has been reported by Golombok and her colleagues (1983), Green (1978), and by Green and his colleagues (1986). Reports by both parents and children suggest normal development of peer relationships. For example, as would be expected, most school-aged children reported same-sex best friends and predominantly same-sex peer groups (Golombok et al., 1983; Green, 1978). The quality of children's peer relations was described, on average, in positive terms by researchers (Golombok et al., 1983) as well as by lesbian mothers and their children (Green et al., 1986). No data on the children of gay fathers have been reported in this area.

Studies of relationships with adults among the offspring of lesbian and gay parents have also yielded a generally positive picture (Golombok et al., 1983; Harris & Turner, 1985/86; Kirkpatrick et al., 1981). For example, Golombok and her colleagues (1983) found that children of divorced lesbian mothers were more likely to have had recent contact with their fathers than were children of divorced heterosexual mothers. Another study, however, found no differences in this regard (Kirkpatrick et al., 1981). Harris and Turner (1985/86) studied the offspring of gay fathers as well as those of lesbian mothers; parent-child relationships were described in positive terms by parents in their sample. One significant difference between lesbian and gay parents, on the one hand, and heterosexual parents, on the other, was that heterosexual parents were more likely to say that their children's visits with the other parent presented problems for them (Harris & Turner, 1985/86).

In the Golombok et al. (1983) study, children's contacts with adult friends of their lesbian mothers were also assessed. All of the children were reported to have contact with adult friends of their mothers, and the majority of lesbian mothers reported that their adult friends were a mixture of homosexual and heterosexual adults.

Lesbians Choosing Motherhood:
A Comparative Study of Lesbian and Heterosexual Parents and Their Children

DAVID K. FLAKS ET AL.

From Developmental Psychology *31, no. 1* (1995)

This is the best recent survey on lesbian mothering. The results of its comparison of heterosexual and lesbian mothers are striking. If anything, Flaks finds lesbian mothers to be more conscientious than their heterosexual counterparts.

It is within the context of the developing literature on planned lesbian-mother families that the present research project was conducted. Its purpose was to expand what is known about these families, with an eye toward addressing the expressed concerns of family court judges and legislators (Falk, 1989). This study focused specifically on lesbian couples raising children born to them through donor insemination. By defining the experimental sample in this way, we eliminated the potentially confounding variables of single parenting, parental separation, and adoption.

Several features of this study make it unique among research on planned lesbian-mother families. First, this is the only study to separately assess the impact on boys and girls of being raised in a lesbian home. In addition, in the area of planned lesbian-mother families, this is only the second study to compare lesbian mothers and their children with a matched control group of heterosexual parents and their children and to corroborate parental assessments of the children by soliciting independent teacher ratings. Furthermore, this study represents the first effort to examine lesbian-mother families by using a broad range of outcome measures, including intellectual and behavioral assessments of the children, as well as evaluations of the parents' relationship quality and parenting skills. Each of these areas was chosen because it has been the subject of negative judicial assumptions about lesbian-mother families. . . .

In all, 15 lesbian-mother families and 15 heterosexual-parent families participated in this study, most of whom resided in the Pennsylvania area. . . . [M]ost of the parents in both groups were well-educated, and almost all had at least part-time employment outside of the home. The lesbian parents were somewhat older on average than the heterosexual parents. In addition, the lesbian and heterosexual couples had relationships of similar length, with the lesbian couples having been together for an average of 12.7 years (ranging from 7.5 to 18 years), and the heterosexual couples had been together for an average of 12.8 years (ranging from 8 to 20.5 years). The couples had also lived together for similar amounts of time: The lesbian couples had shared a residence for an average of 11.9 years (ranging from 5.5 to 18 years), and the heterosexual couples had lived together for an average of 11.2 years (ranging from 6 to 17 years).

Demographics of the 15 focal children in the lesbian- and heterosexual-parent samples were also similar. Both groups consisted of 8 girls and 7 boys. The focal children in both groups had a mean age of 5.8 years, with a range of 3.1 to 8.3 years, respectively, in the lesbian-mother group and 3.2 to 7.9 years, respectively, in the heterosexual-parent group. . . .

Notwithstanding this study's specific features, its results are entirely consistent with prior research on planned lesbian-mother families (McCandish, 1987; Patterson, 1994; Steckel, 1985, 1987). Like earlier research, results of this study are consistent with the conclusion that the children of lesbian and heterosexual parents are remarkably similar, specifically in the areas of intellectual functioning and behavioral adjustment. In each of these areas, no gender differences were found; scores for both boys and girls in the lesbian- and heterosexual-parent groups were extremely similar, and each group compared favorably with the standardization samples for the instruments used. Furthermore, of the 24 comparisons made between the children in the two groups, 17 actually favored the children of lesbian parents, a fact that diminishes the likelihood that differences were not found because of problems associated with small sample size. Rather, given the direction and magnitude of these results, it is more probable that the two groups of children and parents were comparable in the areas assessed.

Like their children, the two groups of parents evaluated in this study also revealed similarities. In the area of relationship quality, no differences were found between the groups, although the lesbian couples received higher scores in every area of dyadic adjustment. Moreover, both the lesbian and heterosexual couples were comparable in overall dyadic adjustment to the married couples in Spanier's (1976) normative sample, suggesting satisfactory relationship quality in both groups.

Only in the domain of parenting skills awareness were differences found between the two groups of couples. Analysis using the Parent Awareness Skills Survey revealed that the lesbian couples were more aware of the skills necessary for effective parenting than were their heterosexual counterparts. Specifically, the lesbian couples proved to be superior in their ability to identify the critical issues in child-care situations and to formulate appropriate solutions to the problems they noticed. With further analysis, however, it was revealed that these differences were related to the parents' gender rather than to their sexual orientation: Both heterosexual and lesbian mothers demonstrated an awareness of parenting skills that was superior to that of heterosexual fathers. Although this result may suggest that the heterosexual fathers were less capable in their ability to handle child-care problems, it may also represent a gender difference in their likelihood to verbalize their ideas about parenting. The latter conclusion is supported by an examination of the actual responses of the participants on the parenting skills measure. The verbatim records of the fathers were substantially shorter than those of the three groups of mothers. Further research is necessary for one to compare the parenting skills of parents on the basis of gender, preferably relying on observational data.

What are the implications of these results? Healthy developmental outcomes for the children in this and other studies of lesbian families support the view of Patterson (1992) and others that neither father presence nor parental heterosexuality is crucial for healthy child development. Such a conclusion, although uncontroverted in the research literature, remains controversial because it challenges widely accepted psychoanalytic and social learning theories of child development. Because such theories rely on traditional family structures to define the factors that promote children's development, they are not able to account easily for successful outcomes in nontraditional families, particularly those in which there is no opposite-sex parent in the home. Evidence of the type presented here, which suggests that well-adjusted children of both sexes can be raised in families of varying configurations, will hopefully provide an impetus for a reevaluation of the parental qualities most important for optimal child development. To accommodate the findings of this and other studies of lesbian families, it would appear that theories of child development will have to take into account the preeminence of process variables over structural ones in predicting the most desirable family environment for raising children (Patterson, 1994). . . .

A Review of Data Based Studies Addressing the Effects of Homosexual Parenting on Children's Sexual and Social Functioning

PHILIP A. BELCASTRO ET AL.

From the Journal of Divorce and Remarriage 20
(1993)

An opposite view of the social science data. Belcastro and his colleagues see most of the studies as essentially useless, ruined by lack of external validity and the biases of their authors. The truth is, the authors argue, we still don't know for sure what effect gay parents have on the development of children.

Abstract Part of the intellectual and political movement to provide homosexuals equal rights and opportunities under the law extends to homosexuals and bisexuals seeking custody of their biological children after divorce and/or custody of an adopted child. Family courts take into consideration parents' sexual orientation when considering custody decisions. To date, the data based research on children reared by homosexual parents is sparse. A search of the published literature identified fourteen data based studies which addressed some aspect of homosexual parenting and its effects on children. Each study was evaluated according to accepted standards of scientific inquiry. The most impressive finding was that all of the studies lacked external validity, and not a single study represented any sub-population of homosexual parents. Three studies met minimal or higher standards of internal validity, while the remaining eleven presented moderate to fatal threats to internal validity. The conclusion that there are no significant differences in children reared by lesbian mothers versus heterosexual mothers is not supported by the published research data base.

As a preface to the discussion, we have an obligation to comment on the real and ideal standards of scientific research utilizing human subjects. It is easy for a critic to demand ideal scientific standards. However, the reality of inadequate funding, population inaccessibility and incomplete behavioral constructs renders the goal of pure validity an ideal. On the other hand, such limitations cannot be ignored when proposing cause and effect via the scientific method.

The most impressive finding is that all of the studies lacked external validity. Furthermore, not a single study remotely represented any sub-population of homosexual parents. This limitation, in terms of scientific inference, is imposing.

With only three exceptions (i.e., Green et al., 1986; Hoeffer, 1979; Puryear, 1983) the studies' designs presented moderate to fatal threats to their internal validity. Seven studies did not utilize a control group and only three studies satisfactorily attempted to match comparison groups (i.e., Green et al., 1986; Hoeffer, 1979; Puryear, 1983). All of the studies utilized marginally acceptable sample sizes. Also, it was possible for a bisexual to enter either the homosexual or heterosexual groups in each study. With only one exception (i.e., Rees, 1979), of those studies utilizing a control group matched to a lesbian group, a considerable proportion of the lesbians were cohabiting with sexual partners and this same factor, cohabitation, was not true for the comparison heterosexual group. Another mutual limitation of these studies was one identified by Rees (1979), namely, lesbians' political and legal desire to present a happy, well-adjusted family to the world.

An importune weakness for these studies was the construction of the independent variable. As pointed out there was no control for bisexuals being classified as homosexuals. Furthermore, there was no control, save Rees (1979), for establishing a single-parent household. The gay households samples were a pieced-together patchwork of gay lovers, former spouses, custody rights quirks, and extended genetic and step-family units. The contamination of the independent variable resulted in the absence of even a single study comprised of a group of single-parent homosexual households matched to a group of single-parent heterosexual households.

The majority of studies also suffered from internal validity flaws such as inadequate instrumentation and disparate testing conditions that, unlike the external validity problems, were well within the researchers' control. In some cases the researchers argued that any information, regardless of quality, is better than none. We disagree and contend that improperly gathered data is scientifically defective.

Finally, based upon the researchers' interpretation of the data and at least in one case censorship of the data, most were biased towards proving homosexual parents were fit parents. A disturbing revelation was that some of the published works had to disregard their own results in order to conclude the homosexuals were fit parents. We believe that the system of manuscript review by peers, for minimum scientific standards of research, was compromised in several of these studies.

On the positive side, three of the studies demonstrated a minimum or higher standard of internal validity; two of which were dissertations. Although additional faults could be cited for these studies, their basic design and analyses were acceptable. In the interest of economy, only the variables that discriminated between the groups statistically, and were directly related to the three general concerns of family courts, are noted.

Green et al., 1986

- Daughters of lesbian mothers were more likely to cross-dress than daughters of heterosexual mothers.
- Daughters of lesbian mothers were more likely to choose traditionally masculine jobs than daughters of heterosexual mothers.
- Daughters of lesbian mothers were more likely to be above average in rough-and-tumble play than daughters of heterosexual mothers.
- Daughters of lesbian mothers were more likely to play with trucks than daughters of heterosexual mothers.
- Daughters of lesbian mothers were more likely to play with guns than daughters of heterosexual mothers.
- Children of lesbian mothers were more likely to be interested in play-acting and role-taking than children of heterosexual mothers.
- Lesbians' daughters were more likely to choose male activities than daughters of heterosexual mothers.
- Lesbians' sons were more likely to have a strong preference for female activities than heterosexual mothers' sons.
- Daughters of mothers who were active in lesbianism or feminist organizations were more likely to be interested in male occupations and desired to be like a man when they grew up.

(Please note: The authors blocked on several variables resulting in cells with < 5 subjects, and these results were omitted from the above list.)

Hoeffer, 1979

- Lesbians' daughters were more likely to score higher on sex-typed masculine activities than daughters of heterosexual mothers.

- Lesbians' daughters were less likely to view themselves as androgynous than daughters of heterosexual mothers.
- Lesbians' daughters were less likely to have female valued traits than daughters of heterosexual mothers.
- Lesbian mothers were less likely to encourage their sons and more likely to encourage their daughters in sex-role behavior than heterosexual mothers.
- Lesbians' sons were more likely to have female-valued traits than sons of heterosexual mothers.
- Lesbian mothers were less likely to encourage play with sex-typed toys for their children than heterosexual mothers.
- Lesbian mothers were more likely to report male peers influencing their sons than heterosexual mothers.
- Lesbians' daughters were more likely to have significant contact with male teachers than daughters of heterosexual mothers.

Puryear, 1983

- Lesbian children were more likely to draw the family as involved in separate activities than children of heterosexual mothers.
- Lesbian children were less likely to draw the father as being involved in activities with themselves than children of heterosexual mothers.
- Lesbian children were less likely to draw activities between mother and child that showed cooperation than children of heterosexual mothers.
- Lesbian children were less likely to draw activities between father and child that showed cooperation between the two, than children of heterosexual mothers.
- Lesbian children were less likely to draw activities between child and "other adult" that showed cooperation, than children of heterosexual mothers.

- Lesbian mothers were less likely to rate their children's relationship with their father as good than children of heterosexual mothers.

A pitfall is to consciously or unconsciously judge these differences on a moral basis. That is not the intent of this review. What is possible, given the collective limitations of these three studies, is to conclude that there appears to be some significant differences between children raised by lesbian mothers versus heterosexual mothers in their family relationships, gender identity and gender behavior. The most defined trend is that daughters of lesbian mothers are more likely to value and exhibit male sex-typed traits than daughters of heterosexual mothers. A second trend is that children of lesbian mothers are less likely to perceive their family as an interactive family unit and their father as cooperative, than children of heterosexual mothers. One critical concern of the courts is whether children of gay parents are more likely to adopt a homosexual lifestyle. Unfortunately, only one study utilized a post-adolescent sample in order to render any estimate. Paul (1986) surveyed adult offspring of gay and bisexual households and reported 23.5 percent of the subjects homosexual. However, his sample was seriously flawed.

In our view, the statement that there are no significant differences in children reared by homosexual parents versus heterosexual parents is not supported by the published research base. The converse also remains unproven.

The ultimate outcome of answering these research questions is not just whether there are differences but whether those differences are desirable or undesirable societal outcomes. This leads to the moral decision of whether society has a right to prevent nurturing of children and ultimately adults who are more tolerant and personally receptive to (1) homosexuals; (2) homosexual behaviors; and (3) homosexual relationships.

Some essential refinements to the research question are necessary. We will not reiterate the recommendations for the reviewed studies with the exception of the need for representative samples, and adult offspring samples from homosexual households. Future studies need to isolate and precisely construct comparison groups that equate the homosexual rearing family unit with the heterosexual rearing family unit in all essential aspects of the experience including (1) parental lovers with parenting roles; (2) length of exposure to the homosexual family unit at various childhood developmental stages; and (3) divorced/separated parents' family role and contact with offspring. The classification of parents' sexual orientation should be qualitatively measured for the entire time frame of their children's lifetime. Parents' sexual orientation should be blocked on homosexual, heterosexual, or bisexual. A comprehensive lifetime sexual behavior profile should be constructed on children from homosexual households and their heterosexual cohorts. There is a pressing need to study children raised by homosexual fathers and in turn determine any differences in outcomes regarding children raised by lesbian mothers versus homosexual fathers, and also their heterosexual cohorts. Lastly, in order to address the question of whether homosexual parents rear homosexual children, it is necessary to examine the lineage of homosexuals.

Coming Out to My Children
ANTIGA

Homophobia at Home
BAYLAH WOLFE

From Politics of the Heart: A Lesbian Parenting
Anthology, 1987

Two reflections on the rejection lesbian mothers sometimes experience at the hands of their own children.

COMING OUT TO MY CHILDREN

I thought that I was waiting
until
they could handle it
before telling them.

When I did
both daughters wondered why
it had taken me so long
both sons pretended that
they hadn't heard.

The pain
of the oldest daughter was spoken:

"Mom, I wish you weren't a Lesbian."
The pain
of the youngest son was hidden until
he was hospitalized
so drunk
he could not say his name.
When he could speak
they asked for my phone number
and he answered:
"Don't call her. She's a Lesbian."

HOMOPHOBIA AT HOME

Homophobia has been a profound challenge to me, particularly as it manifested itself in my relationships with my two children, Julie and Steve. I came out as a lesbian twelve years ago, after leaving a white middle-class marriage. Together with Julie and Steve, I lived in a Long Island suburb, and became a "known" lesbian after appearing on a television program about lesbian mothers. Because of this exposure, the children experienced varying degrees of homophobia: my lover's fifteen-year-old daughter was physically roughed up, accompanied by taunts of *lezzie* and *queer;* Steve lost a friend after his friend found out. Mostly the homophobia played itself out in subtle attitudinal ways. During this time, I did not waver in asserting my right to be out.

Six years ago, after breaking up with my lover, I planned a move to Brooklyn. Julie and Steve, then fourteen and eleven, were frightened at the prospect of this move. I tuned in to the fact that they had been through some very rough years which included the divorce, my coming out crisis, and adjusting to living with my lover and her two children. My heart went out to them, and I decided to make a compromise. I told them I would keep a low profile as a lesbian so that they could make new friends without fear of exposure to homophobia. Since they felt me caring about their feelings, this compromise served to rebuild trust and was a kind of healing between us. I agreed to restrict lesbian posters to my bedroom. I was discreet in the neighborhood.

Despite all of this, in the four years we had been here, Julie and Steve still chose to walk ten paces behind me on the street. They rarely brought friends home. Julie could not look me in the eye at school plays and concerts. They never told any friend, no matter how close, that they had a lesbian mother. Rather than easing up as they became connected in the city, they seemed more rigid in their homophobia. They slipped into the expectation that I would remain closeted in their presence, although they never fully trusted that. This provided a false level of sameness for them and increased a painful alienation between us. I ached from their denial of me and my friends. . . .

One evening two years ago, I could no longer bear my complicity in protecting Julie and Steve's insecurities, their fear of difference. I took a stand. I told Julie I would be happy to attend her high school graduation the following week, but if she wanted me there, I would be wearing a lesbian mother button. During the next few days, Julie, Steve, and I had many painful conversations. Steve, in particular, thought I was being very unfair. I told him I would no longer erase myself, that I planned to wear my lesbian mother button around the neighborhood.

I felt alternately anxious, sad, and strong. I often played Alix Dobkin's song, "A Mother Knows," which is about Alix's love for her daughter and about the work of being a feminist-lesbian mother. This comforted me and challenged Julie. On the night before her graduation, Julie broke down, wept, engaged her courage, and invited me. We were closer to each other than we had been in a long time.

That was the beginning of Julie's facing and feeling the reality of my lesbianism. She began the painful and scary task of unraveling her homophobia and her strong fear of disapproval. Almost immediately, she told two friends that she had a lesbian mother, and she attended her first Gay Pride march wearing a sign which read, I AM THE DAUGHTER OF A LESBIAN DEALING WITH MY HOMOPHOBIA.

Steve had a more difficult time. As Julie and I were leaving for her graduation, he said, "I'm going to kill myself." It is excruciating to hear one's child make this statement. I did not think he was literally suicidal at the time, but something in him had to die—some illusion of sameness, some illusion of control. He was so threatened by my refusal to be invisible that he chose to live with his father, a move he had wanted previously but did not know how to actualize. Now he could present his father with a good reason: his mother was flaunting her lesbianism. We each felt separate agonies.

On the evening Steve left, a violent thunderstorm erupted suddenly. I sat at an upstairs window, encircled by loving sisters, as we watched Steve, Julie, and their father make endless trips to the car in the pouring rain, with a fifteen-year accumulation of things. Lightning illuminated their comings and goings. We did not say goodbye. My lover told me the storm was an expression of my clarity, anger, and tears.

I wrote Steve a letter a few weeks later, telling him that while I was hurt by his homophobia and how he used it, I respected his decision and wished him well in his new life. I let him know that I would still be there for him, albeit in a different way. Nevertheless he was very distant, and there was a great strain between us that first year.

Now he stays with me two days a week, and while he is still embarrassed by my lesbianism, he is slowly dealing with his homophobia. I am grateful for the movement in our relationship. He knows what my bottom lines are, and I have learned to respect his pace. Recently, he surprised me: he expressed how much he enjoys his time with me now. After searching for what he called the right verb, he said, "It is more healing here. I am more relaxed. I can be myself. We talk about meaningful things." He said all this hesitantly and with a twinkle in his eye, then added, "I can't believe I just said this." He has become introspective, and his growth brings me great joy.

Parenting by Gay Fathers
JERRY J. BIGNER AND FREDERICK W. BOZETT

From Homosexuality and Family Relations, *edited by Frederick W. Bozett and Marvin B. Sussman, 1990*

A recent sociological survey of gay fathers.

When gay fathers are compared with nongay fathers in their responses to the Iowa Parent Behavior Scale, the gay fathers are found to be more strict and to consistently emphasize the importance of setting limits on children's behavior (Bigner & Jacobsen, 1989b). They report going to greater lengths than nongay fathers in promoting cognitive skills of children by explaining rules and regulations. As such, they may place greater emphasis on verbal communication with children. Gay fathers tend to be less traditional or more authoritative with children and to be somewhat strict in the execution of their control over children. Generally, gay fathers are found to be more sensitive and responsive to the perceived needs of children than nongay fathers. Gay fathers also appear to go to extra lengths to act as a resource for activities with children. They seem no different from nongay fathers in their expression of intimacy toward children except that they appear less willing to be demonstrative toward their partner in their children's presence than are nongay fathers (Bigner & Jacobsen, 1989b).

Several explanations can be suggested that address the differences and similarities in parenting behavior of gay and nongay fathers. First, gay fathers may feel additional pressures to be more proficient at their parenting role than nongay fathers. Factors that might motivate them to be "better" fathers could include (1) stronger feelings of guilt about their role in fathering children, based on an increased sensitivity about their sexuality; and (2) sensitivity to the belief that they are "in the spotlight" or expected to perform better due to a fear that visitation or custody decisions could be challenged because of their sexual orientation. Second, these findings suggest that gay fathers may be less conventional and more androgynous than nongay fathers. As such, they may incorporate a greater degree and combination of expressive role functions than more traditionally sex-role oriented nongay fathers. These expressive role functions are found more conventionally in the traditional female mothering role. The cultural stereotype of the father role among traditional males is that they (1) generally are not interested in children or in child-rearing issues; (2) view the occupational role as their primary parenting identity; (3) are less competent caregivers than women; and (4) are less nurturant than women toward children. It is possible that nongay fathers adopt this as their parenting style while gay fathers may demonstrate a blending of the qualities traditionally associated with both mother and father role images.

What is the quality of parent-child relations for those men who are gay and yet remain married and/or closeted and do not reveal their homosexuality to children? Researchers find that these relationships often are of less quality than those found among fathers who are open and honest with their children regarding their homosexuality (Bozett, 1987b; Miller, 1979a). Gay fathers who have disclosed their homosexuality to their children and to others tend to live a relatively stable lifestyle that may involve a domestic type of relationship with another man who often is a permanent partner, they tend to spend quality time with their children, and are dependable sources of caregiving (Miller, 1979a). . . .

A Mother's Son?

Bottoms v. Bottoms. From the Court's Ruling, Court of Appeals of Virginia, June 1994

> *Sharon Bottoms's fight against her own mother for custody of her child became a* cause célèbre *in the same-sex marriage wars. Here's the ruling in the case, which went in Sharon Bottoms's favor. The reader should be aware that Bottoms was ultimately denied custody of her child, because she sold her story for $75,000 and a cut of the profits to Home Box Office, which produced a movie about the case in 1996.*

In 1989, Sharon Bottoms married Dennis Doustou. They separated when Sharon was pregnant with their son, who was born in 1991. The 1991 divorce decree awarded custody of the child to Sharon Bottoms. Doustou has not been actively involved in his son's life since the divorce. During the three years following the divorce, Sharon Bottoms dated another man, lived with her cousin, lived with two lesbians, and in 1992, began living with April Wade. During this time, Sharon Bottoms had legal custody of her son, but she frequently relied on her mother, Kay Bottoms, to keep and care for the child. Kay Bottoms estimated that she had kept the child most of the time after his birth.

In January 1993, Sharon Bottoms informed her mother that her son would be spending less time at her mother's house because of Tommy Conley's presence there. Tommy Conley was Kay Bottoms's live-in male companion. The two had lived together and reared Sharon Bottoms from the time Sharon was a child. Sharon Bottoms explained to her mother that she was taking her son out of the household because while she, Sharon, was growing up, Tommy Conley had sexually abused her over eight hundred times. Kay Bottoms was shocked and upset by the accusations, but she later decided that the accusations were not altogether unfounded.

Shortly after the conversation between Sharon and Kay Bottoms, Kay filed a petition with the juvenile and domestic relations district court seeking custody of her grandson. She asked Tommy Conley to move out of the house during the custody dispute because her lawyer "thought it would be best." The circuit court ultimately granted Kay Bottoms custody of her grandson, and this appeal followed. . . .

The trial court ruled that because Sharon Bottoms lives in a sexually active lesbian relationship and engages in illegal sexual acts, she is an unfit parent as a matter of law. The trial court held as follows:

> Sharon Bottoms has . . . admitted . . . that she is living in a ho-
> mosexual relationship. . . . She is sharing . . . her bed with . . .
> her female lover. . . . Examples given were kissing, patting, all
> of this in the presence of the child. . . . There is no case di-
> rectly on point concerning all these matters. In the case of
> *Roe v. Roe,* it's certainly of assistance to me in reaching a deci-
> sion here today. I will tell you first that the mother's conduct is
> illegal. . . . I will tell you that it is the opinion of the court that
> her conduct is immoral. And it is the opinion of this court that
> the conduct of Sharon Bottoms renders her an unfit parent.
> However, I also must recognize, and do recognize, that there
> is a presumption in the law in favor of the custody being with
> the natural parent. And I then ask myself are Sharon Bottoms'
> circumstances of unfitness . . . of such an extraordinary nature
> as to rebut this presumption. My answer to this is yes [under]
> *Roe v. Roe.* . . . I further find that in addition to this, there is
> other evidence . . . which is unrebutted of the cursing, the ev-
> idence of the child standing in the corner.

The trial judge granted custody to Kay Bottoms and visitations on Mondays and Tuesdays to Sharon Bottoms, provided
that no visitations be in the home shared with April Wade or in
April Wade's presence. . . .

The most that can be said against Sharon Bottoms, insofar as
her parenting is concerned, is that on two occasions she spanked
her son "too hard," on occasion she swore in his presence, she
had him stand in a corner, and on occasion she had failed to
change his diaper as soon as conditions required. Sharon Bottoms had lived in four different residences in different relationships in a three-year period, and she had not been regularly
employed. On one occasion, Sharon Bottoms had left her son
with Kay Bottoms, the grandmother, for a week without inform-
ing the grandmother how she could be reached.

Although Sharon Bottoms's parenting during this three-year period was far from ideal, she was not indifferent to her child's well-being. Her disciplining of the child, even if by some standards considered intemperate or inappropriate, was not abusive. Her lifestyle in moving several times in a short period, in being unemployed for a time, and in failing to inform her mother of her whereabouts for a week were not acts of neglect or abuse sufficient to render her an unfit custodian. At all times, Sharon Bottoms either cared for the child or assured that proper care was provided for the child. No evidence suggested that any of Sharon Bottoms's actions resulted in psychological, emotional, or physical harm to the child or that her actions constituted neglect or abuse.

The psychological evaluations admitted into evidence indicated that Sharon Bottoms's son is a "happy, well-adjusted youngster" with an "out-going, engaging manner . . . capable of forming and sustaining both emotional and social attachments to others." The psychological reports concluded that Sharon Bottoms is "warm" and "responsive" with her son and that "[he] behave[s] as if entirely secure and at ease with his mother, [being with her is] . . . very familiar and comfortable . . . for him."

The trial judge based his finding of Sharon Bottoms's parental unfitness on the fact that she is living in an open lesbian relationship with April Wade and that the two engage in sodomy, an illegal sexual act, in the home where the child would reside. Certainly, those facts, which define the nature of the relationship between a custodial parent and a resident of the household where the child would reside, are the most critical and significant factors in this case for determining whether this parent is unfit or whether continued parental custody will be harmful or deleterious to the child. All factors must be considered, but in this instance, the open lesbian relationship and illegality of the mother's sexual activity are the only significant factors that the court considered in finding Sharon Bottoms to be an unfit parent.

We agree with the trial court that the nature of the relationship between a parent and the parent's live-in companion where the child resides may affect the type of conduct and behavior to which a child will be exposed and, thus, profoundly affect the child. The Supreme Court of Virginia has expressly said that a lesbian "lifestyle" is one factor "to [be] . . . considered in determining [a woman's] fitness as a mother." A parent's behavior and conduct in the presence of a child influences and affects the child's values and views as to the type of behavior and conduct that the child will find acceptable.

The fact that a parent is homosexual does not *per se* render a parent unfit to have custody of his or her child. Thus, the fact that a mother is a lesbian and has engaged in illegal sexual acts does not alone justify taking custody of a child from her and awarding the child to a non-parent, even though an award of custody may be only temporary. The fact that a parent has committed a crime does not render a parent unfit, unless such criminal conduct impacts upon or is harmful to the child, or unless other special circumstances exist aside from the parent's conduct that would render continued custody with the parent deleterious to the child.

A parent's sexual behavior, particularly a parent's sexual indiscretions, in a child's presence is conduct which may render a parent unfit to have custody of a child. A parent's private sexual conduct, even if illegal, does not create a presumption of unfitness. In order for the state or a third party to take custody of a child from its natural parent, more is required than simply showing that a parent has engaged in private, illegal sexual conduct, lacks ideal parenting skills, or is not meeting society's traditional or conventional standards of morality. A court will not remove a child from the custody of a parent, based on proof that the parent is engaged in private, illegal sexual conduct or conduct considered by some to be deviant, in the absence of proof that such behavior or activity poses a substantial threat of harm to a child's emotional, psychological, or physical well-being. . . .

Even when a natural parent falls short of society's accepted standards of behavior, such as the parents in *Mason, Ferris* and *Phillips,* unless proof of harm to the child or evidence of neglect or abuse is shown, the state will not intervene to take custody of a child from its natural parent.

In Sharon Bottoms's case, the trial court found that Sharon Bottoms engaged in illegal sexual activity and that her open lesbian relationship rendered her an unfit parent "as a matter of law." The trial court erroneously adopted a *per se* approach in finding Sharon Bottoms to be an unfit parent without finding that she engaged in conduct or exposed her son to conduct that would be harmful to him. In declaring as a matter of law that Sharon Bottoms is an unfit parent, the trial court misapplied the Supreme Court's decision in *Roe v. Roe.*

First, the *Roe* case does not stand for the proposition that a homosexual parent is *per se* unfit to have custody of a child. The Court stated in *Roe,* "[a]lthough we decline[d] to hold that every lesbian mother or homosexual father is *per se* an unfit *parent* . . . [this] father's continuous exposure of the child to his immoral and illicit relationship renders him an unfit and improper custodian as a matter of law."

Second, the *Roe* decision has little or no application to this case because *Roe* involved a dispute between two parents over which was the preferred custodian. In *Roe,* the presumption of parental fitness had no application. In *Roe,* the court was only required to determine that, as between the parents, the child's best interests would be best served by granting custody of the child to the mother rather than to the father, who was engaged in a homosexual relationship to which the child was openly exposed. Although aspects of Sharon Bottoms's behavior were similar to the father's conduct in *Roe* because Sharon Bottoms had hugged and kissed and displayed some affection toward her lesbian partner in the presence of her child, the father in *Roe* had exposed his daughter to more intimate behavior of a sexual nature, which had an impact upon the child. In *Roe*, the nine-year-old daughter was visibly distressed by her father's homosexual relationship after she witnessed the two men "hugging and kissing and sleeping in bed together." In *Roe*, the father had parties at his house where other homosexuals would "engage in similar behavior in the child's presence." Although Sharon Bottoms resides with April Wade in an open lesbian relationship, no evidence showed that they engaged in illegal sexual behavior in the child's presence. No evidence showed that the child has or will suffer any emotional or psychological distress as a result of the relationship. Where a parent exposes a child to an illicit sexual relationship, as in *Roe,* the Supreme Court has upheld denying a parent custody; however, where parents have shielded the child from illegal heterosexual adultery, as in the *Ford* and *Sutherland* cases, we have held the parents not to be unfit. . . .

Why I'm Glad I Grew Up in a Gay Family
PAULA FOMBY

From Mother Jones, *May/June* 1991

A voice rarely heard from in this context: the child's.

I grew up in the closet, waiting for my mother to come out first. When I was thirteen, she told me that she was a lesbian and confessed what I had assumed, that the woman who had lived with us for four years was her lover. I cried; when I remember it, I picture myself running away from her and down the street.

Being the child in a gay family, for me, meant telling lies. My mother asked me not to tell my friends that she was gay, comparing the embarrassment to a secret we shared about an eraser I had once stolen from a stationery store. There was little danger that I would say anything. Through high school, I constructed my social life around the fact that my mother and her lover were asleep by ten o'clock, making sure I had no guests in our house, who might see them go to bed. Should anyone actually see them disappear behind the same closed door, I was quick to invent an explanation. If my mother and Connie overheard the stories I made up, they never said anything, taking this, I suppose, as my method of defense.

Children have clear signals about what it means to be gay— where I lived, a limp wrist, a high-pitched voice, a purple polo shirt for boys, and anything leaning toward hippie fashion for girls. To be gay was to be stupid; the two words were literally synonymous. I was slow to understand that the shared bed in my house and the insults made in the cafeteria line were all supposed to be part of the same thing.

The hardest part of having a gay mother was accepting homosexuality and all its consequences before I even knew what that involved. I loved my mother and Connie, but I cringed at the mention of the Gay Pride parade, and I looked at their gay friends skeptically, eager for reasons to dislike them. I never said anything, valiantly trying to support a cause I didn't even want to discuss with my friends. As long as they kept it quiet, I was content; otherwise, I hated the danger their social lives posed to mine.

In order to live peaceably, I accepted my mother's lifestyle a long time ago; feeling comfortable with it has come more recently. My first efforts to defend gays were destructively self-conscious. I gave a speech to a high-school class about gay rights, but when a student asked if I was gay, I was quicker than I should have been to say no. In college, I alienated myself at a party by screaming at somebody who resented heterosexual-hating gays. My argument lacked basis and logic, but I felt threatened, as if they were somehow pointing a finger at my mother. This constant tension between defending gays while defining myself as straight finally articulated itself when I realized that there are not simply gay couples with children; there are gay families, where everyone must deal with the prejudice surrounding homosexuality.

The fact that there is no real definition of the gay family is obvious when I try to explain Connie. To dismiss Connie as an entity existing in our house only for my mother's sake negates the impact she's had on more than half of my life. She has been a part of my decisions, she has purchased my groceries, she has entertained my ambitions. She has been far more than a roommate to me, and I love her, want to protect her, and make her happy. I know also what she means to my mother—they are wedded in everything but the legal sense.

Each person in my family has matured into what it means to be gay individually. My mother and Connie have become more involved in the gay community since I left home. Seeing them take pride in their relationship makes me more proud to talk about them, and I have met people who say "it's pretty cool" to come from such a unique family. My willingness to discuss coming from a gay family results as much from the support of friends and college teachers as it does from my unchanging belief, idealized in all families, that my mother always does the right thing. . . .

CHAPTER EIGHT

A Slippery Slope?

THE POLYGAMY AND ADULTERY DEBATE

Curiously, perhaps, a major subsidiary argument related to same-sex marriage turned into a full-scale fight. Several leading conservatives—including former education secretary Bill Bennett and Washington Post columnist Charles Krauthammer—chose to oppose same-sex marriage partly on the grounds that they believed that there was no rational or moral distinction between sanctioning polygamy and legalizing same-sex marriage. Their arguments are reproduced below—as are impassioned responses from me and Jonathan Rauch.

Linked to polygamy was the notion that gay men are inherently more promiscuous than straight men and that a same-sex marriage would therefore inevitably be more likely to involve adultery than would a heterosexual marriage; and so gay unions would demean the institution as a whole. So polygamy and adultery became part of a distinct line of argument against same-sex marriage that continues still.

This chapter concludes with an extract from The Homosexual-ization of America, *in which gay writer Dennis Altman celebrates precisely the polygamous gay male impulses that so alarm Bennett and Krauthammer. The essay appeared in 1982—before the AIDS epidemic exploded, and before the issue of same-sex marriage came to redefine the cultural and political self-understanding of many lesbian and gay Americans.*

Leave Marriage Alone
WILLIAM BENNETT

From Newsweek, *June 3, 1996*

If we allow same-sex marriage, why not polygamy? or incest?

There are at least two key issues that divide proponents and opponents of same-sex marriage. The first is whether legally recognizing same-sex unions would strengthen or weaken the institution. The second has to do with the basic understanding of marriage itself.

The advocates of same-sex marriage say that they seek to strengthen and celebrate marriage. That may be what some intend. But I am certain that it will not be the reality. Consider: the legal union of same-sex couples would shatter the conventional definition of marriage, change the rules which govern behavior, endorse practices which are completely antithetical to the tenets of all of the world's major religions, send conflicting signals about marriage and sexuality, particularly to the young, and obscure marriage's enormously consequential function—procreation and child rearing.

Broadening the definition of marriage to include same-sex unions would stretch it almost beyond recognition—and new attempts to expand the definition still further would surely follow. On what principled ground can Andrew Sullivan exclude others who most desperately want what he wants, legal recognition and social acceptance? Why on earth would Sullivan exclude from marriage a bisexual who wants to marry two other people? After all, exclusion would be a denial of that person's sexuality. The same holds true of a father and daughter who want to marry. Or two sisters. Or men who want (consensual) polygamous arrangements. Sullivan may think some of these arrangements are unwise. But having employed sexual relativism in his own defense, he has effectively lost the capacity to draw any lines and make moral distinctions.

Forsaking all others is an essential component of marriage. Obviously it is not always honored in practice. But it is the ideal to which we rightly aspire, and in most marriages the ideal is in fact the norm. Many advocates of same-sex marriage simply do not share this ideal; promiscuity among homosexual males is well known. Sullivan himself has written that gay male relationships are served by the "openness of the contract" and that homosexuals should resist allowing their "varied and complicated lives" to be flattened into a "single, moralistic model." But that "single, moralistic model" has served society exceedingly well. The burden of proof ought to be on those who propose untested arrangements for our most important institution. . . .

The Role of Nature
HADLEY ARKES

*From the hearing of the House Judiciary Committee,
May 15, 1996*

> *Here Amherst political science professor Hadley Arkes makes
> the same point as Bennett, but he defends it more philosophi-
> cally. His point is that marriage is rooted in nature, not con-
> vention, and that nature requires the union to be procreative
> in possibility. Lose that principle, and everything else is lost
> with it.*

The categories of the Constitution must be filled in with a substance of what we are talking about, and it becomes impossible to speak about marriage and sexuality in these cases without
using the "N" word, nature. We understand that this is not about
love. There are abiding relations of love between brothers and
sisters, parents and children, and in the nature of things those
loves cannot be diminished as loves because they are not attended
by penetration or because they are not expressed in marriage.

Marriage has something to do preeminently with the establishment of a framework of lawfulness and commitment for the
begetting and nurturance of children. This is the plainest connection between the idea of marriage and what has been called
the natural teleology of the body, the fact that we are all, as the
saying goes, engendered. We are men and women, there are
only two people, not three, only a man and woman can beget a
child. There is a coherence in this scheme that is not impaired in
the least when the couple are incapable of bearing children.

But my main point is this, if we detach marriage from that natural teleology of the body, on what ground of principle to the law consigns marriage to couples, on what ground would the law say no to people who profess that their love is not confined to a coupling, but woven together in the larger ensemble of three or four. I think our previous speakers have already indicated they are not aware of any ground of principle in which the law would say no. If that arrangement were made available to ensembles of the same sex, it would have to be made available to ensembles of mixed sexes, which is to say we would be back, in principle, to the acceptance of polygamy.

I want to make clear that I am not offering a prediction. I am not saying that if we accept gay marriage we will be engulfed by polygamy and incest and other exotic arrangements. I am raising a question of principle about the ground on which the law says no. It couldn't simply say, that is not what we do here, because that answer suffices right now.

Let me go further. Let me say, I would not impute to the people on the other side of this question, even the remotest interest in promoting polygamy or anything more exotic, but this much can be said properly about their position, that it has at the heart of their rhetorical strategy and the logic of their arguments to deny that there is any defining ground in nature for sexuality, or any defining limits in nature for sexuality, and it is their strategy to keep pushing that to the limit to keep establishing the point that all these relations are ultimately matters of convention. That we know we can count upon, that there will be activists out there testing the limits and pushing it to the next level, and we know we can count on it precisely for the reasons expressed here, that no one on the panel seems to be quite clear about the ground of principle on which the law would say no. . . .

Three's a Crowd

A N D R E W   S U L L I V A N

From The New Republic, *June 17, 1996*

A riposte to Arkes and Bennett. Note in particular the point that if promiscuity is the issue, then lesbian marriage—on conservative grounds—should have more moral legitimacy than heterosexual marriage.

It wasn't that we hadn't prepped. Testifying on the Hill was a first for me, and those of us opposing the "Defense of Marriage Act" had been chatting for days about possible questions. But we hadn't quite expected this one. If a person had an "insatiable desire" to marry more than one wife, Congressman Bob Inglis of South Carolina wanted to know, what argument did gay activists have to deny him a legal, polygamous marriage? It wasn't a stray question. Republican after Republican returned gleefully to a Democratic witness who, it turned out, was (kind of) in favor of polygamy. I hastily amended my testimony to deal with the question. Before long, we were busy debating on what terms Utah should have been allowed into the Union and whether bisexuals could have legal harems.

Riveting stuff, compared to the Subcommittee on the Constitution's usual fare. But also revealing. In succeeding days, polygamy dominated the same-sex marriage debate. Both Bill Bennett and George Will used the polygamy argument as a first line of defense against same-sex marriage. In the *Washington Post* and *Newsweek,* Bennett in particular accused the same-sex marriage brigade of engaging in a "sexual relativism" with no obvious stopping place and no "principled ground" to oppose the recognition of multiple spouses.

Well, here's an attempt at a principled ground. The polygamy argument rests, I think, on a couple of assumptions. The first is that polygamous impulses are morally and psychologically equivalent to homosexual impulses, since both are diversions from the healthy heterosexual norm, and that the government has a role to prevent such activities. But I wonder whether Bennett really agrees with this. Almost everyone seems to accept, even if they find homosexuality morally troublesome, that it occupies a deeper level of human consciousness than a polygamous impulse. Even the Catholic Church, which believes that homosexuality is an "objective disorder," concedes that it is a profound element of human identity. It speaks of "homosexual persons," for example, in a way it would never speak of "polygamous persons." And almost all of us tacitly assume this, even in the very use of the term "homosexuals." We accept also that multiple partners can be desired by gays and straights alike: that polygamy is an activity, whereas both homosexuality and heterosexuality are states.

So where is the logical connection between accepting same-sex marriage and sanctioning polygamy? Rationally, it's a completely separate question whether the government should extend the definition of marriage (same-sex or different-sex) to include more than one spouse or whether, in the existing institution between two unrelated adults, the government should continue to discriminate between its citizens. Politically speaking, the connection is even more tenuous. To the best of my knowledge, there is no polygamists' rights organization poised to exploit same-sex marriage to return the republic to polygamous abandon. Indeed, few in the same-sex marriage camp have anything but disdain for such an idea. And, as a matter of social policy, same-sex marriage is, of course, the opposite of Bennett's relativism. Far from opening up the possibilities of multiple partners for homosexuals, it actually closes them down.

Bennett might argue, I suppose, that any change in marriage opens up the possibility of any conceivable change in marriage. But this is not an argument, it's a panic. If we're worried about polygamy, why not the threat of legally sanctioned necrophilia? Or bestiality? The same panic occurred when interracial marriage became constitutional—a mere thirty years ago—and when women no longer had to be the legal property of their husbands. The truth is, marriage has changed many, many times over the centuries. Each change should be judged on its own terms, not as part of some seamless process of alleged disintegration.

So Bennett must move to his next point, which is that homosexuals understand the institution of marriage so differently than heterosexuals do that to admit them into it would be to alter the institution entirely. To argue this, he has to say that gay men are so naturally promiscuous that they are constitutively unable to sustain the monogamous requirements of marriage and so fail to meet the requirements of membership. He has even repeatedly—and misleadingly—quoted my book, *Virtually Normal*, to buttress this point.

Bennett claims that I believe male-male marriage would and should be adulterous—and cites a couple of sentences from the epilogue to that effect. In context, however, it's clear that the sentences he cites refer to some cultural differences between gay and straight relationships, as they exist today before same-sex marriage has been made legal. He ignores the two central chapters of my book—and several articles—in which I unequivocally argue for monogamy as central to all marriage, same-sex or opposite-sex.

That some contemporary gay male relationships are "open" doesn't undermine my point; it supports it. What I do concede, however, is that, in all probability, gay male marriage is not likely to be identical to lesbian marriage, which isn't likely to be identical to heterosexual marriage. The differences between the genders, the gap between gay and straight culture, the unique life experiences that divide as well as unite heterosexuals and homosexuals, will probably create an institution not easily squeezed into a completely uniform model. And a small minority of male-male marriages may perhaps fail to uphold monogamy as successfully as many opposite-sex marriages. But what implications does that assertion have for the same-sex marriage debate as a whole?

Bennett argues that nonmonogamous homosexual marriages will fatally undermine an already enfeebled institution. He makes this argument for one basic reason: men are naturally more promiscuous, and male-male marriages will legitimize such promiscuity. But this argument has some problems. If you believe that men are naturally more promiscuous than women, then it follows that lesbian marriages will actually be more monogamous than heterosexual ones. So the alleged damage male-male marriages might do to heterosexual marriage would be countered by the good example that lesbian marriages would provide. It's a wash. And if you take the other conservative argument—that marriage exists not to reward monogamy but to encourage it—then Bennett is also in trouble. There is surely no group in society, by this logic, more in need of marriage rights than gay men. They are the group that most needs incentives for responsible behavior, monogamy, fidelity, and the like.

I'm not trying to be facetious here. The truth is, I think, marriage acts both as an incentive for virtuous behavior—and as a social blessing for the effort. In the past, we have wisely not made nit-picking assessments as to who deserves the right to marry and who does not. We have provided it to anyone prepared to embrace it and hoped for the best. . . .

When John and Jim Say "I Do"
CHARLES KRAUTHAMMER

From Time, *July 22, 1996*

The wrangle continues, with Krauthammer (again) charging Sullivan with providing no coherent, moral basis for allowing same-sex marriage and not polygamous marriage.

Gay marriage is coming. Should it?

For the time being, marriage is defined as the union (1) of two people (2) of the opposite sex. Gay-marriage advocates claim that restriction No. 2 is discriminatory, a product of mere habit or tradition or, worse, prejudice. But what about restriction No. 1? If it is blind tradition or rank prejudice to insist that those who marry be of the opposite sex, is it not blind tradition or rank prejudice to insist that those who marry be just two?

In other words, if marriage is redefined to include two men in love, on what possible principled grounds can it be denied to three men in love?

This is traditionally called the polygamy challenge, but polygamy—one man marrying more than one woman—is the wrong way to pose the question. Polygamy, with its rank inequality and female subservience, is too easy a target. It invites exploitation of and degrading competition among wives, with often baleful social and familial consequences. (For those in doubt on this question, see Genesis: 26–35 on Joseph and his multimothered brothers.)

The question is better posed by imagining three people of the same sex in love with one another and wanting their love to be legally recognized and socially sanctioned by marriage.

Why not? Andrew Sullivan, author of *Virtually Normal: An Argument About Homosexuality,* offers this riposte to what he calls the polygamy diversion (*New Republic,* June 7): homosexuality is a "state," while polygamy is merely "an activity." Homosexuality is "morally and psychologically" superior to polygamy. Thus it deserves the state sanction of marriage, whereas polygamy does not.

But this distinction between state and activity makes no sense for same-sex love (even if you accept it for opposite-sex love). If John and Jim love each other, why is this an expression of some kind of existential state, while if John and Jim and Jack all love each other, this is a mere activity?

And why is the impulse to join with two people "morally and psychologically inferior" to the impulse to join with one? Because, insists Sullivan, homosexuality "occupies a deeper level of human consciousness than a polygamous impulse." Interesting: this is exactly the kind of moral hierarchy among sexual practices that homosexual advocates decry as arbitrary and prejudiced.

Finding, based on little more than "almost everyone seems to accept," the moral and psychological inferiority of polygamy, Sullivan would deny the validity of polygamist marriage. Well, it happens that most Americans, finding homosexuality morally and psychologically inferior to heterosexuality, would correspondingly deny the validity of homosexual marriage. Yet when they do, the gay-marriage advocates charge bigotry and discrimination.

Or consider another restriction built into the traditional definition of marriage: that the married couple be unrelated to each other. The Kings and Queens of Europe defied this taboo, merrily marrying their cousins, with tragic genetic consequences for their offspring. For gay marriage there are no such genetic consequences. The child of a gay couple would either be adopted or the biological product of only one parent. Therefore the fundamental basis for the incest taboo disappears in gay marriage.

Do gay-marriage advocates propose to permit the marriage of, say, two brothers, or of a mother and her (adult) daughter? If not, by what reason of logic or morality?

The problem here is not the slippery slope. It is not that if society allows gay marriage, society will then allow polygamy or incest. It won't. The people won't allow polygamy or incest. Even the gay-marriage advocates won't allow it.

The point is why they won't allow it. They won't allow it because they think polygamy and incest wrong or unnatural or perhaps harmful. At bottom, because they find these practices psychologically or morally abhorrent, certainly undeserving of society's blessing.

Well, that is how most Americans feel about homosexual marriage, which constitutes the ultimate societal declaration of the moral equality of homosexuality and heterosexuality. They don't feel that way, and they don't want society to say so. They don't want their schools, for example, to teach their daughters that society is entirely indifferent whether they marry a woman or a man. Given the choice between what Sullivan calls the virtually normal (homosexuality) and the normal, they choose for themselves, and hope for their children, the normal.

They do so because of various considerations: tradition, utility, religion, moral preference. Not good enough reasons, say the gay activists. No? Then show me yours for opposing polygamy and incest.

Marrying Somebody
JONATHAN RAUCH

Unpublished

In an essay submitted to Time *but rejected for publication, Rauch argues that marriage is inherently about uniting with one other person, and, given that definition, same-sex marriage does not represent a slippery slope at all.*

I'm not surprised—who could be?—by the furor over homosexual marriage, which Hawaii's courts may (or may not) legalize. . . .

What does surprise me is the line that opponents are taking. When the fuss about gay marriage began, I assumed the main case against it would revolve around adoption rights. In fact, the main objection has turned out to be, essentially, this: If homosexuals can get married because they love each other, why not polygamy? Why not incest? A man may love several women, after all, or his mother.

People who use this line of attack seem to regard it as a trump card, a devastating objection. In *Time* magazine, Charles Krauthammer declared that marriage is two-sex for the same reasons—tradition, religion, utility, morality—that it is two-person. "Not good enough reasons, say the gay activists," he gloated. "No? Then show me yours for opposing polygamy and incest." Ha!

All right, I'll show him, and it isn't difficult.

The hidden assumption of the argument which brackets gay marriage with polygamous or incestuous marriage is that homosexuals want the right to marry anybody they fall for. But, of course, heterosexuals are currently denied that right. They cannot marry their immediate family or all their sex partners. What homosexuals are asking for is the right to marry, not anybody they love, but *somebody* they love, which is not at all the same thing.

Heterosexuals can now marry any of millions of people; even if they can't marry their parents or siblings, they have plenty of choice. Homosexuals want the same freedom, subject to the same restrictions. Currently, however, they have zero marital choice (unless, of course, they try to fool heterosexuals into marrying them—a bad idea for a lot of reasons). To ask for a comparably, but not infinitely, broad choice of partners is not unreasonable.

Do homosexuals actually exist? I think so, and today even the Vatican accepts that some people are constitutively attracted only to members of the same sex. By contrast, no serious person claims there are people constitutively attracted only to relatives, or only to groups rather than individuals. Anyone who can love two women can also love one of them. People who insist on marrying their mother or several lovers want an additional (and weird) marital option. Homosexuals currently have no marital option at all. A demand for polygamous or incestuous marriage is thus frivolous in a way that the demand for gay marriage is not.

Suppose, though, that someone insists that he can't be happy without several husbands, and that this is a basic constitutive need for him. Or suppose he says he can't be happy unless he marries a close relative. For argument's sake, let's say we believe him. Shouldn't at least this person be allowed to marry two wives, or his father?

No. The reason is that, from society's point of view, the main purpose of marriage is not, and never has been, to sanctify love. If the point of marriage were to let everybody seek his ultimate amorous fulfillment, then adultery would be a standard part of the marital package. In fact, society doesn't much care whether spouses love each other, as long as they meet their marital obligations. The purpose of secular marriage, rather, is to bond as many people as possible into committed, stable relationships. Such little societies-within-society not only provide the best environment for raising children, they also domesticate men and ensure that most people have someone whose "job" is to look after them.

Polygamy radically undermines this goal, because if one man has two wives, it follows that some other man has no wife. As Robert Wright notes in his book *The Moral Animal,* the result is that many low-status males end up unable to wed and dangerously restless. Over time, a society can sanction polygamy only if it is prepared to use harsh measures to repress a menacing underclass of spouseless men. In that respect, the one-partner-each rule stands at the very core of a liberal society, by making marriage a goal that everyone can aspire to. Gay marriage, note, is fully in keeping with liberalism's inclusive aspirations. Polygamy absolutely is not.

Incest, of course, may produce impaired children. But incestuous marriage is a horrible idea for a much bigger reason than that, a reason that holds even for sterile (or homosexual) couples. Imagine a society where parents and children viewed each other as potential mates. Just for a start, every child would grow up wondering whether his parents had sexual designs on him, or were "grooming" him as a future spouse. Holding open the prospect of incestuous marriage would devastate family life by, effectively, legitimizing sexual predation within it.

Faced with such arguments, the Krauthammer school retreats to a last stand. OK, they say, "you still can't give any principled reason why adult *homosexuals* shouldn't be allowed to form legal unions of three or more. Once gay marriage is legal, how are you going to prevent that?" But no homosexuals that I know of want the right to marry two or more same-sex partners, and society has no earthly reason to sanction such a frivolous right anyway. This is like arguing, "Once gay marriage is legal, how can you stop people from marrying their dog?" To such an argument, the appropriate response is Don't be ridiculous.

The rather peculiar idea underlying the "If gay marriage, then polygamy" argument is that, at bottom, there really is no very good reason to be against polygamy—you just have to be blindly against it, and ditto for gay marriage. But there are ample grounds to oppose polygamous and incestuous marriage, grounds that have nothing to do with whether gay people will be allowed to partake of society's most stabilizing, civilizing institution. I don't ask to break the rules that we all depend on. I just want to be allowed to follow them.

Sexual Freedom and the End of Romance
DENNIS ALTMAN

From The Homosexualization of America,
1982

A pre-AIDS defense of the religious right's nightmare: a culture in which monogamy is not expected in relationships. Note, however, that this describes gay male culture before same-sex marriage became an imaginable option.

While the idea that all lesbians seek totally monogamous relationships while all gay men reject monogamy is clearly a myth, it does seem clear that among gay men a long-lasting *monogamous* relationship is almost unknown. Indeed both gay women and gay men tend to be involved in what might be called multiple relationships, though of somewhat different kinds. For many lesbians, especially those affected by feminist precepts, the very exaggeration of this paragraph by Charlotte Waters sums it up:

> Once upon a time Deardra loved Carol. Deardra also loved Margo, Toni and Kathy, but was just coming out of a primary relationship with Jan and so didn't want to get into anything heavy with anyone. Carol loved Deardra and also Margo and sometimes Renalda, but she didn't give a hang about Toni and she hated Kathy's guts. Actually, Carol loved Deardra best, but Deardra wasn't into loving anyone best and claimed she was equally noncommitted to them all.

For gay men a parallel case is described by Edmund White:

> The gay male couple inhabiting the seventies is composed of
> two men who love each other, share the same friends and in-
> terests and fuck each other almost inadvertently once every
> six months during a particularly stoned, impromptu three-
> way. The rest of the time they get laid with strangers in a con-
> text that bears the stylistic marks and some of the reality of
> s-and-m.

Both these descriptions are caricatures, but they do catch
one of the features common to a great many gay relationships,
namely a degree of fluidity that allows for considerable variety
and autonomy. What often appears to straight critics as an obses-
sion with sex is more accurately a preoccupation with construct-
ing relationships that can meet our needs for both security and
independence, commitment and variety.

A great deal of the gay writing of the past decade has been
concerned, both explicitly and implicitly, with the construction
of new relationships: just to cite Kate Millett's *Sita*, Michael
Denneny's *Lovers*, Marie-Claire Blais's *Nights in the Under-
ground* (subtitled *An Exploration of Love*), plays like Robert
Patrick's *T-shirts* and Jane Chambers's *Last Summer at Bluefish
Cove* makes the point. Again there is a difference between
female and male writing; much lesbian writing has been concerned with the development of nonpossessive multiple relationships (which underlies Sally Gearhart's fantasies in *The
Wanderground* or Monique Wittig's *Les Guérillères*), while gay
men seem caught between the two myths of finding everlasting
true love and happiness in the same person and constant excite-
ment through sexual adventures. These myths are not as incom-
patible as one might think; much of the tension present in

contemporary male gay writing stems from the attempt to reconcile the traditional image of romantic love and the reality of present-day sexuality, with its demands for constant variety and performance.

The most explicit discussion of the problem is *Faggots*, a Rabelaisian account of contemporary New York fag life that disguises a serious discussion of sexual ethics. Larry Kramer is, in fact, a traditional romantic who believes in monogamous coupling and is upset by its disappearance in the world of fast sex, drugs, and Fire Island—"Our sexual fantasies are ruining us," says one character, speaking (it would seem) for Kramer himself—but his novel poses, nonetheless, very real questions. It is, I suspect, a quite unrealistic novel in its desires, but not necessarily a homophobic one; Kramer just wants the sort of relationship that is less and less possible even outside the rarefied world of Fire Island.

Kramer is, however, fairly exceptional; in practice most gay males accept that fidelity to a relationship is not to be measured in sexual terms. A large-scale study of gay male couples in San Diego concluded that every couple together more than five years had outside sexual contacts as a recognized part of the relationship. As David McWhirter and Andrew Mattison put it: "We never heard the word 'cheating' or 'faithful' applied to outside sex, even though outside relationships caused pain. And many couples reported that sex outside the relationship enhanced or reinvigorated the sexual contact when they were back with their partner.

Just because there *are* no real social sanctions to support gay couples (indeed, it is often easier to remain closeted if one is not in a relationship) and no clear role definitions as to who should do what, it is easier for gay couples to experiment with unusual arrangements, and to maintain relationships that allow more flexibility and freedom than the norm. The absence of gay marriage (except among a very small group who have used gay churches for such purposes) means that it is easier for homosexuals to develop other ways of living than conventional coupledom; there has been considerable discussion, in the new gay writings, of the advantages and disadvantages of a whole range of possible living and sexual arrangements.

In their study of homosexuals in San Francisco Bell and Weinberg did find a number of men in "closed couple" relationships and concluded they were happier than those in "open couple" ones. However, an examination of their definitions reveals that the difference is not a simple one of monogamy versus promiscuity; having defined "closed couples" as those in which the partners "tend to look to each other rather than to outsiders for sexual and interpersonal satisfactions," it is not very difficult to "prove" that people in such relationships are more satisfied with them. For all its protestations of tolerance and understanding, Bell and Weinberg's book is heavily influenced by conventional assumptions about relationships and happiness.

It is my hunch that the illusion of love is more important for homosexual couples than for heterosexual ones, because without it there is much less reason to persist with the relationship, and this becomes truer as the overt gay world grows and there is less fear of never meeting anyone else. At the same time, while homosexuals may well have more illusions than do straights about love, they also have fewer illusions about permanence (I still remember my shock when one of my lovers said to me, early in our affair, "When we finish . . . ," and I recognized the chance of his being right). In a study of lesbian couples Donna Tanner noted that, despite the fact that the majority of women had been involved in at least one previous "paramarriage," several respondents considered their relationship a long-term commitment: they exchanged rings and provided for their partners in case of death through insurance policies and wills. On the other hand, while most of these relationships were monogamous, there was also an acceptance of the possible end of the relationship that differed from the marriage model. "I guess," said one woman, "we are of the mind that we should make it go as long as it goes, and when it stops going we should be reasonable enough to say that it is over and move on."

Both lack of marriage and exclusion from the heterosexual world of conventional families tend to make friendship all the more important for homosexuals; while sociologists in recent years have shown some interest in gay coupling, they have tended to completely miss the significance of friendship among both gay women and gay men. Over the years numbers of people have said to me that they place more importance on their friends than on their lovers, and what many gay lives miss in terms of permanent relationships is more than compensated for by friendship networks, which often become de facto families. (Emily Sisley has described one such network in her story, "The Novel Writers.") Former lovers often are drawn into such networks, so that many gays are surrounded by a rich network of friends (often originally sexual partners) and past and present lovers, which can be far more supportive than are most nuclear families.

I don't want to appear to deny the negative side of gay relationships; it does seem, at least among male homosexuals, that there is often a real fear of commitment and a quite unrealistic level of expectations that dooms many men to never finding a satisfactory relationship. While it is tempting to claim that this reveals something about inherent differences either between gays and straights or between women and men, I suspect it is largely a reflection of social pressures; the low level of self-esteem among many homosexuals hardly helps in establishing the mutual trust and tolerance on which relationships must be based. Nonetheless there is much in the gay experience of relationships that is of more general relevance. It is not just that gay relationships are a threat to the dominant family structures that conservatives are desperately trying to bolster up. (This theme is found in much gay writing; John Reehy sees acceptance of homosexuality as leading to a questioning of "not heterosexuality itself, no, but the stagnant conformity of much of his tribal society.") The attempts of homosexuals to create new forms of relationships can also be seen as part of a more general search to resolve universal problems. Under present conditions no one can be very sure of having solved the problem of how best to order one's personal life.

CHAPTER NINE

Whose Life Is It Anyway?

THE REAL WORLD OF LOVE AND MARRIAGE

In the political, moral, and social debate about same-sex marriage, it's all too easy to forget the human dimension. This is not, after all, a debate about whether, for the first time ever, lesbians and gay men are to have long-term relationships. They already do. Same-sex marriage exists in life; it simply doesn't exist in law. What this chapter hopes to do is show a variety of interpretations of that experience—from Dudley Clendinen's account of his fast-changing neighborhood in Baltimore to Ann Landers's all-too-recognizable inability to approve of the sanctifying of the relationship, even if she is tolerant of its existence. An account of an interracial lesbian marriage ceremony is followed by Doug Ireland's sketch of a French lover whom he lost to AIDS and a discriminatory immigration system. Kathy Duggan expresses a surprising need for the emotional and financial closure of divorce. Henry Alford recounts a hilarious tale of setting up an actual wedding between two men in New York

City. Finally Joseph Landau describes how important the institu-tion of marriage may be for the full integration of gay and straight life and the role it might play in blunting the often reductive power of identity culture .

Jack and Bob, Going to the Chapel
DUDLEY CLENDINEN

From the New York Times, *August 7, 1996*

Dudley Clendinen chronicles the changing face of a Baltimore neighborhood.

When I was a boy, the men in my neighborhood had names like Charlie, Wilbur, Jimmy, Homer, T. Paine, Frank, Marvin, Gus and Sam. They had served in World War II and come back to Tampa, Florida, to settle down. In the morning, they went off to jobs in sales, journalism, banking, law, accounting, dentistry and politics. At night, they came home to women named Mildred, Mary, Bobbie, Nell, Jean, Patti, Cile, Georgie and Martha. They were married to them. They had to be. It was the South.

The couples lived in single houses. They had children by birth or adoption. The children had dogs. The adults had cocktails. And most of them went to church or temple, belonged to the same clubs, read the same newspapers and magazines, visited back and forth, voted in every election and did not divorce or speak of homosexuals in polite conversation. It was the 1950s.

In the 1990s, some of the offspring of those marriages lead different lives. I live in Baltimore, in the neighborhood of Bolton Hill, not far from where Francis Scott Key wrote the national anthem, where Gertrude Stein, as a medical student, carried on her first affair and where F. Scott Fitzgerald finished *Tender Is the Night.*

Bolton Hill is now a more urban, more eclectic neighborhood. The couples live in brick row houses, two by two. We have fewer children and fewer cocktails.

But we work, we worship, we visit back and forth, we fly the flag and pay our taxes. Most of us vote. Some of us have dogs, and many of us belong to the neighborhood swim and tennis club. There are three categories of club membership: single, family and household—meaning any two adults who live together. It's convenient for couples who aren't legally married— some because they choose not to marry and some because the law won't let them.

The men have names like Ted, Dudley, Jack, Hoult, John, Bob, Mike, David and Dion. They work at jobs in government, banking, teaching, architecture, medicine and journalism. So do the women. Ted comes home at night to Mary Jo, and Hoult to Nancie, and Bob to Doris and Dion to Jean.

But Dudley comes home to Stephen, Jack to Bob, John to Peter, Mike to Dean and David to Joe. There are also Pat and Mary, a doctor and carpenter, in church on Sunday.

The culture is changing. In the house where Fitzgerald sat in a second-floor study, locked in marriage to his mad wife, Zelda, writing the doomed love story of Nicole and Dick, Jimmy now lives in sanity with Will. A block away, in a house where a nonfiction Dick had lived with his wife, Robin, Michael now has a life with Andy. They had a wedding. And Dick got a divorce and now lives with Scott.

It is not as if this were something new. Almost a century ago, Gertrude Stein left 215 East Diddle Street for Paris, where she met, wooed and secretly wed Alice B. Toklas.

Gertrude and Alice had only each other's blessing. Michael and Andy, when they married on a snowy hill in Ohio, had the blessing of a friendly Roman Catholic priest. David and Bruce were joined by a captain on the deck of a sailing boat in the Aegean Sea.

None of them, of course, had the official blessing of Church or State. Four years ago, on the Fourth of July, two women and their wedding party gathered at the altar of the Memorial Episcopal Church. The slate roof and squat stone tower loom just a block beyond the windows of Scott Fitzgerald's writing room. The women were in gowns, the men in black tie.

The Rev. Bill Rich, assistant rector at Memorial, officiated at the ceremony. Vows were exchanged, the organ thundered and in a hotel downtown that night the couple, their families and friends danced, drank from an open bar and watched as a parasol of fireworks rose from the harbor and lit the sky in celebration.

It was a short euphoria. The priest could not by Episcopal liturgy or Maryland law pronounce them married. Although the rector of the parish had approved and the vestry and bishop were aware, the event stirred a furor among conservative Episcopalians, who tried to strip the bishop of his office and Bill Rich of his priestly robes.

For almost two hours Bill Rich stood alone at an inquisition, facing a small grim sea of one hundred questioning, accusing fellow priests. The crisis passed, but the bishop ordered a moratorium on blessing the unions of homosexuals.

In truth, the moratorium has not held. Love will out, and quietly, in private settings across the diocese of Maryland, as across the nation, blessings have taken place.

For twenty-six years, beginning with two men in Minneapolis named Jack Baker and Mike McConnell, there has been a public campaign for marriage as a basic right. And more and more not just in marriage but in birth and death as well, churches here and there have been responsive.

Tenderly, with ancient ritual and holy water, the baby of a lesbian couple, faithful Catholics, was baptized here on Bolton Hill, in the white marble sanctuary of Corpus Christi Church. With dignity last year, the Jesuits at St. Ignatius Roman Catholic Church memorialized the life of Don Daniels, with a plain speech by his lover and open emblems of his life as a gay man.

Proudly, in its June bulletin, the Baltimore Hebrew Congregation announced the election of a new assistant rabbi, Peter Kessler, welcoming him—and his male partner, a mechanical engineer—to town.

And regularly, beneath the slender, towering brown stone spire of First and Franklin Street Presbyterian Church, male and lesbian couples are joined in holy union by the Rev. Harry Holfelder. It happens ten or twenty times a year. Mark and Brad had a formal ceremony there before Christmas, with 140 guests, three quarters of them heterosexual.

Why do these couples do it?

Why does anyone? Quietly, for two years, a small committee of laymen and women, priests and doctors, gay and nongay, have been working on Project Blessing. The committee grew from Memorial Church, from the loving spirit of its rector, the Rev. Barney Farnham, and the inspiration of John Payne, a member of Memorial, a doctor at Johns Hopkins and a trustee of the Episcopal Divinity School in Cambridge, Mass.

Sanctioned by the trustees of the Divinity School, approved by the bishops of ten Episcopal dioceses and more than thirty parishes from California through Indiana to New Jersey, the project would authorize the blessings of gay and lesbian unions in a limited number of churches. But those couples—and all heterosexual couples who ask to be married in those same churches—would have to agree to answer a battery of questions over a period of five years. From all those questions and answers, we may learn something about why it is important to some people, gay or straight, to stand up and have their love and commitment blessed in public, in a holy setting. Judging from the cloud of noise that has blown up around the political issue of same-sex marriage, it is a need that politicians—most of them married, some of them running for president—find incomprehensible. Perhaps they should ask their wives.

"Darling, why do you think it matters to be married?"

And, "Darling, tell me what politician would you trust to judge our love?"

I Earned This Divorce
KATHY DUGGAN

From The New York Times, *July 25, 1996*

There is also the flip side to the right to marry: lesbian and gay relationships need the clarity of legal divorce.

The woman who once stood with me before an altar, promising to share her life with me, is now holding my computer hostage until I give her the VCR. Though the Defense of Marriage Act, passed last week by the House, bars federal recognition of gay marriages, I find myself wishing our marriage was legal for a reason I never anticipated. I want a divorce.

I don't just mean I want to end my marriage. I did that two years ago. I'm single now, having learned how to cook for one and attend weddings alone.

What I want is a forum where I can act out all the anger, frustration and disappointment of a failed relationship. One where I can hand responsibility for the haggling over our possessions to a professional—a lawyer who can be ruthless on my behalf when I'm likely to just dissolve into tears and say, "No, really, you take the flatware." I want a ritual that takes apart our relationship as deliberately as we put it together.

Mary and I were the perfect couple. Unfortunately, together we made lousy individuals. From the start, people often got us confused. We chalked it up to being the same height and having similar coloring, but the truth is our identities were slowly merging into one.

Oblivious to the consequences of our fused identities, in September 1991 we gathered family and friends at a ceremony in my girlhood church, had a backyard reception and then left for a honeymoon in Provincetown, Massachusetts.

Though we knew we were just as married as any husband and wife, we chose not to use the language of heterosexual marriages. We believed that to use such words as "wedding," "marriage" and "wife" would trivialize that there was no legal or religious recognition.

So we decided on life partner and labeled the relationship a domestic partnership. (I'm still stunned by how many people thought we had opened a small business together.) We struggled over a suitable alternative to the word "wedding." For lack of anything better, we finally just called our ritual exchange of vows "the ceremony."

Taking sacred vows did not help our individuality problems.

After two and a half years, I left Mary and found myself in a semantic void. I could call her my ex-lover, but I rarely called her my lover when we were together—the illicit undertones the word carries were the last thing I wanted. "Former life partner" sounds like something Shirley MacLaine would say.

When a relationship that was only marginally recognized comes to an end, it is almost as though it never existed. When filling out forms, I can no more check the box labeled "divorced" than I could have once checked "married." Invisible as we may have been as a couple, Mary and I at least had each other to affirm our relationship.

Some gay men and lesbians have come up with ceremonies of dissolution to mark the radical changes in their lives, but I couldn't imagine planning such an event. For heterosexual couples, the legal process of filing for divorce can serve that function. Oh, sure, Mary and I attended to a few legal matters. But telling coworkers, "Well, we shredded the health-care proxies last night," just doesn't carry the same weight as saying, "Well, I signed the divorce papers last night."

I sometimes jokingly refer to Mary as my first wife. I hope to marry again, and I hope that by the time I do, my partner and I will be able to do it legally. Right now though, I want a divorce.

Ann Can't Give Her Blessing to This Marriage

ANN LANDERS

From the Chicago Tribune, *July 21, 1996*

The pro-gay advice columnist draws the line.

Dear Ann Landers:

Last year, I married the woman of my dreams. She is funny, intelligent, loving, caring, exciting and gentle. Ours is a full and rewarding life together. We have traveled to several states for both business and pleasure. We go to church, get together with friends and relatives, and share the household chores. We have known both good times and bad, and our commitment to one another is stronger now than ever.

So why am I writing to you? Because I hope you will help educate a few million people today. Our marriage, blessed by a minister and approved by many friends and family members, is not legal in the United States. And if Congress has anything to say about it, we may never have a chance to make it legal. You see, Ann, I am also a woman.

My wife and I are hardworking professionals who pay our taxes and vote regularly. We pay our bills on time and are law-abiding citizens. However, we are not accorded all the civil rights that most Americans assume to be their privilege. Because we are not legally married, we have none of the legal rights married couples enjoy, such as gaining immediate access to a loved one in case of an emergency, sharing insurance policies at reduced rates, holding property together, filing joint tax returns, and so on.

We are not seeking "special rights." We simply want the same rights every other American couple has: the right to be free from discrimination in housing and employment, the right to legal protection from harassment and, most importantly, the right to marry whomever we choose and to enjoy the benefits of marriage.

A supportive word from you would give us broader acceptance and might possibly help us with a few legislators. How about it, Ann?

—A Loving Wife

Dear Loving Wife:
I believe same-sex couples should be entitled to the legal rights that married couples enjoy, including the ones you stated: gaining immediate access to a loved one in case of an emergency, sharing insurance policies at reduced rates, owning property together, and filing joint income tax returns. I also believe that same-sex couples should be free from discrimination in housing and employment and should have the right to legal protection against harassment. But, my friend, that is as far as I want to go. I define marriage as a union between a man and a woman.

Before you gay-rights folks land on me with both

feet, I would like to remind you that I have been supportive of your movement for many years, have withstood a great deal of criticism in the process and have risked the wrath of some editors and publishers. I cannot support same-sex marriage, however, because it flies in the face of cultural and traditional family life as we have known it for centuries. And that's where I must draw the line. Sorry.

Love and Marriage
CATHERINE TUERK

From The Flagpole, *the newsletter of Parents, Friends, and Families of Lesbians and Gays of the Metropolitan Washington, D.C., area, October 1996*

The mother of a gay son responds to Ann Landers.

It came to me out of the recesses of my mind as I was walking in the park on a fine Saturday morning. A chant returned to my conscious memory as I watched myself in my mind's eye taking my turn at jumping rope in my Pennsylvania hometown:

First comes love, then comes marriage.
Here comes Cathy with a baby carriage.

Perhaps this time-worn rhyme surfaced as a result of a recent Ann Landers column. She was asked by a reader to help others realize that this sequence of desires (love→marriage→baby) is the same among all human couples whether they are homosexual or heterosexual. The reader noted that the desire for marriage naturally follows in a love relationship, and that the wish for a baby carriage is very likely to come next. Thus, the reader told Landers, our society institutionalizes this natural series of events, providing structures that reinforce and support the bonding of adult human beings, and it is only logical that loving homosexual couples would want what heterosexual couples already enjoy.

Ann Landers, however accepting she is of the gay community, noted that she is unable to support the concept of gay marriage because she views marriage as an institution reserved exclusively for people of opposite genders. I understand her position. Gay-accepting and supportive people—myself included—have had at some point a negative visceral response to the idea of same-sex marriage. It seemed to mar the "ideal" of the institution. Then I realized that this concern about leaving marriage "unsullied" has raised its ugly head many times before in our society, such as when we grappled with the idea of inter-racial marriage. Now we need to redefine marriage as the institutionalized recognition of love and commitment between *any* two people.

Thinking about all this, I am struck by how far we have come within and without the gay community. The older generation of gay people tended to define their feelings as an "identity"—"I am a gay person, whatever that means." That generation, the "Stonewallers," came out in an explosion of sexuality, the area of their lives that epitomized their oppression by, and symbolized their differences from, heterosexuals. Thus, if "Black is Beautiful," then "Gay Sexuality is Good."

My son once told me that, while the previous gay generation may have been about sex, his generation is about love. His statement was supported by a forty-something gay man whom I met at a Whitman Walker volunteer dinner five years ago. He was raised in a small rural town where his father was a prominent civic leader. From an early age he had felt that something was "wrong" with him. When he reached adolescence, he somehow found the right street corner on which to stand every Saturday night. He waited there, this bewildered young man, with no resources to help him understand his feelings, until someone in a car would pick him up. It was dark and they never spoke, but something sexual always happened, after which he would be dropped off at the same corner. There he would see other people coming and going. Eventually he would return home to live with his fear and shame. One day in a small college town, he found his way to a gay bar. "I looked around," he said, "and saw the faces of gay men. I realized that I found some of them attractive and some unattractive. When I spoke to them I found that I liked some of them and some of them I didn't. That was the first time I realized that I could feel love; up until that moment, I thought that men like me could have sex, but that love could only happen between a man and a woman."

I've told that story many times. It is a poignant reminder of our profound ignorance about the normal personhood of gay people, a state of affairs that still exists today in our society. Several years ago, when I told my neighbor that my son and his boyfriend had split up, she said, "What do you mean 'boyfriend'? Don't you mean the man he has sex with?" I was stunned. This is a well-educated woman who has always been very accepting of our son, but she truly, like most heterosexuals, did not understand.

Some parts of our society—because of gays in the military and other issues—are beginning to realize that gay people feel love for each other just as heterosexual people do. Thanks to Ann Landers and other like-minded public figures, as society gets healthier and less homophobic, our gay children can develop healthy self-esteem and move into relationships that mirror the commitment of heterosexual couples. First comes love, then comes marriage—having one's relationship recognized by society *is* the next logical step.

Gospel Under the Chuppah
YAEL LEE SILVERBERG-WILLIS

From Ceremonies of the Heart: Celebrating Lesbian Unions, *1990*

> *Silverberg-Willis has written a first-person account of an interracial, intercultural lesbian marriage: where traditionalism and pluralism meet.*

Luana Silverberg-Willis is my wife and soul mate. . . .
Luana grew up in Minneapolis as a Black woman with a mother and two brothers. Her economic level while growing up was working class, and she attended Catholic schools through college. She danced and taught dance for nineteen years and, in 1983, came to California to get her master's degree in dance education at Mills College in Oakland. It was at this point that she and I met.

My name is Yael Silverberg-Willis. I am twenty-nine years old, studying to be a nurse-midwife, and I am also a powerful woman. I grew up in an upper-middle-class home in New York. My family is culturally very Jewish, with a large and active extended family. My nuclear family consists of a father, mother, and four sisters. We were very close until, at age eighteen, I came out to them. At that point, the family went through major changes. In 1981, I left the East Coast to find myself, lesbian role models, and support for my life choices, since I had received little of that from my family. In 1983, I was facilitating a lesbian support group at the Pacific Center for Human Growth, and Luana joined the group.

We courted. I had never done that before. Many women "fall in love" so quickly, but Luana and I romanced. Each date ended with my walking her to her car and kissing her on the hand. We were both nervous and felt like teenagers. Somehow, though, it seemed worth it. Months later, I felt it was time to express some of the overpowering feelings inside of me. I invited her over to my apartment. I sang her the Holly Near song "Sit With Me," and we kissed.

Our relationship has always stressed communication and humor. We play like kids and have a talent for being able to change things that are hard by merely mentioning them. Our brand of love is also a passionate one; we never take the other person for granted. People often think that we are in the first months of our relationship because flowers, poems and gifts are such mainstays for us. Actually, we have been together for over five years; our secret is romance, passion and change.

On December 29, 1986, during the Afro-American holiday of Kwanzaa, I asked Luana for an even deeper statement of our commitment and love for each other. Kwanzaa is a beautiful seven-day holiday which stresses seven principles for maintaining and thriving as a Black community. The twenty-ninth of December is dedicated to familyhood, so the date felt very appropriate. I prepared a beautiful meal and had champagne, roses and a ring with my Hebrew name engraved on it. By dessert I hadn't said a word; I was terrified! Finally, I asked her to create with me a ceremony of love, a commitment of time and dedication to each other. I told her to take her time in deciding. Five minutes later she had said yes! I almost died. . . . Now what? We wanted to call people—but whom? We weren't in the mood to call people who would need convincing that we weren't mad; this isn't an easy issue for either the straight or lesbian communities. Thank God for one of our friends, Carol Charlot, who knew the exact script we needed to hear.

So how do we set the date? Who will perform it? What is it we want to say? And to whom? In what style? And what about our families? We decided to do it in the summer; that was far enough away not to feel so threatening. For reasons that were both practical and romantic, August 9, 1987, became the date. We are family members in a gay synagogue called Sha'ar Zahav, so we decided to have our synagogue's rabbi, Yoel Kahn, perform the ceremony. After we talked to him, we knew that he would meet our needs perfectly. While understanding my desire for a Jewish ceremony, he also voiced the concern that we create a ceremony in which Luana's needs would be fully met as well. We loved him from that point on. We met with him once a month for six months as he led us through lessons of personal growth, dream sharing and conflict resolution. Later we would understand that this process was, in fact, the wedding.

As extravagant women, we decided to have a formal event. We each wanted to wear dresses, and we decided that our attendants would wear black tuxedos. As we moved into gear, it became evident that we would each have to deal with our emotions around not having our families there to help with the process. There was no emotional and, of course, no financial support. It was through putting together this enormous event that we gradually changed our definition of "family." Every need that arose was answered by a core group of friends. One embroidered our chuppah (the canopy under which we were married), another planted all the flowers, another arranged all the bouquets, another baked a three-tier carrot cake and ran our reception. There was also a bridal shower and a bachelorette party; the community was getting ready for a much needed public statement of powerful love and commitment.

I had decided not to tell my family until two months prior to the ceremony. Luana and I had had little luck in getting any positive responses from them, and we didn't want six full months of negative feelings. Why did I tell them at all? Because I wasn't going to hide my passages. The only members of either family who were supportive were Luana's youngest brother, Robert, and my Aunt Terry. Luana decided to have her brother walk her down the aisle, and I chose to go it alone.

The writing of the ceremony was the most difficult part. We worked hard to create a ceremony which integrated our individual cultures as well as our beliefs as a couple. Linda Tillery sang gospel under the chuppah, we drank wine from a kiddush cup and a kikombe (unity) cup from Kwanzaa, and we wrote our own interpretation of the Jewish seven blessings which spoke of our eight most important values. We created a ketubah (a Jewish marriage license) and called our ceremony a kiddushin (a sanctification ceremony), not a wedding. We put together a pamphlet which explained the ritual objects we were using as well as our beliefs. This was important, because our friends' cultures are as diverse as ours.

Ritual is integral to the survival of a people. Support and

love are integral to making that survival healthy. We learned, as did our friends, that we must look beyond the limited definitions that exist in both the gay and straight communities. Our ceremony left all one hundred and fifty guests changed. There was such an extraordinary feeling of love filling the synagogue; there wasn't a dry eye left, and everyone's perspective was broadened.

When we entered the local women's bar several days after the wedding, we received a standing ovation. People are proud of those who are willing to take a chance toward love, the chance to build a structure that can withstand the hostilities of this society. Luana and I are a part of that new structure, and we continue to grow as well as to fall more and more in love. Hopefully our children will experience the openness of our love, and they will feel able to be a part of changing this society into a more loving and nonjudgmental place.

Remembering Hervé
DOUG IRELAND

From The Nation, *June 24, 1996*

A memoir of a love riven for want of the right to marry.

Hervé was a native Parisian with an infectious sense of humor and a passion for serious literature—his favorite authors were Gombrowicz, Musil and Genet—who at fifteen had fled the double homophobia of parents who were both working-class Catholic and Communist. When I went to live in France in the eighties, we were introduced by a filmmaker friend—Hervé was twenty-one then—and I was captivated by his intelligence and rebellious spirit. He had a wry attitude toward politics that befitted an addicted reader of *Le Canard Enchaîné*, a visceral compassion for the poorest and most oppressed of any color, an evergreen anger at injustice and a contempt for bourgeois hypocrisies.

After a year of constant companionship, we decided that our emotional commitment to each other would be lifelong, and in the ensuing decade we often talked about what it would be like to grow old together, making plans for a cottage in Brittany and, perhaps, for raising a child. Alas, these dreams were cut short when Hervé was diagnosed with H.I.V.

Hervé wanted to see the States before he died, and so I returned to New York to lay the groundwork for his joining me. Not long after, however, George Bush ordered the iniquitous ban on immigration by H.I.V.–positive people, subsequently codified into law by the signature of President Clinton. So Hervé could spend only three months at a time here on a tourist visa. He might have been able to stay illegally and escape detection, but fighting his illness required increasing medical attention.

I was fortunate enough to be working at the time for a newspaper with nondiscriminatory spousal health insurance—*The Village Voice*—but the insurance companies require that one be a legal resident to benefit from such coverage. France's socialized medicine, on the other hand, provided Hervé with first-rate care. So, while he was condemned to visits of a few months until his malady forbade travel, I was cruelly denied the right to be his caregiver. Forbidden by law the loving presence and moral support that are so crucial to fighting AIDS, Hervé lost the will to live; a few weeks from now will mark the second anniversary of his death. I was not able to be at his bedside when the end came.

A heterosexual couple in similar circumstances could have

avoided this anguished separation by marrying: Hervé and I would have done so if we could, not because we felt any need to seek the blessings of the state for our relationship but simply to secure legal protection for our right to be together. Our story may be less than common, but the reason that same-sex marriage is such an urgent issue for lesbians and gays—even those of us with radical sexual politics—is that it affords a host of civil guarantees that heterosexual couples take for granted. . . .

My Gay Wedding
HENRY ALFORD

From New York *magazine, June 17, 1996*

An account of setting up a same-sex wedding in New York City. The author is accompanied on his quest by his mother.

On the road to equality, we may encounter pebbles. In my case, it went like this: I was trundling briskly toward the Waldorf Astoria, where, in my capacity as journalist and interested citizen, I was about to claim that my boyfriend and I were getting married soon and that we were interested in holding our ceremony and reception at the hotel. At my side was my sixty-six-year-old Republican mother, a willing accomplice whose presence I hoped would inject my scenario with realism. Several blocks away from the Waldorf, I shared with Mom my long-held opinion that a truly resplendent wedding would include a performance by Cirque du Soleil. Mom said she was unfamiliar with that group; I explained that it is a Franco-Canadian circus troupe that performs without animals. Mom looked slightly concerned. "With 'out' animals?" she asked.

"Without animals," I clarified.

"Oh, I thought you meant with gay animals," she said, relieved. "That sounded very interesting."

Moments later, on meeting our Waldorf contact—a clean-cut, polished corporate fellow in his early thirties named Jim—I asked him whether, when I had called and set up our appointment to inspect the hotel's wedding facilities, I had explained that the ceremony was to celebrate the union of two men. "No, you didn't," he said, somewhat haltingly. An awkward pause. I asked, "Is that okay?" He said it was. Indeed, on our ensuing tour of the hotel, this charming gentleman made every indication that it was. To dispel all doubt, however, I was moved to ask him whether he had ever booked a gay function before; he said he had not but that he had a friend who worked at the Yale Club, where a recent party had celebrated the life partnership of two women.

When we stopped in at the Starlight Roof to marvel over its Art Deco splendor, Mom took one look at the room's twenty-four-foot ceilings and announced, "This would be good for your circus performers." As the words *circus performers* had not yet come up in the conversation with our man from the Waldorf, it was with a certain amount of curiosity and suspicion that he looked to me for an explanation; I sheepishly told him that I planned to have Cirque du Soleil perform during the reception's dinner. The man tried to process this information aloud: "So you're marrying your boyfriend. And then the circus is coming to town." I nodded in a way that I hoped was reassuring; I was suddenly glad that earlier that day Mom had appraised my outfit as "very Potential Big Rentals." The man continued, "Next you're going to tell me that there'll be contortionists."

"No—no contortionists," I wanted to say, "but possibly a kick line of slightly nelly elephants and tigers."

No, my boyfriend and I are not, in fact, about to wed. I am not actually going to broker the Waldorf's introduction to the Danskin crotch panel. But given the likelihood that within the next year or so, lesbian and gay couples in Hawaii will be marrying legally—a prerogative currently denied in all fifty states—I have started my advance work. . . .

Clearly, I am ready for gay marriage. But is the world? Eager to find out, I set out on a series of quests. The first was a search for a site in which I would feel comfortable holding a supposed commitment ceremony honoring my boyfriend and me. Mom and I headed to the delegates' dining room at the United Nations, shown to us by two personable young women employed by Restaurant Associates, a company that books and plans events at various Manhattan locations. I told these women—as I would tell all of our contacts at sites—that I wanted to have my wedding on a weekend a few months hence; at all locations, our event would be the only one scheduled.

As Mom and I took in the room's handsome East River views, the women reacted enthusiastically to the details of my proposed nuptials. I mentioned plate-spinning; they did not flinch. When our conversation turned to the topic of wedding videotaping, I said that that irritating practice would not be necessary: "One of our guests is a performance artist, sort of a gay Anna Deavere Smith, and he's going to re-enact the wedding Off Broadway." One of the women responded, "He's going to re— he's going to re-enact the wedding Off Broadway?! *Wow!*" Her colleague exclaimed, "We'll want tickets to *that!*" The first added, "That's *adorable.*"

When I asked one of the women whether it would be "okay" if my male friends danced with one another to loud disco music, she assured me it would; she said, "It's your party, and dance how you want to," adding that the U.N. security guards would tell us to turn down the music if its volume became oppressive. When her colleague subsequently took Mom and me across town to look at the lovely Sea Grill at Rockefeller Center, I asked what would happen at that location if my friends, as often occurs at clubs where there is a preponderance of gay men, took their shirts off while dancing. Our Sea Grill contact allowed as how this would not be a problem, particularly as the wedding could be thrown only on a Sunday, when there wouldn't be "many people around."

Having decided, during the course of our visits, that my boyfriend, Jess, and I should travel to our hypothetical ceremony by carriage and dress as Amish farmers, I told our contact at the Equitable Center that the theme of our wedding was "Pennsylvania Dutch–meets–Cirque du Soleil." I asked whether we could decorate either of the function rooms she showed us; she said, "You can't staple or glue anything." When I explained that my decorating plans involved the dramatic display of a large, slightly rusted nineteenth-century farming implement, she said simply, "As long as you don't touch the artwork."

Four locations seemed especially gay-friendly. Although Mom and I did not visit the town house that the National Society of Colonial Dames runs on Seventy-first Street—our party of one hundred was much too large for them, and they prefer not to host weddings—the colonial dame I spoke with said she had no problem with a gay event: "It probably doesn't include children, which is usually one of my objections." Mom and I were greeted warmly in the East Village at Lucky Cheng's, whose jaunty director of operations, Rusty, assured us that although her transvestite wait staff had never "done Amish" before, they had much experience in highly elaborate theme weddings; Mom said of the more elegant, gay-owned Townhouse restaurant on East Fifty-eighth Street, "Not the Waldorf. But a bargain."

The location I felt most comfortable in—indeed, the location I would choose were I actually getting married—was aboard the *Honey Fitz,* a ninety-two-foot-long yacht that has served five presidents, many of whose photographs adorn the yacht's cabin. Mom and I boarded near the World Financial Center; while descending the boat's staircase, Mom announced that she was pretending to be Marion Davies. I told our contact, John, that I was marrying my boyfriend; he earnestly uttered, "Beautiful." When I asked, somewhat disingenuously, whether a gay-themed event would discomfit any of the ship's crew, he said that the ship's captain had grown up on Fire Island and thus had "seen everything." My "Pennsylvania Dutch–meets–Cirque du Soleil" idea seemed as nothing when we learned that the yacht had picked up twenty drag queens in Weehawken for the premiere of the movie *Wigstock.* I was thrilled by the yacht and its pedigree; Mom was more cautious. "Stormy weather is a big possible worry," she said. "And it's hell on the circus performers."

My wedding enjoyed a less-than-enthusiastic response at only two locations. One we did not visit. On a whim, I had called the throbbing nexus of gay New York—the Chelsea Gym—and asked whether I could throw the wedding amid the weightlifting equipment; I was told, "We can't accept that proposal . . . I'm sorry, hon." The other was a place where I once attended a fun bachelor party—New York's oldest steakhouse, the Old Homestead, located on Fourteenth Street at Ninth Avenue. As we sat in the restaurant's dark foyer with our contact—a better-looking Joe Pesci—I asked him whether "the gay aspect" of the wedding made him uncomfortable. He responded, "Can I give you some advice? Don't ask that." I apologized; Mom, clutching her Metropolitan

Museum of Art gift bag as if she feared that it might be ripped from her arms by a fast-moving vehicle, asked, "Does that offend you?" He said, "Well, yeah. It's just not an issue. I'd be happy to do your party." But would he be, really? Our subsequent tour of the premises was tense in the extreme; I would not have told him about my little friends in brightly colored leotards even at gunpoint. Mom, once we had departed: "I would say, 'Definitely no.'"

Who would be the officiant at my same-sex wedding? Although I am, at heart, agnostic, and thus would be most inclined to have a civil ceremony, I can imagine a scenario—particularly one in which my wedding was bankrolled by my family—wherein I might be disposed to call upon a person of the cloth. In this second quest, I turned, as I always do in moments of religious doubt, to the Yellow Pages. I called all three of the Episcopal churches listed in the NYNEX community directory for Chelsea, Greenwich Village, and Vicinity. Only St. Peter's in Chelsea was willing to perform the ceremony—I was told that the rector at St. John's on Waverly Place "does not perform unions," because "he would get in a lot of trouble with the mission"; Mother Rockman at the Church of the Ascension on Fifth Avenue said she could not because "there isn't any service outlined by the church for that." Both parties apologized profusely; both parties suggested that I contact either Dignity or Integrity, the organizations for gay and lesbian Catholics and Episcopalians.

To their credit, none of the church people with whom I broached the possibility of my friend's Off Broadway reenactment of the wedding were bothered by the idea; one interfaith minister, when asked, "Would it make you uncomfortable if my friend 'did' you?" responded, "Only if it were unflattering." I also contacted several clergypeople listed in the Manhattan phone directory not under CHURCHES but under WEDDING CHAPELS and WEDDING CLERGY. "First of all, let me say that nothing legal is going on here," the first of these, a Unitarian clergyman, cautioned me rather sternly. He then read me a proviso that he said would have to be read at the ceremony—a statement of the wedding's nonlegality. "I don't want to have some enterprising D.A. who's trying to make a name for himself hear about the wedding, show up, and then decide to prosecute," he told me. I explained that I was thinking about having the ceremony on a boat; the clergyman said he would have to raise his $300 fee "because you're taking me out of circulation." However, it became clear that he would rather not go on a cruise around Manhattan if he didn't have to; his conversation was heavily peppered with the phrase *hop off*.

"What do you mean 'a commitment ceremony'?" an interfaith minister asked me; I explained, "Between two men." I told him that the ceremony was to be on a boat off Manhattan; he said, "To be very truthful, I'm not interested in this. It's too much time for me." However, when I explained that I had budgeted $500 or $600 for the officiant, the minister's spirits rallied. He told me that he had once married a pair of transvestites on a TV talk show. "You know how I did that?" he said. "I did that by not looking at them." I asked him what the significance of his not looking at the couple was; he said he couldn't because he might have burst out laughing. "The way I see it," he told me, "it's in the genes. People have those desires because they were born that way. It's not your fault."

"It's not a fault," I said.

"It's *not* a fault. It's a characteristic of their nature because of their genes. . . . Society frowns, but I don't have to. I accept people for who they are."

"So—you're tolerant?" I tried to anticipate his point. He continues, "Yeah. And I mean, you're not going to be dancing in drag at the wedding." I replied that no, in fact, we might be, particularly as we know many "show people." He said, "That's okay.

But not at the ceremony. Once you're at the reception, that's another story. But at the ceremony, it's going to be straight."

"I don't like the word *straight*."

"I'm sorry for *straight*. I meant *serious*."

For our last investigation of the prerequisites of union, I called the St. Moritz hotel and actually booked a honeymoon suite ($295) and an additional room for our best man ($125). When we arrived, it was unclear whether the thirteen minutes it took for our harried clerk to check us in was a result of the fact that I wanted the best man's room to be on the same floor as the honeymoon suite, or of the fact that our best man was our lesbian friend Adrienne. He was unable to give us rooms on the same floor; he did, however, hand me something labeled HONEY-MOON DREAM PACKAGE COUPON KIT. Empowered with this booklet of three coupons, I felt like Charlie Bucket in *Charlie and the Chocolate Factory*.

The three of us assembled in the honeymoon suite—a pageant of various hues of green whose provenance Jess pinpointed as "émigré Eva Gabor." Adrienne noted, "A great big bed for having sex in!" Jess, however, remarked that the presence of a television in each of the honeymoon suite's two rooms denoted the management's lack of optimism, Jess called room service to exchange our first coupon for a bottle of champagne and petits fours. The kitchen was out of petits fours—would we take cake? Jess asked for "something savory." Potato chips were offered. We took potato chips. Later we ordered room service. I told our waiter, "We just got married!" He looked first at me, then at Adrienne; I pointed at Jess and said, "No, *we* just got married!" He smiled in a confused manner and threw himself into his duties with a somewhat manic vigor.

Later that night, unable to sleep, I went down to the lobby at 4:10 A.M. and, holding out my second coupon—the one labeled A LOVELY SOUVENIR GIFT FROM THE ST. MORITZ—told the clerk that I was in the honeymoon suite with my new husband. "I don't think the marriage is working out," I said. "My husband is—well, he's ignoring me. Nothing's happening. So I thought maybe a gift would perk me up." The clerk asked somewhat sternly, "What is it that you want, sir?" I told him. "The gift, I'd like to get the gift." He told me I would have to wait till morning. (I did, and received mugs.)

Jess and I awoke five hours later, whereupon we tangled with the epistemological question posed by the third coupon: whether to have "complete breakfast for two in bed" or "breakfast as [sic] Rumpelmayer's." The second choice, of course, was the more alluring; and so, imagining ourselves in the tourist-clogged restaurant of a large midtown hotel, we went downstairs, where we ate both as and at Rumpelmayer's. "We just got married," I told our Latin waiter. "Hey, it's a free country!" he said, throwing his arms up in the air in bewilderment. "You do what you want to do!"

I have seen the future, and it is tolerant. Fabulousness will prosper. While traditionalists will always claim that gay marriage is both frivolous and threatening (the former because it blesses unions society has no vested interest in, particularly given the high rate of childlessness among gay couples, and the latter because it thus makes folly of the institution of marriage itself), I would argue that this folly-making is chief among its strengths. To wit: Good-bye, blurry wedding videos shot by your out-of-town cousin with the shakes . . . hello, videography that screams "Dorothy Chandler Pavilion." Good-bye, Pachelbel's Canon and endless selections of *The Prophet* . . . hello, "It's Raining Men" and a sound collage of Thelma Ritter backchat. Good-bye, alcohol-fueled anomie and thirty-seven-year silences over the breakfast table . . . hello, kimonos and sobbing in a foreign language.

To many minds, the gay community and its supporters were

not well enough prepared for the 1993 debate about gays in the military. On the issue of legalized marriage, we have more lead time. We must assemble, don berets, and demand that if gay people can't marry, then straight people can't decorate. We must, in short, even the score. Because it's our turn to be deluged with a torrent of Uncle Ben's. It's our turn not to do the catering.

Marriage as Integration
JOSEPH LANDAU

Unpublished

Researcher Joseph Landau explains why one central institution could bring gays and straights together.

Advocates and opponents of same-sex marriage speak two very different languages, the former employing a discussion about rights, the latter the pursuit of common goods. And in this, the debate reflects the crucial tension that has animated political theory throughout modernity. Yet the case for same-sex marriage cannot be truly made without meeting head-on the arguments of those presumed "traditionalists" who cite a long list of disasters that will be wrought by same-sex marriage. What we need, in short, is an argument for same-sex marriage that can speak in terms of goods, one of which is the social good of cultural integration.

The very fact that lesbian women and gay men want to be a part of the institution of marriage complicates many stereotypes distancing life-long commitment, monogamy, and children from the wants and desires of gay individuals. But the quest for marriage amounts to much more than a radical statement of self-definition; marriage, once broadened to include gays and lesbians, would bring a diverse population together under one common institution. It would provide outlets for living that stretch beyond the segregated world of homogeneous, same-sex communities or "ghettos" (such as the Castro district of San Francisco or Manhattan's Chelsea) and a nongay, "mainstream" or "straight" culture on the other. Today, homosexuality is often culturally severed from non-urban areas, an idea that helps anti-gay marriage advocates plausibly argue that homosexuality is inherently anti-family.

Separated from one another, both gays and straights today enjoy the comforts of a relatively homogeneous style of life. Neither group needs to confront the other directly, for the most part. Yes, places exist where gay men and lesbians coexist harmoniously with their straight counterparts. Many stories from the mainstream press have recently reported an ever-growing number of gay and lesbian parents who raise children in the traditionally straight suburbs. But since the first time that homosexuals were classified exclusively according to sexual orientation, a strict dichotomy between heterosexual and homosexual, or straight and gay, has become rooted in the language of human definition. These identities gained tremendous vigor and have now become associated with a number of defining characteristics. Stereotypes have emerged which both undergird the presumed exclusivity of those identities while all the while invigorating their dominance. A culture of literature, music, and fashion has emerged which has sharpened these supposed differences. The effect of this change has been particularly strong on the young, who often adopt new styles of hair, dress, attitude, speech, and behavior as part of their newfound identity. So from an early age, the cultural distinctions emerge, eclipsing real self-expression, exploration, and risk, stifling genuine human difference. Individuality, once churned through the mill of identity, is reduced to the lowest level of the banal.

Young gays and lesbians are particularly susceptible to the orthodoxy of the gay enclave. They may look back on their childhoods and cringe at the memory of having been ostracized. Ambivalence about the past leads to a wholesale rejection of it, and armed with a new rhetoric of gay/lesbian liberation, they can become downright hostile to what they see as straight society.

Though it may at first be healthy for gay men and lesbians to either adopt new styles of living or choose to live in urban ghettos, without which a thriving gay and lesbian culture could not flourish, it can also be personally limiting. A person is more than his sexuality, and the gay and lesbian subculture cannot sustain a person over an entire lifetime. One cannot live a complete life without being part of the broader culture at the same time.

This is why marriage is so important. It provides an identical institution in which gay and straight love can be expressed. The effects of same-sex marriages will be tremendous: since marriage is so clearly related to where and how people live, it provides a venue through which the boundary between the two communities will be lifted. It slowly allows for lesbians and gay men to move back into the "straight" sector of society with the same self-understanding and self-esteem as their heterosexual peers. There will for the first time be a common language in which to describe both sorts of lives, a language in which concealment and euphemism is no longer embedded. Young men and women coming to terms with their own feelings of homosexuality will have an understanding of the normalcy and legitimacy of homosexual relationships, bringing an end to the shame and silence that is such an unnecessary source of trauma for so many. People will, to coin a phrase, be judged less by the accident of their orientation than by the content of their character. The public debate over homosexuality, now so burdened by the lack of integration between gay and straight members of society, will be transformed by newfound interaction.

Make no mistake: deprived of marriage rights, gays and lesbians will not be able to venture back into mainstream culture. The message sent by a second-class citizenship, undone to a degree by the private sector's active willingness to extend domestic partnership benefits, is too heavy to surmount. It contributes to the message that identity is more fundamental than the common sentiment of love, that gay relationships are, at heart, simply lesser than heterosexual ones, a sentiment that shrinks, rather than enlarges, the entire human experience.

CHAPTER TEN

After Hawaii, What?

THE FUTURE OF THE LEGAL
AND POLITICAL BATTLE

Much of the national debate in 1996 and 1997 was fueled by the notion that a ruling in Hawaii in favor of same-sex marriage rights would mandate legal same-sex marriage across the country. But as Professor Larry Kramer points out in the first article of this chapter, that was never likely to be the case. In controversial marriage recognition cases, states have always been able to invoke what is known as a "public policy" exception to marriages in another state. That means that when one state's marriages offend a deeply held belief or well-grounded public policy of another state, that state need not be obliged to recognize marriages performed in the sister state. In the field of law known as "conflict of laws," it seems clear that this nonrecognition process would regularly occur in the context of the extremely explosive issue of same-sex marriage.

Nevertheless, there are exceptions to the nonrecognition rule.

As Andrew Koppelman points out, there are precedents with regard to interracial marriage that show that, even when the public policy of one state is deeply offended by a marriage in a sister state, those marriages have still sometimes been upheld. Evan Wolfson suggests that the constitutional right to travel might be infringed by non-recognition, and Professor Seth Kreimer argues that the incentive to retain important family bonds might also be regarded as a sufficient reason to uphold same-sex marriages across state borders. Professor Thomas Keane shows that in the critical case of California, the tradition of recognizing other states' marriages—even the most controversial ones—is extremely deep. Finally, David Frum, recognizing the legal force of these arguments, suggests that the ,only way for anti–same-sex marriage advocates to stem the tide is by reviving anti-sodomy statutes to create intolerable obstacles to state recognition of same-sex marriages sanctioned in other states. In the myriad of cases that are likely to be argued across the country in the coming months and years, who knows which of these arguments will finally win or lose the day? But here, at least, are some of the factors that will shape the future.

How Other States Can Ignore Hawaii
PROFESSOR LARRY KRAMER

From "How About a Nice Hawaiian Punch?: Same-Sex
Marriage, Conflict of Laws, and the Unconstitutional
Public Policy Exception." Yale Law Journal,
vol. 106, no. 7 (1997)

*Here, Professor Larry Kramer—not that Larry Kramer, the
playwright and AIDS activist, but the one who is one of the
most authoritative conflict-of-laws experts in the country—argues that, as a matter of legal precedent, the Full Faith and
Credit clause does not mandate same-sex marriage across the
country. Kramer also argues, elsewhere in the paper, that the
"public policy exception" to the Full Faith and Credit clause,
which ensures that a state can refuse to recognize a marriage
sanctioned by another state, is, however, nonsensical and, in
his view, unconstitutional.*

> Concern that a decision to legalize same-sex marriages
> would result in gay couples from the mainland traveling to
> Hawaii to wed has led conservatives in at least 19 states to
> seek new state laws denying recognition to such unions.
> Without specific laws, states would be obliged under the
> United States Constitution to recognize same-sex mar-
> riages performed in another state.
>
> —*The New York Times*, Sunday, July 28, 1996

The newspapers have been filled with stories like this in recent
months, reporting how states are scrambling to avoid an obligation they will supposedly be placed under if Hawaii makes

same-sex marriages legal. Horrified conservatives feverishly imagine a world where gay and lesbian couples, by marrying in Hawaii, can force their home states to recognize the union fully and for all purposes. Even some legal experts make this assumption, and Congress is actually thinking about jumping in to save states from this lamentable fate with the cynically named "Defense of Marriage Act," which seems well on the way to a promised presidential signature (talk about cynical).

On the one hand, these stories are enough to drive anyone familiar with conflict of laws crazy. As presently interpreted, the Constitution almost never requires states to enforce the marriage laws of other states (though where the Constitution does apply, states obviously cannot avoid it by enacting "specific laws" to the contrary). The brouhaha over Hawaii's anticipated legalization of same-sex marriages is therefore a big dud from a conflict of laws perspective. There simply is no problem: other states do not have to recognize such marriages, and they do not need special laws or federal legislation to make that clear. But more on this below. . . .

Before doing anything else, we need to make sure we understand the basic rules governing choice of law in marriage cases. To fully recapitulate the law in this area would actually take some time—no surprise really, since nothing in conflicts law is ever neat or tidy. There are just too many states making independent decisions and too many different variations of each problem to consider. For present purposes, however, we can work with the following paradigmatic situation: A and B live in State X, which does not recognize their right to marry; they travel to State Y, which does, and immediately after the ceremony (and a brief honeymoon) they return to State X to resume their lives together. How would State X view their marriage?

As a general matter, every state recognizes the validity of a marriage valid where it was celebrated (i.e., where the marriage contract was made). This "place of celebration" rule is not, of course, carved in stone or revealed from heaven. States do not have to adopt it, and nothing in the Constitution precludes them from following a different rule (say, for example, applying the law where the parties are domiciled when they get married). But a variety of considerations—in particular, widely shared policies that favor validating marriages consummated in good faith and enabling partners to know with certainty whether their marriage is valid—have led states to conclude that the best rule is one recognizing marriages legal where celebrated. This has long been the rule in every state of the United States, and it continues to govern pretty much without regard for whether a state adheres to the traditional jurisdiction-selecting rules or opts for one of the fancier modern approaches.

Its general convenience notwithstanding, every state recognizes situations in which it abandons the place of celebration rule. Many states, for example, will recognize a marriage that is invalid in the state where it was celebrated if it is valid where the parties are domiciled. Conversely, some states will refuse to recognize a marriage that is valid where it was celebrated if the partners went there solely to evade restrictions imposed in their domicile. Surprisingly, this entirely reasonable exception is rarely used, and its appearance often depends on how quickly a marriage is challenged and whether the challenger is one of the partners or some other interested party. Even where the rule against deliberate evasion is codified, courts have construed it narrowly and found ways to uphold most marriages.

By far the most common exception to the place of celebration rule is for marriages deemed contrary to the forum's strong public policy—and this again seems to be true regardless of how a state handles its choice-of-law problems. Of course, public policy is not violated every time the forum's law differs from that of the place of celebration—otherwise, the exception would swallow the rule. Rather, as in other contexts where "public policy" is used to avoid a conflicts rule, the exception applies (in Judge Cardozo's well-known formulation) only where another state's law violates "some fundamental principle of justice, some prevalent conception of good morals, some deep-rooted tradition of the common weal." Although invocation of the public policy exception varies somewhat from state to state, a number of common situations are found in marriage law. Typically, states turn to public policy in connection with issues like remarriage after divorce, incest, polygamy, and marriage by minors.

Two refinements should be noted in how public policy is used in marriage cases. First, the exception is not employed as an overly blunt tool, but is selectively refined in application. Rather than repudiate the place of celebration rule in every case that would be incest under forum law, courts in many states recognize that some differences are more matters of degree than of fundamental policy. A state that permits second cousins to marry may be more willing to recognize a law extending the privilege to first cousins than one permitting siblings to do so; a state that permits sixteen-year-olds to marry may apply another state's law permitting fifteen-year-olds to do so, but not one extending the right to nine-year-olds. States may also be more likely to ignore public policy considerations for couples with legitimate expectation interests: there is an obvious difference between a couple that recently married outside the state in order to evade its marriage restrictions and a couple that moved into the state after living together for twenty years in a place that recognized their union.

Second, many courts distinguish between the validity of a marriage and the ability to enjoy its "incidents." There was a time when courts treated marriage as a simple yes-or-no, up-or-down proposition: a marriage was either valid—in which case it was valid for all purposes—or it was not—in which case it was invalid for all purposes. More recently, and with increasing frequency, courts have been willing to draw finer lines, applying the place of celebration rule to the question of validity while saving the public policy exception for particular "incidents" of being married. The right to cohabit, for example, is a usual incident of being married, but not a necessary one. A man married to two wives in India might be able to move to New York without being prosecuted for bigamy, but New York might forbid the three of them from living together. At the same time, the surviving wives might both be permitted to inherit as spouses under the state's law of succession.

Two relevant generalizations can be made about choice of law in marriage cases. First, the place of celebration rule governs the vast majority of cases. Exceptions exist, but these are used with considerable reluctance, even when embodied in statutes. Second, the vast majority of the small subset of cases in which the place of celebration rule is not applied are decided on public policy grounds. Other exceptions exist, but these are seldom invoked and typically appear in conjunction with a public policy objection. (A state may, for example, allow parties to marry elsewhere solely to evade its restrictive law unless they do so in order to get the benefit of a law deemed contrary to the forum's strong public policy.) As same-sex marriages become an issue, then, we can expect reluctant states to turn to the public policy doctrine to protect their interests. . . .

With these principles in mind, we can predict the likely operation of the public policy doctrine in same-sex marriage cases. With or without explicit authorization from state legislatures, courts are relatively free to make an exception to the place of celebration rule for same-sex marriages. They are most likely to do so, moreover, in cases like my initial hypothetical, where a couple travels to Hawaii to get married with no intention of changing domiciles. If applied, the exception will almost certainly lead to a declaration that such marriages are invalid.

It is at least possible that some courts will choose not to classify same-sex marriages as falling within the public policy exception, which may explain why so many states are hurrying to codify the principle. A number of commentators have, in fact, argued valiantly that public policy can and should be narrowly construed in the context of same-sex marriages. These efforts might even succeed in persuading a few courts or legislatures, though I suspect they are as futile as they are well intended. Call me a cynic, but my guess is that same-sex marriages will continue to be, shall we say, frowned upon in most states for at least the foreseeable future. And given the discretion and flexibility inherent in the public policy doctrine, arguments that it is not always applied in similar or even "worse" situations probably will not matter much. The simple fact is that public policy is readily available for use in nullifying same-sex marriages performed in Hawaii, and it is probably naive not to expect most states to use it.

The Miscegenation Precedents

ANDREW KOPPELMAN

"Same-Sex Marriage, Choice of Law, and Public Policy," from Quinnipiac Law Review
vol. 16 (1997)

Law professor Andrew Koppelman points to a couple of fascinating legal precedents that could yet bring Hawaiian same-sex marriages to the rest of the country. Those precedents have to do with race.

The closest historical analogue to the radical moral disagreement that will shortly divide the states [on same-sex marriage] is the divide between states that permitted and those that forbade marriage between whites and blacks. Miscegenation prohibitions were in force since the 1660s, but only after the Civil War did they begin to function as the central sanction in the system of white supremacy. At one time or another, forty-one American colonies and states enacted them.

The miscegenation taboo was held in the Southern states with great tenacity; it was close to the psychological core of racism. "Although such marriages were infrequent throughout most of U.S. history, an enormous amount of time and energy was nonetheless spent in trying to prevent them from taking place" (Peggy Pascoe). When they defended the prohibition, Southern courts were at least as passionate in their denunciations as modern opponents of same-sex marriage.

> The purity of public morals, the moral and physical develop-
> ment of both races, and the highest advancement of our cher-
> ished southern civilization, under which two distinct races are
> to work out and accomplish the destiny to which the Almighty
> has assigned them on this continent—all require that they
> should be kept distinct and separate, and that connections
> and alliances so unnatural that God and nature seem to forbid
> them, should be prohibited by positive law, and be subject to
> no evasion. (*Kinney v. Commonwealth* (1878).)

Yet even in this charged context, the Southern states did not
make a blunderbuss of their own public policy. Their decisions
concerning the validity of interracial marriages were surprisingly
fact-dependent. They did not utterly disregard the interests of
the parties to the forbidden marriages, but weighed them
against the countervailing state interests. Where those state interests were attenuated, Southern courts sometimes upheld
marriages between blacks and whites.

Three classes of choice-of-law problems arose involving interracial marriages. The first were cases in which parties had
traveled out of their home state for the express purpose of evad-
ing that state's prohibition of their marriages, and thereafter immediately returned home. Despite some early authority to the
contrary, Southern courts always invalidated these marriages.
Second were cases in which the parties had not intended to
evade the law, but had contracted a marriage valid where they
lived, and subsequently moved to a state where interracial marriages were prohibited. These were the most difficult cases, and
the Southern courts divided on how to deal with them. Finally,
there were cases in which the parties had never lived within the
state, but in which the marriage was relevant to litigation conducted there. Typically, after the death of one spouse, the other
sought to inherit property that was located within the forum

state. In these cases, the courts invariably recognized the marriages.

The earliest case involving an attempt to evade a prohibition on interracial marriage, *Medway v. Needham,* arose in Massachusetts in 1819. A mulatto man and a white woman, both domiciled in Massachusetts, had gone to Rhode Island, where interracial marriage was legal, in order to evade their home state's prohibition on their marriage. The court upheld the marriage, emphasizing, as modern authorities do, the importance of certainty and uniformity with respect to the existence of a marriage. A contrary rule would involve "extreme inconveniences and cruelty"; the rule it adopted "must be founded on principles of policy, with a view to prevent the disastrous consequences to the issue of such marriages, as well as to avoid the public mischief, which would result from the loose state, in which people so situated would live." The court acknowledged that there would have to be limits to its holding.

> If without any restriction, then it might be that incestuous marriages might be contracted between citizens of a state where they were held unlawful and void, in countries where they were not prohibited; and the parties return to live in defiance of the religion and laws of their own country. But it is not to be inferred from a toleration of marriages which are prohibited merely on account of political expediency, that others, which would tend to outrage principles and feelings of all civilized nations, would be countenanced.

The leading American treatise on conflict of laws defended the result in *Medway,* but it was criticized by others, was never followed in any miscegenation case, and was later overruled by statute. The principal counterargument was that states had a right to govern within their own territories. As a ruling in

Virginia in 1885 put it, "In the very nature of things every sovereign state must have the power to prescribe what incapacities for contracting marriage shall be established as the law of the state among her own citizens, and it follows, therefore, that when the state has once pronounced an incapacity on the part of any of its citizens to enter into the marriage relation with each other, that such capacity attaches itself to the person of the parties, and although it may not be enforceable during the absence of the parties, it at once revives with all its prohibited power upon their return to the place of domicile."

The distinction drawn by *Medway* between moral and political prohibitions was also criticized. Raleigh Minor, law professor at the University of Virginia and author of an important 1901 treatise on the conflict of laws, agreed with the Massachusetts court (many Southern jurists did not) that the miscegenation prohibition did not rely on universal considerations of morality, but he thought that the state's political interest in maintaining the supremacy of the white race could be very strong. "[M]atters of political expediency may become of as tremendous importance as matters of moral expediency. It must be remembered that at the date of this decision (1819) there were (and still are) comparatively few negroes in Massachusetts, and the policy which dictated this statute had ceased to be of great importance." Despite the result in *Medway*, "under precisely similar circumstances it has been held by the courts of the Southern States, where negroes are numerous and marriages between them and the whites are regarded justly as most contrary to public policy and expediency, as well as utterly repugnant to the sentiment of the people, that marriages of this sort will not be sustained in the domicile and forum, though validly contracted by its citizens in another jurisdiction. . . ."

This anti-evasion principle was, however, only applied in cases where the parties were domiciliaries of the forum at the

time of marriage. In cases where they had been domiciled elsewhere at the time of the marriage, and even in one case where
they had left the forum before the marriage, intending to reside
elsewhere, and after marrying had decided to return to the
forum, the marriage was held valid. Even Minor, whose sympa-
thy for Southern racism has already been illustrated, thought
that "if the parties remove from the State of their domicile, with
the *bona fide* intent to become *domiciled* in another State, and
having settled there then marry according to its laws, the marriage, though prohibited by the law of their first domicile, will be
deemed valid everywhere, *even in the first domicile,* should they
afterwards return thither either temporarily or permanently."

One obvious difficulty with drawing the lines in this way was
that a marriage would be valid or not, depending on whether the
parties, at the time of the marriage, intended to return to the
domicile that prohibited their marriage. The difficulties of determining such intent led Joseph Story to endorse a blanket rule
validating all such marriages. It is, he wrote,

> far better to support marriages celebrated in a foreign country
> as valid, when in conformity with the laws of that country, al-
> though the rule may produce some minor inconveniences,
> than, by introducing distinctions as to the designs and objects
> and motives of the parties, to shake the general confidence in
> such marriages, to subject the innocent issue to constant
> doubts as to their own legitimacy, and to leave the parents
> themselves to cut adrift from their solemn obligations when
> they may become discontented with their lot.

The more serious objection was that the Southern states
would have to tolerate some interracial cohabitation within their
borders after all. There are only two cases in which this result
was threatened, and they reach opposing results.

State v. Bell involved a white man and a black woman who married in Mississippi, where they then resided, and later moved to Tennessee, where the husband was arrested and tried. He pleaded the Mississippi marriage as a defense. The state supreme court rejected the defense, complaining that under it

> we might have in Tennessee the father living with his daughter, the son with the mother, the brother with his sister, in lawful wedlock, because they had formed such relations in a state or country where they were not prohibited. The Turk or Mohammedan, with his numerous wives, may establish his harem at the doors of the capitol, and we are without remedy. Yet none of these are more revolting, more to be avoided, or more unnatural than the case before us.

The only other reported case in which a validly married interracial couple changed domiciles and moved to a state that prohibited their marriage is *State v. Ross*. A white citizen of North Carolina, which prohibited interracial marriage, traveled in May 1873 to South Carolina, where she married a black man who lived there. At that time, South Carolina did not prohibit interracial marriage. In August of the same year, they both moved to North Carolina, where they were tried for fornication and adultery. A divided state supreme court held that the South Carolina marriage was a valid defense to the charge.

The court rejected the state's claim that the female defendant had sought to evade the law, because it had not proven that, at the time of the marriage, she had intended to return to North Carolina.

> It is difficult to see how in going to South Carolina to marry a negro, without an intent to return with him to this State, she

could evade or intend to evade the laws of this State. Our laws have no extra territorial operation, and do not attempt to prohibit the marriage in South Carolina of blacks and whites domiciled in that State.

The court conceded that interracial marriages were "revolting to us and to all persons, who, by reason of living in States where the two races are nearly equal in numbers, have an experience of the consequences of matrimonial connections between them." This sentiment was not, however, shared by all Christian nations. "The general rule is admitted that a marriage between citizens of a foreign State contracted in that State and valid by its laws is valid everywhere where the parties might migrate, although not contracted with the rites required by the law of the country into which they come and between persons disqualified by such law from intermarrying." Because of the strong interest in uniformity, marriages not deemed odious to all had to be given extraterritorial recognition by all. Because the civilized world was not united in rejecting interracial marriages, North Carolina had a duty to join the rest of civilization in enforcing the common rule. "The law of nations is a part of the law of North Carolina. We are under obligations of comity to our sister States."

Two judges dissented, insisting on the forum state's right to govern itself. "If such a marriage solemnized here between our own people is declared void, why should comity require the evil to be imported from another State? Why is not the relation severed the instant they set foot upon our soil?" If this consequence is inconvenient to some, "individuals who have formed relations which are obnoxious to our laws can find their comfort in staying away from us." In coming to North Carolina and asking that their marriage be recognized, the dissent argued, the defendants were asking for more than North Carolina's own citizens were entitled to.

It is courteous for neighbors to visit, and it is handsome to allow the visitor family privileges and even give him the favorite seat; but if he bring his pet rattlesnake or his pet bear or spitz dog, famous for hydrophobia, he must leave them outside the door. And if he bring smallpox the door may be shut against him. . . .

The Right to Travel
EVAN WOLFSON

From "Winning and Keeping Equal Marriage Rights: What Will Follow Victory in Baehr v. Lewin," *published by Lambda Legal Defense and Education Fund, May 20, 1996*

Another chink in the federal anti–same-sex-marriage armor. What if a legally married gay couple are traveling elsewhere in the United States? Isn't their marriage constitutionally recognized by other states while they are in transit?

A state's refusal to recognize a marriage validly contracted under the laws of Hawaii would place a direct and tangible obstacle in the path of interstate migration and burden people's now-not-merely-abstract right to marry, thus implicating other constitutional provisions relating to due process, the right to travel and move freely throughout the nation, equal protection (sex discrimination as well as sexual orientation discrimination), interstate commerce, and privileges and immunities, as well as the fundamental right to marry itself. For example, a married couple in Hawaii who wished to travel in or to another state would essentially have to choose between their marriage and their right to travel.

The rights to marry and to have that marriage recognized are of fundamental importance, both in and of themselves, and in part because marital status includes substantial economic and practical protections and benefits, upon which may depend the couple's ability to live as they want, raise children as they want, or even subsist. By refusing to recognize a couple's marriage, a state would, for example, "unduly interfere with the right to migrate, resettle, find a new job, and start a new life." *Shapiro v. Thompson.* . . .

In *Shapiro,* the [U.S. Supreme] Court grounded the right to travel in the Equal Protection clause and employed strict scrutiny analysis. The Court stated: "Since the classification here touches on the fundamental right of interstate movement, its constitutionality must be judged by the stricter standard of whether it promotes a compelling state interest." At issue in *Shapiro* were state and federal provisions denying welfare benefits to persons who had not resided within the jurisdiction for at least a year. The requirement both deterred and penalized travel. In addition, none of the government's reasons were found to be compelling. The Court said that families could not be "denied welfare aid upon which may depend the ability . . . to obtain the very means to subsist," solely because they were members of a class which could not satisfy a one-year residency requirement.

See also *Edwards v. California*, which involved California's attempt to slow travel into the state by prosecuting citizens who knowingly brought into the state any indigent nonresident. The Supreme Court unanimously upheld the constitutional right to cross state lines, but disagreed on the constitutional provision abridged. The majority relied on the Commerce clause as prohibiting "attempts . . . of any single state to isolate itself from difficulties common to all of them . . . by the single expedient of shutting its gates to the outside world." . . . The two concurrences found the Privileges and Immunities clause of the Fourteenth Amendment to be the applicable constitutional text, and focused on individual rights in finding that right to free movement between states is a right of national citizenship. Mobility, Justice Douglas argued in his concurrence, is basic to any question of freedom of opportunity and to prevent the indigent from seeking new horizons would "contravene every conception of national unity." This takes on even greater force when linked to marriage.

Whatever cluster of constitutional grounds ultimately proves successful, it is clear that those opposing recognition of same-sex couples' marriages are advocating a position that could do great damage not only to the individual couples and children involved, but also to the institution of marriage, family relationships, and the links and mobility vital to our federal union. For all these reasons, the position that the Constitution mandates full faith and credit for validly contracted marriages is right and should be developed. . . .

The Right to Travel and Family Values
SETH F. KREIMER

From "Territoriality and Moral Dissensus: Thoughts on Abortion, Slavery, Gay Marriage and Family Values," from Quinnipiac Law Review, Vol. 16 (1997)

> *Law professor Seth Kreimer takes Wolfson's argument a step further. What about the rights of children of a legally married couple who move from Hawaii to another state? Do those children lose their legitimacy when their parents move? Don't children have a right to a stable home and legal parents anywhere in the United States? The constitutional precedents suggest they do.*

The analysis thus far treats the issue of nonrecognition of same-sex marriages as a denial of legal entitlements as to which individuals migrating from Hawaii and Pennsylvania residents are similarly situated. The fact, however, is that an exercise of Pennsylvania's authority to deny recognition to marriages of unconventional immigrants as they cross its boundary involves more than a refusal to recognize an abstract legal capacity. For Hawaiian emigrants, the denial of marital recognition means rending a family bond which has already been established. If courts recognize that the question is whether there is a right to migrate as an existing family, the analysis dons a different aspect. We might call this the "family values" approach.

To put the strongest case, assume a same-sex couple who have children in Hawaii moves to Pennsylvania, and the biological parent dies. Would Pennsylvania be entitled to treat the children as wards of the state and the surviving spouse as a stranger to the children she has raised as a lawful parent? There is certainly precedent suggesting that a refusal to recognize a family unit in such circumstances raises constitutional doubts. The destruction of a long-standing family unit is an evil that demands justification, and the imposition of that evil as a consequence of migration is in tension with the mobility of national citizenship conferred by the Fourteenth Amendment and the federal structure, and the proposition that a state may not penalize the exercise of those rights.

It is reasonably clear that the effort to dismember an existing family initially recognized by domestic law would require justifications more substantial than a mere policy preference for alternative living arrangements by the state. This constitutional protection is not limited to families whose existence is initially sanctioned by law. In *Stanley v. Illinois,* the children of Joan and Peter Stanley, an unmarried couple who raised their children jointly for eighteen years, were determined to be wards of the state upon the death of their mother. Faced with the state's claims that by defining an unmarried father—an Illinois resident—not to be a "parent," it could ignore the existing relationship between father and children, the court declared "the interest of a man in the children he has sired and raised undeniably warrants deference, and absent a powerful countervailing interest, protection." Justice White acknowledged that "family relationships unlegitimized by a marriage ceremony . . . involve family bonds as warm, enduring and important as those arising within a more formally organized family unit."

Mr. Stanley was entitled to invoke constitutional protection for his existing family unit in the absence of prior legal recognition on the basis of both his ongoing caretaking relationship and biological bonds. Subsequent cases hold that biology is not sufficient to establish constitutional protection for the parent-child relationship, but that the crucial element is "full commitment to the responsibilities of parenthood." A father whose connections with his biological child are not solemnized by marriage, but who nonetheless "grasps the opportunity" to develop a relationship with his children, and "accepts . . . responsibility for the child's future," is entitled to "enjoy the blessings of the parent-child relationship and make uniquely valuable contributions to the child's development." One whose relationship remains merely "potential," rather than "developed," can claim no constitutional protection.

Certainly, in the case of same-sex couples who have married and established families with children in Hawaii, the parent-child relationships are as "warm, enduring and important" as those within a "developed" nonmarital family of different sexes. Indeed, the parents have sought legal recognition for the relationship seeking the "protection . . . provided by the laws that authorize formal marriage." Under existing law, a state that sought to ignore a biological parent-child relationship because of hostility to the law under which marriage was solemnized would be on dubious constitutional ground. The question is whether, in the absence of biological connections, a prior legal recognition in another state, combined with an ongoing caretaking relationship is sufficient to invoke constitutional protection.

One building block is *Smith v. Organization of Foster Families for Equality and Reform*, where the court "assumed" that foster parents—who had no biological connection with the children entrusted to their care—could invoke a protectable liberty interest in the ongoing relationship. Justice Brennan commented that "the importance of the family relationship to the individuals involved and to the society stems from the emotional attachments that derive from the intimacy of daily association and from the role it plays in promoting a way of life through the instruction of children. . . . At least where a child has been placed in foster care as an infant . . . and remained continuously for several years in the care of these same foster parents, it is natural that the foster family should hold the same place in the emotional life of the foster child and fulfill the same socializing functions as a natural family." By this measure, an existing legally recognized family with same-sex parents clearly partakes of the family values that invoke constitutional protection when they migrate to a new state.

Likewise, in *Michael H. v. Gerald D.* Justice Scalia's plurality opinion upheld California's decision to prefer legally sanctioned relationships to biological ties. California's domestic relations law excluded a biological father from parental rights where the mother sought to invoke the presumption of paternity arising out of her ongoing legal marriage with another man. Justice Scalia read prior federal precedent to accord constitutional protection to "relationships that develop within a unitary family," typified by a "marital family." He relied on a tradition of protecting "the marital family" against the claims of outsiders, the "aversion to declaring children illegitimate," combined with the importance of protecting an "extant marital family" to uphold California's decision to exclude the biological father from parental rights. Despite its impact on the interests of the biological father and his child, California was free to preserve the "integrity of the traditional family unit."

Again, if the court recognizes the importance of protecting a legally constructed "marital" family against the disruption by a biological, but nonmarital parent, it should recognize the magnitude of the loss imposed where a same-sex "marital family" formally established in Hawaii is subjected to the penalty of dissolution upon migration.

In the case of a Hawaiian emigrant family with children, moreover, the argument for recognition is strengthened by the interests of children who will lose the legal relationship to one of the only two parents they have ever known because of the receiving state's refusal to recognize the existence of an existing marital family. Even in the case of a family where the parental union remains intact, the child suffers a significant deprivation. In the case of death of one parent or dissolution of the existing marriage, the effect on the child could be traumatic.

While the parents themselves could avoid the threat of a Pennsylvania dissolution by remaining in Hawaii, for the children involved, there is no choice. To deprive them of existing family ties because of their parents' decision to migrate is in tension with the constitutional stricture against imposing burdens on children because of their parents' actions. Thus, the court has regularly invalidated "classifications that burden illegitimate children for the sake of punishing the illicit relations of their parents, because visiting this condemnation on the head of an infant is illogical and unjust." Likewise, the court in *Plyler v. Doe* was unwilling to sanction the exclusion of the children of illegal immigrants from public schools; while their "parents have the ability to conform their conduct to societal norms" and presumably the ability to remove themselves from the State's jurisdiction, the children . . . "can affect neither their parents' conduct nor their own status." Like nonmarital children, children of same-sex couples face potential social difficulties even in the absence of state discrimination triggered by their parents' actions. Like the children of illegal immigrants, they stand liable to be deprived of parental relationships not because of what they have done but because of who their parents are; indeed what their parents have done was entirely legal in their previous state of residence.

This focus on "family values" is more than an exercise in hypothetical construction. While relatively few bona fide Hawaiian residents are likely to emigrate with their children to the mainland in the next few years, other jurisdictions have begun to recognize same-sex couples as parents without Hawaii's constitutional fanfare. For the more numerous families that have established their relations in these states in contemplation of continued legal relationships, the disruptive potential of exclusionary legislation is equally severe. Where one state's laws establish family units involving same-sex couples precisely in order to provide both tangible and psychic benefits to children of stable families, to deprive children of those benefits because of their parents' decision to migrate to a new state raises constitutional objections of the first order.

I realize, of course, that this is hardly an airtight legal argument. On one front, it is clear that the court has thus far invoked the value of the "marital family" as a method of justifying government decisions, rather than a basis for challenging them. Justice Scalia has cautioned, for a plurality, against "turning around" the approval in *Michael H.* of "favored treatment" of traditional family relationships into "a constitutional requirement that a state must recognize the primacy of those relationships." Establishing the legal premise that a legally recognized nonbiological family that has developed intimate emotional linkages has a constitutional interest in remaining intact is an extrapolation from current doctrine.

On a second front, the recognition of a constitutional interest does not mean that it will prevail. States are, in appropriately severe cases, entitled to dismember even traditional families in the interests of protecting children. The family values argument puts directly at issue the factual premise that it is a grave deprivation to sunder childrens' relationship with their nonbiological parent in a same-sex marriage. The premise is not likely to go unchallenged, for there are certainly states that will maintain that gays and lesbians are per se unfit parents.

But this challenge is, it seems to me, an opportunity. Unlike the appropriate definition of "marriage," the issue can be joined on a basis which both is susceptible to concrete proof and allows advocates to dramatize the human costs of nonrecognition. I am not sure what proof would disabuse a judge of an intuition that "marriage" is by definition the union of a man and a woman; it is quite clear, however, how to present evidence that children are in pain. The extant studies suggest that the state will have a hard case to make, and it will rapidly become clear the extent to which animosity toward gays and lesbians is at work.

The argument from family values has the virtue of focusing attention on the real human costs associated with a denial of recognition to extraterritorial same-sex marriages. If there is something wrong with these denials, it is not primarily an affront to Hawaii's sovereign interests. It is the practical cruelty of dismembering a family that has been legally joined, and the denial of equal respect in refusing to acknowledge a legally sanctioned relationship on the basis of invidious animus. Relatively rarely can constitutional intervention establish loving relationships, but the argument from family values at least provides the hope of focusing on the reasons to prevent the states from extinguishing those loving relationships which already exist.

The Example of California
THOMAS M. KEANE

From *"Aloha Marriage? Constitutional and Choice*
of Law Arguments for Recognition of Same-Sex
Marriages." From The Stanford Law Review,
February 1995

> *The largest state in the union—and the one with the closest*
> *ties to Hawaii—has an extremely consistent record of always*
> *recognizing marriages of a sister state. Here is a preview of the*
> *legal precedents in the state that could set the agenda for what*
> *happens in the rest of the country.*

In addition to analyzing legislative declarations of state policy regarding homosexuality, one can examine cases involving analogous marriage-recognition issues to determine the relative strength of a state's marriage validation policy. For example, although California law does not permit same-sex marriage, California's courts have concluded that the state has a very strong marriage validation policy. California validated out-of-state mixed-race marriages seventy-three years before it overturned its own antimiscegenation statute, and it has long recognized marriages between people too young to marry in California but legally married elsewhere. Even a bigamous marriage and a marriage in violation of a California communicable disease control law have been validated. What's more, the state even validates marriages by California residents who deliberately evade California law. California's validation policy is so strong that it would be very difficult to argue the existence of a state policy against same-sex marriage strong enough to support invalidation. This conclusion is buttressed by California's explicit validation statute, its lack of a sodomy law, its employment antidiscrimination law, and the state constitution's explicit guarantee of privacy.

Unlike California, however, some states have either weak marriage validation policies or none at all. If a state consistently denied recognition to out-of-state marriages which were contrary to local law, without regard for the characteristics of the marriage or the policy underlying the local ban, that state or a private party would probably have a strong argument for invalidating same-sex marriages, particularly if the state has other indicia of a strong policy against homosexuality. Few states, however, can be said to refuse recognition consistently to locally illegal out-of-state marriages. Frequently, the factual context of an action appears to weigh as heavily in the courts' decision making as any general state policy against recognition.

The Courts, Gay Marriage, and the Popular Will
DAVID FRUM

From the Weekly Standard, *October 30, 1996*

A young conservative bemoans what he sees as the inevitability of same-sex marriage. And he posits a post-Hawaii strategy: reinforcement of antisodomy laws.

During the great debate over ratification of the Equal Rights Amendment, Phyllis Schlafly used to cause sophisticated eyes to roll with her prediction that the amendment would inspire the courts to create a new right of gay marriage. It was just twenty years ago, but this warning then seemed so self-evidently ludicrous as to blast Schlafly's credibility among journalists and other respectable folk.

It turns out Schlafly was right. It's on grounds of sex discrimination, not discrimination against homosexuals, that the plaintiffs in *Baehr v. Lewin*, the now-famous case involving gay marriage in Hawaii, may win the right to wed. And it's because claims of sex discrimination are involved that the Defense of Marriage Act, which has passed both houses of Congress and is due to be signed by the president this week, may prove vulnerable.

As liberal as the Hawaiian courts are, even they refused to swallow the argument that a gay couple refused a marriage license had been discriminated against because they were homosexual. The Hawaiian Supreme Court's May decision in *Baehr v. Lewin* conceded that the local constitution could not be stretched as far as that. But, the court went on to chirrup, the constitution could be stretched in a different direction: Hawaii's practice of denying marriage licenses to men who want to marry men and women who want to marry women constituted *sex* discrimination. Sex discrimination is prohibited under the Hawaiian state constitution. And with that, the Hawaiian Supreme Court sent the case back to the trial courts to give the state an opportunity to justify this discrimination.

Other plaintiffs in other states have tried this argument but were rebuffed because state courts hesitated to read equal-rights clauses in their state constitutions about sex as literally as they read equal-rights clauses about race and religion. Judges have felt constrained to recognize what most sensible non-judges recognize: that sex is not analogous to race, that there are important differences between men and women the law must respect and honor. Most of us would be troubled if we learned that in traffic accidents between whites and nonwhites, the courts of our state found in favor of white drivers 95 percent of the time. But only a fanatic would be troubled to find that the local courts found for the mother in 95 percent of child-custody disputes.

Alas, American lawyers being what they are, it was only a matter of time before five such fanatics found themselves in control of a state supreme court somewhere. It happened to be Hawaii's. *Baehr v. Lewin* probably won't receive its final adjudication until 1998 or 1999. But everyone should prepare for the worst. The Hawaiian courts will subject the state's arguments to the standard of scrutiny that lawyers call "strict": strict in theory, the old dictum runs, but fatal in fact.

It was to insulate the other forty-nine states from the caprice of the Hawaiian judiciary that Congress adopted the Defense of Marriage Act.

It has become commonplace to argue that the Defense of Marriage Act violates the Constitution—specifically, the Full Faith and Credit clause, which appears in Article IV. Never before in the annals of American history has that clause been so cited; advocates of gay marriage claim that Article IV would require every state to accept the validity of a Hawaiian homosexual wedding. And because the Defense of Marriage Act authorizes states to deny the validity of that wedding, advocates of gay marriage contend that it is unconstitutional.

That argument is flimsy. Here's the clause in full: "Full faith and credit shall be given in each State to the public acts, records, and judicial proceedings of every other state. And the Congress may by general laws prescribe the manner in which such acts, records, and proceedings shall be proved, and the effect thereof." The language is clear: The Constitution does grant Congress plentiful authority over the mutual legal obligations of the states.

So the Defense of Marriage Act is safe from Article IV. But it is vulnerable nonetheless, because it arguably falls afoul of the Supreme Court's strict new interpretation of the U.S. Constitution's guarantee of sexual equality.

What a minute, you might wonder. What guarantee of sexual equality is that? Didn't the Equal Rights Amendment lose? Amazingly, the answer is—yes, it did, but that doesn't matter anymore. America's judges are not the sort of people to let a little thing like the defeat of a constitutional amendment stop them from radically reconstructing society.

In the mid-1970s, the Supreme Court decided to ignore the verdict of the ratifying process that denied the ERA a place in the Constitution. Instead, it began interpreting the Fourteenth Amendment as if ERA had prevailed. At first, in a ritual nod to constitutional politesse, the justices observed some caution. Plaintiffs who complained they had been denied the equal protection of the laws because of their sex would get a slightly cooler judicial reception than plaintiffs making a similar complaint about race. Sex became a new, "intermediate" category of scrutiny. But in practice, "intermediate" scrutiny soon proved indistinguishable from the "strict" scrutiny of race-discrimination cases.

And this spring, when it decided to mandate the gender integration of the Virginia Military Institute, the Supreme Court finally and frankly inscribed the rejected ERA into the Constitution. The court laid down the rule that in all but the most extreme instances, the law must refuse to take any notice of the differences between the sexes.

Taking notice of the difference between the sexes is, however, precisely what the Defense of Marriage Act is meant to do. So, sometime after 1998 or 1999, there will be a new court battle. Two men or two women married in Hawaii will seek to force another state to recognize their relationship. When that state cites the Defense of Marriage Act and resists, the act's constitutionality will be challenged. If Justice Ruth Bader Ginsburg still commands a majority for the extreme understanding of the Fourteenth Amendment she displayed in the VMI case, the Defense of Marriage Act may well go down.

Especially since this Supreme Court seems to have quietly decided that sexual orientation is itself a category worthy of special attention, like race or—now—sex. It's hard to understand exactly what the court held in its murky and undisciplined ruling this year in *Romer v. Evans*, the Colorado gay-rights referendum case. At a minimum, though, the court has traveled a long way from *Bowers v. Hardwick*, the 1986 "sodomy" case that recognized the right of states to criminalize homosexual behavior. In *Romer v. Evans*, the court denied a state the right to exclude homosexuals from the special protection of its civil-rights laws.

The court's reasoning in *Romer v. Evans* bodes especially ill for the Defense of Marriage Act. The Colorado referendum, the Supreme Court said, was invalid because it was motivated by an "animus" against homosexuals. It offered no evidence of such animus; apparently the mere fact that homosexuals were the unique targets of the law proved it. And of course, homosexuals are the unique targets of the Defense of Marriage Act too.

Does this mean the defense of traditional marriage is doomed? Far from it—provided that Americans and their lawmakers are prepared to muster their resolve now. The great precedent here is the court's attempt to outlaw the death penalty in 1974. Over the following two years, more than thirty states rewrote their criminal laws in ways designed to satisfy the court's stated objections to the capital penalty. Confronted with a powerful national consensus, the Supreme Court backed down. And while it has never reconciled itself to the death penalty—while it and the lower federal courts still sabotage the penalty's application to the utmost of their ability—it has accepted the sentence's ultimate constitutionality.

And so here. American courts and law schools have been hugely influenced by the teachings of Ronald Dworkin, who has argued that the American Constitution should be interpreted in terms of "evolving standards of decency." Translate that to "cramming down the throat of a hostile public as much liberalism as possible short of impeachment." It's the job of state legislators and Congress to help the judiciary understand where that line will be drawn.

The need to draw that line is why the Senate's close vote on the bill sponsored by Sen. Ted Kennedy to forbid employment discrimination against homosexuals—devised as an effort to derail or defang the Defense of Marriage Act and brought to a vote the same day—was so misguided.

True, the bill went down to defeat by a one-vote margin. But at a moment when the courts are trying to decide how much they can get away with, it was (to say the least) spectacularly unhelpful to the cause of marriage and the family for the Senate to send the courts so ambiguous a signal. Some senators, with their instinct for horse-trading, may have seen the Kennedy bill as a reasonable compromise—they could vote for the Defense of Marriage Act *and* the Kennedy bill and thus appear broadminded. But courts don't operate by horse-trading; courts operate by taking principles to their logical (or, nowadays, their most extreme possible) conclusion.

That's what has happened north of the border. Inspired by the same sympathetic motives as the forty-nine senators who voted in favor of the Kennedy anti-discrimination bill, eight of the ten Canadian provinces gave homosexuals the benefit of their anti-discrimination statutes in the 1980s. Since then, Canadian courts—who are even more impressed with the output of America's radical law professors than U.S. courts—have gone to work, Dworkin-style, fabricating something extraordinarily close to gay marriage. Governments are obliged to pay pensions, relocation expenses, and other benefits to the "partners" of homosexual civil servants; homosexuals may sue each other for support after their relationships dissolve; they may adopt each other's biological children; and they may even adopt children as couples. And whenever a government objects (usually pretty insincerely) to the latest innovation, the courts cite the jurisdiction's own human-rights statutes for justification.

States and Congress need to begin now making unmistakably clear the seriousness of their commitment to marriage and the family. Sixteen legislatures have already affirmed their commitment to the traditional understanding of marriage; pressure should be brought on the remaining states to do the same. Hawaiians may need to amend their constitution.

In extremis, states may even want to consider one final, distasteful expedient: reaffirming or re-enacting sodomy laws. In the best spirit of tolerance, half the states repealed their sodomy laws in the early 1970s, and the other half stopped enforcing them. That was the right thing to do: These laws not only invade precious rights of personal privacy, they confer dangerously arbitrary powers on the police as well.

But the fact is, these laws remain constitutional. And—should the courts ever make it necessary—they can serve as a legal weapon of last resort. First, in a state with a sodomy law, gay marriage could not be legally consummated. Second, a state with a sodomy law can, if challenged in court to defend its "sex discrimination" in a gay-marriage case, do what Colorado and

Hawaii could not in defending their "discriminatory" legislation: cite a compelling state law-enforcement interest, the prevention of a criminal act. Third, and most serious, the reaffirmation by states of a sodomy law would signal the courts that their attack on marriage risks triggering a legal convulsion even grimmer than that touched off by the decision in *Roe v. Wade*.

Americans are a tolerant people. The overwhelming majority generously upholds the good old principle of live and let live. In recent years, homosexuals have asked for better police protection, hundreds of millions of dollars for AIDS research, equal treatment in the workplace, and an end to the sneering spirit of cruelty in which their condition was too often discussed in the past. And by and large their requests have been granted. Millions of Americans already cheerfully accept that their homosexual friends enter into romantic relationships, and wish them nothing but happiness. To an unprecedented degree, Americans give the most generous possible answer to E. M. Forster's haunting question: Is there so much love in the world that you want to deny anyone any portion of it? And in giving that generous answer, they have helped to form a more generous country.

But Americans are also deeply attached, as they should be, to the fundamental institutions of Judeo-Christian civilization. They are living in the third decade of a crime and welfare crisis largely attributable to the collapse of marriage. They are coming to appreciate the damaging consequences of casual divorce to two generations of children. They sense, if they do not understand, that marriage is an institution that rests on a recognition of the cultural and biological differences between men and women, and that the call for gay marriage is the culmination of the intellectual and political campaign to deny and suppress those differences. They feel—they are right to feel—anger and outrage when it's proposed to them to abolish marriage and replace it with a new unisex partnerhood, casually entered into and as casually dissolved.

And the sooner and more bluntly the people's representatives confront the courts with the power and permanence of those feelings, the more likely it is that American society will be spared a destructive and unnecessary conflict.

ABOUT THE CONTRIBUTORS

Henry Alford is the author of the humor collection *Municipal Bondage*.

Dennis Altman teaches in the politics department at La Trobe University in Melbourne, Australia, and is the author of *Homosexual: Oppression and Liberation* (New York University Press).

Antiga is a writer and workshop creator.

Hannah Arendt, a historian and political philosopher, died in 1975.

Aristophanes was a Greek dramatist who lived from c. 448–c. 388 B.C.

Hadley Arkes is the Ney Professor of Jurisprudence at Amherst College and a contributing editor at *National Review*.

Philip A. Belcastro is the chairman of the department of Physical Education, Health, Recreation and Dance at B.M.C.C.—City University of New York.

William Bennett, a fellow at the Hudson Institute and the Heritage Foundation, is the codirector of Empower America.

Jerry J. Bigner is a professor in the department of Human Development and Family Studies at Colorado State University.

Elizabeth Birch is the executive director of the Human Rights Campaign.

Harry Andrew Blackmun was an associate justice of the U.S. Supreme Court from 1971 to 1994.

Sonny Bono is the U.S. representative from the 44th district of California.

Frederick W. Bozett, a professor in the Graduate Program in the College of Nursing at the University of Oklahoma, died in 1990.

Frank Browning is the author of *Queer Geography: Journeys Toward a Sexual Self* (Crown).

Robert Byrd is a U.S. senator from West Virginia.

Dudley Clendinen is a freelance writer living in Baltimore, Maryland and a former national correspondent for *The New York Times*.

William Orville Douglas was an associate justice of the United States Supreme Court from 1939 to 1975. He died in 1980.

Kathy Duggan is a freelance writer living in New York City.

About the Contributors

Mary C. Dunlap is a writer and director of the Office of Citizen Complaints in San Francisco, California.

Jean Bethke Elshtain is the Laura Spelman Rockefeller Professor of Social and Political Ethics at the University of Chicago.

Paula Ettelbrick is legislative council at the Empire State Pride Agenda.

David K. Flaks, Psy. D., is a psychologist licensed in Pennsylvania and New Jersey.

Paula Fomby was an intern at *Mother Jones* in 1991.

Barney Frank is the U.S. representative from the 4th district of Massachusetts.

David Frum is a contributing editor at *The Weekly Standard* and the author of *What's Right* (HarperCollins).

E. J. Graff is a freelance writer in Massachusetts and is working on a book, *What is Marriage For?*

Phil Gramm is a U.S. senator from Texas.

Deborah M. Henson is a clerk at the Louisiana Supreme Court and a part-time psychotherapist.

Melville J. Herskovits was a professor of anthropology at Northwestern University from 1927 to 1963. He died in 1963.

Ralph Hexter is a professor of Classics at the University of California at Berkeley.

Bret Hinsch is an associate professor at the National Chung Cheng University, Taiwan.

Henry Hyde is the U.S. representative from the 6th district of Illinois.

Bob Inglis is the U.S. representative from the 4th district of South Carolina.

Doug Ireland is a contributor to *The Nation* and a former *Village Voice* contributor.

Jeffrey John is a parish priest and theology lecturer in London.

Rabbi Yoel J. Kahn was rabbi of Congregation Sha'ar Zahav in San Francisco from 1985 to 1996, and is now completing his Ph.D. at the Graduate Theological Union in Berkeley, California.

Thomas M. Keane is an associate at Paul, Weiss, Rifkind, Wharton & Garrison in New York City.

Anthony McLeod Kennedy is an associate justice of the U.S. Supreme Court.

Andrew Koppelman is an assistant professor of politics at Princeton University.

Larry Kramer is a professor of law at New York University Law School.

About the Contributors

Charles Krauthammer is a syndicated columnist.

Seth F. Kreimer is a professor of law at the University of Pennsylvania.

Joseph Landau is a researcher in Washington, D.C.

Ann Landers is a syndicated columnist.

John Lewis is the U.S. representative from the 5th district of Georgia.

James McGough is an epidemiologist specializing in AIDS research with the Seattle–King County Department of Public Health. He lives in Seattle, Washington.

Michel de Montaigne was a French essayist who lived from 1533 to 1592.

Sandra Day O'Connor is an associate justice of the U.S. Supreme Court.

Camille Paglia is a professor of humanities at the University of the Arts in Philadelphia.

Charlotte Patterson is a developmental psychologist at the University of Virginia.

Plato, a disciple of Socrates, was an Athenian philosopher who lived from c. 427 to 347 B.C.

Katha Pollitt is an associate editor at *The Nation*.

Richard A. Posner is the chief judge of the 7th U.S. Circuit Court of Appeals in Chicago and the author of *A Guide to America's Sex Laws* (University of Chicago).

Lewis Franklin Powell, Jr., was an associate justice of the U.S. Supreme Court from 1972 to 1987.

Dennis Prager is a lecturer, writer, and KABC Radio talk show host in Los Angeles, California.

Jonathan Rauch is the author of *Demosclerosis: The Silent Killer of American Government* (Random House).

Chuck Robb is a U.S. senator from Virginia.

William Safire is a *New York Times* columnist.

Antonin Scalia is an associate justice of the U.S. Supreme Court.

Amy E. Schwartz is a member of the *Washington Post* editorial page staff.

Jay Alan Sekulow is the chief counsel for the American Center for Law and Justice.

Brent D. Shaw is a professor of classical studies at the University of Pennsylvania.

Yael Lee Silverberg-Willis was studying midwifery in San Francisco in 1990 and is no longer together with Luana Willis.

About the Contributors

William S. Skylstad is the bishop of the Spokane, Washington, diocese.

John Shelby Spong, the Episcopal bishop of Newark, is the author of *Living in Sin?* (Harper San Francisco).

Andrew Sullivan is a senior editor at *The New Republic* and the author of *Virtually Normal: An Argument About Homosexuality* (Vintage).

Cass Sunstein is a professor of jurisprudence at the University of Chicago Law School.

Catherine Tuerk is the president of the D.C. Metropolitan Chapter of PFLAG.

Earl Warren was the chief justice of the Supreme Court from 1953 to 1969. He died in 1974.

Byron Raymond White was an associate justice of the U.S. Supreme Court from 1962 to 1993.

Walter L. Williams is a professor of anthropology at the University of Southern California.

James Q. Wilson is a professor of management and public policy at UCLA.

Baylah Wolfe is a social therapist and a writer.

Evan Wolfson is Marriage Project Director of Lambda Legal Defense and Education Fund.

ACKNOWLEDGMENTS

"The Speech of Aristophanes" from the *Symposium* by Plato, translated by Alexander Nehamas and Paul Woodruff (Indianapolis: Hackett Publishing Company, Inc., 1989). Reprinted by permission.

"A Groom of One's Own?" by Brent D. Shaw (*The New Republic*, July 18 and 24, 1994), copyright © 1994 by The New Republic, Inc. Reprinted by permission of *The New Republic*.

"Same-Sex Unions in Pre-Modern Europe: A Response" by Ralph Hexter (*The New Republic*, October 3, 1994), copyright © 1994 by The New Republic, Inc. Reprinted by permission of *The New Republic*.

"A Strange Brotherhood" by Michel de Montaigne, March 18, 1581, journal entry from *Travel Journal* in *The Complete Works of Montaigne*, translated by Donald Frame (Stanford University Press). Reprinted by permission of Stanford University Press.

"Deviant Marriage Patterns in Chinese Society" by James McGough from *Normal and Abnormal Behavior in Chinese Culture*, edited by Arthur Kleinman and Tsung-Yi Lin (Kluwer Academic Publishers, 1981, pp. 171–201). Reprinted by permission of Kluwer Academic Publishers, Dordrecht, The Netherlands.

"Husbands, Boys, Servants" by Bret Hinsch from *Passions of the Cut Sleeve: The Male Homosexual Tradition in China* by Bret Hinsch, copyright © 1990 by The Regents of the University of California. Reprinted by permission of the Regents of the University of California and the University of California Press.

"A Note on 'Woman Marriage' in Dahomey" by Melville J. Herskovits (*Africa*, the Journal of the International African Institute, Vol. 10, 1937). Reprinted by permission of the International African Institute, London.

"A Normal Man" by Walter L. Williams from *The Spirit and the Flesh* by Walter L. Williams, copyright © 1986, 1992 by Walter L. Williams. Reprinted by permission of Beacon Press, Boston, and Georges Borchardt, Inc., on behalf of the author.

Acknowledgments

"A Comparative Analysis of Same-Sex Partnership Protections" by Deborah M. Henson (*International Journal of Law and the Family*, 1993). Reprinted by permission of Oxford University Press.

Material from *The King James Bible*. Reprinted by permission of HarperCollins Publishers, London.

"Statement on Same-Sex Marriage" by Rev. Joseph L. Charron and Rev. William S. Skylstad (National Conference of Catholic Bishops), copyright © 1996 by the United States Catholic Conference. All rights reserved. Reprinted by permission of the Office for Publishing and Promotion Services, United States Catholic Conference, Washington, D.C.

"Marriage's True Ends" by the Editors (*Commonweal*, May 17, 1996), copyright © 1996 by Commonweal Foundation. Reprinted by permission of *Commonweal*.

"Against Gay Marriage" by Jean Bethke Elshtain (*Commonweal*, October 22, 1991), copyright © 1991 by Commonweal Foundation. Reprinted by permission of *Commonweal*.

"Homosexuality, the Bible, and Us—A Jewish Perspective" by Dennis Prager (*Ultimate Issues*, Vol. 6, No. 2). Reprinted by permission of *Ultimate Issues*, 10573 West Pico Blvd., #167, Los Angeles.

"Blessing Gay and Lesbian Commitments" by John Shelby Spong from *Living in Sin? A Bishop Rethinks Sexuality* by John Shelby Spong, copyright © 1989 by the Rt. Rev. John Shelby Spong. Reprinted by permission of HarperCollins Publishers, Inc.

"The Kedusha of Homosexual Relationships" by Rabbi Yoel H. Kahn from the *CCAR Yearbook XCIV* (New York: Central Conference of American Rabbis, 1989), copyright © 1989 by Yoel H. Kahn. Reprinted by permission of the author.

"Creation and Natural Law" by Jeffrey John from *Permanent, Faithful, Stable: Christian Same-Sex Partnerships* by Jeffrey John, copyright © 1993 by Jeffrey John. Reprinted by permission of the author, Affirming Catholicism, St. Giles Church, London.

"What You Do" by Andrew Sullivan (*The New Republic*, March 3, 1996), copyright © 1996 by The New Republic, Inc. Reprinted by permission of *The New Republic*.

Acknowledgments

"Since When Is Marriage a Path to Liberation?" by Paula Ettelbrick (*OUT/LOOK National Gay and Lesbian Quarterly*, No. 6, Fall 1989). Reprinted by permission of the author.

"Choosing" by Mary C. Dunlap from "The Lesbian and Gay Marriage Debate: A Microcosm of Our Hopes and Troubles in the Nineties" (*Law and Sexuality: A Review of Lesbian and Gay Legal Issues*, Vol. I, No. 63, 1991). Reprinted by permission of *Law and Sexuality*.

"Why We Should Fight for the Freedom to Marry" by Evan Wolfson (*Journal of Gay, Lesbian & Bisexual Identity*, Vol. 1, No. 1, 1996). Reprinted by permission of Plenum Publishing Corporation.

"Why Marry?" by Frank Browning (*The New York Times*, Op-Ed, April 17, 1996), copyright © 1996 by The New York Times Co. Reprinted by permission of *The New York Times*.

"Retying the Knot" by E. J. Graff (*The Nation*, June 24, 1996), copyright © 1996 by The Nation Company, L.P. Reprinted by permission of *The Nation*.

"Connubial Personae" by Camille Paglia (*10 Percent Magazine*, May/June 1995, Vol. 3). Copyright © 1995 by *10 Percent Magazine*. Reprinted by permission of Camille Paglia and *10 Percent Magazine*.

"Crossing the Threshold: Equal Marriage Rights for Lesbians and Gay Men and the Intra-Community Critique" by Evan Wolfson (*New York University Review of Law & Social Change*, Vol. 21, No. 3, 1994–1995, pp. 73–76). Reprinted by permission of the *New York University Review of Law & Social Change*.

"Reflections on Little Rock" by Hannah Arendt (*Dissent*, Vol. 6, No. 1, Winter 1959). Reprinted by permission of *Dissent*.

"The Conservative Case" by Andrew Sullivan from *Virtually Normal: An Argument About Homosexuality* by Andrew Sullivan, copyright © 1995 by Andrew Sullivan. Reprinted by permission of Alfred A. Knopf, Inc.

"The Closet Straight" by Hadley Arkes (*National Review*, July 5, 1993), copyright © 1993 by National Review, Inc. Reprinted by permission of *National Review*, New York.

Acknowledgments

"Against Homosexual Marriage" by James Q. Wilson (*Commentary*, March 1996). All rights reserved. Reprinted by permission of the author and *Commentary*.

"For Better or Worse?" by Jonathan Rauch (*The New Republic*, May 6, 1996), copyright © 1996 by Jonathan Rauch. Reprinted by permission of the author.

"Let Them Wed" by the Editors (*The Economist*, January 6, 1996), copyright © 1996 by The Economist Newspaper Group, Inc. Reprinted by permission of *The Economist*.

"Homosexuality: The Policy Questions" by Richard A. Posner from *Sex and Reason* by Richard A. Posner, copyright © 1992 by the Presidents and Fellows of Harvard College. Reprinted by permission of Harvard University Press, Cambridge, Massachusetts.

"Same-Sex Marriage Nears" by William Safire (*The New York Times*, April 29, 1995), copyright © 1995 by The New York Times Co. Reprinted by permission of *The New York Times*.

"Gay Marriages and the Affirmation of an Ideal" by Amy E. Schwartz (*The Washington Post*, June 3, 1996), copyright © 1996 by *The Washington Post*. Reprinted by permission of The Washington Post Writers Group.

"Gay Marriage? Don't Say I Didn't Warn You" by Katha Pollitt (*The Nation*, April 29, 1996), copyright © 1996 by The Nation Company, L.P. Reprinted by permission of *The Nation*.

"Defending Marriage" by Jay Alan Sekulow (written testimony provided to the House Judiciary Committee from the American Center for Law and Justice, May 15, 1996). Reprinted by permission.

"Children of Lesbian and Gay Parents: Summary of Research Findings" by Charlotte Patterson from *Lesbian and Gay Parenting: A Resource for Psychologists*, copyright © 1995 by the American Psychological Association. Reprinted by permission of the American Psychological Association.

"Lesbians Choosing Motherhood: A Comparative Study of Lesbian and Heterosexual Parents and Their Children" by David K. Flaks et al. from *Developmental Psychology*, Vol. 31, copyright © 1995 by the American Psychological Association. Reprinted by permission of the American Psychological Association.

Acknowledgments

"A Review of Data Based Studies Addressing the Effects of Homosexual Parenting on Children's Sexual and Social Functioning" by Philip A. Belcastro et al. (*Journal of Divorce and Remarriage,* Vol. 20, 1/2, 1993). Reprinted by permission of The Haworth Press, Inc.

"Coming Out to My Children" by Antiga from *Politics of the Heart,* edited by Sandra Pollack and Jeanne Vaughn, copyright © 1987 by Sandra Pollack and Jeanne Vaughn. Reprinted by permission of Firebrand Books, Ithaca, New York.

"Homophobia at Home" by Baylah Wolfe from *Politics of the Heart,* edited by Sandra Pollock and Jeanne Vaughn, copyright © 1987 by Sandra Pollock and Jeanne Vaughn. Reprinted by permission of Firebrand Books, Ithaca, New York.

"Parenting by Gay Fathers" by Jerry J. Bigner and Frederick W. Bozett from *Homosexuality and Family Relations,* edited by Frederick W. Bozett and Marvin B. Sussman (1990). Reprinted by permission of The Haworth Press, Inc.

"Why I'm Glad I Grew Up in a Gay Family" by Paula Fomby (*Mother Jones,* August 16, 1996), copyright © 1996 by Foundation for National Progress. Reprinted by permission of *Mother Jones.*

"Leave Marriage Alone" by William Bennett (*Newsweek,* June 3, 1996), copyright © 1996 by Newsweek, Inc. All rights reserved. Reprinted by permission of *Newsweek.*

"Three's a Crowd" by Andrew Sullivan (*The New Republic,* June 17, 1996), copyright © 1996 by The New Republic, Inc. Reprinted by permission of *The New Republic.*

"When John and Jim Say 'I Do'" by Charles Krauthammer (*Time,* July 22, 1996), copyright © 1996 by Time Inc. Reprinted by permission of Time Life Syndication.

"Marrying Somebody" by Jonathan Rauch, copyright © by Jonathan Rauch. Reprinted by permission of the author.

"Sexual Freedom and the End of Romance" by Dennis Altman from *The Homosexualization of America* by Dennis Altman (1982). Reprinted by permission of Curtis Brown (Aust.) Pty. Ltd.

"Jack and Bob, Going to the Chapel" by Dudley Clendinen (*The New York Times,* Op-Ed, August 7, 1996), copyright © 1996 by The New York Times Co. Reprinted by permission of *The New York Times.*

Acknowledgments

"I Earned This Divorce" by Kathy Duggan (*The New York Times*, Op-Ed, July 25, 1996), copyright © 1996 by The New York Times Co. Reprinted by permission of *The New York Times*.

"Ann Can't Give Her Blessing to This Marriage" by Ann Landers (*The Chicago Tribune*, July 21, 1996). Reprinted by permission of Ann Landers and Creators Syndicate.

"Love and Marriage" by Catherine Tuerk (*Flagpole*, the newsletter of Parents, Families and Friends of Lesbians and Gays of the Metropolitan Washington, D.C., Area, October 1996). Reprinted by permission of the author.

"Gospel Under the Chuppah" by Yael Lee Silverberg-Willis from *Ceremonies of the Heart: Celebrating Lesbian Unions*, edited by Becky Butler, copyright © 1990 by Becky Butler (to be reissued by Seal Press, Seattle, in 1997). Reprinted by permission of Seal Press.

"Remembering Hervé" by Doug Ireland (*The Nation*, June 24, 1996), copyright © 1996 by The Nation Company, L.P. Reprinted by permission of *The Nation*.

"My Gay Wedding" by Henry Alford (*New York Magazine*, June 17, 1996), copyright © 1996 by New York Magazine. Distributed by the Los Angeles Times Syndicate. Reprinted by permission.

"Marriage as Integration" by Joseph Landau, copyright © by Joseph Landau. Reprinted by permission of the author.

"How Other States Can Ignore Hawaii" (originally titled "Same-Sex Marriage, Conflict of Laws, and the Unconstitutional Public Policy Exception") by Larry Kramer (*The Yale Law Journal*, Vol. 106, no. 7). Reprinted by permission of the author and The Yale Law Journal Company and Fred B. Rothman & Company.

"The Miscegenation Precedents" by Andrew Koppelman, from "Same-Sex Marriage and the Conflict of Laws" (*Quinnipiac Law Review*, Vol. 16), copyright © 1997 by Andrew Koppelman. Reprinted by permission of the author and the *Quinnipiac Law Review*.

"The Right to Travel" by Evan Wolfson from "Winning and Keeping Equal Marriage Rights: What Will Follow Victory in *Baehr v. Lewin*?" (Lambda Legal Defense and Education Fund, May 20, 1996). Reprinted by permission of the author.

Acknowledgments

"The Right to Travel and Family Values" by Seth F. Kreimer, from "Territoriality and Moral Dissensus: Thoughts on Abortion, Slavery, Gay Marriage and Family Values" (*Quinnipiac Law Review,* Vol. 16). Reprinted by permission of the author and the *Quinnipiac Law Review.*

"The Example of California" by Thomas M. Keane, from "Aloha, Marriage? Constitutional and Choice of Law Arguments for Recognition of Same-Sex Marriages" (*Stanford Law Review,* 47/499, 1995), copyright © 1995 by the Board of Trustees of the Leland Stanford Junior University. Reprinted by permission of the *Stanford Law Review* and Fred B. Rothman & Co.

"The Courts, Gay Marriage, and the Popular Will" by David Frum (*The Weekly Standard,* September 30, 1996), copyright © 1996 by David Frum. Reprinted by permission of Mildred Marmur Associates Ltd. on behalf of the author.